FAR OUT MAN

FAR
OUT

TALES OF LIFE *IN*

MAN

THE COUNTERCULTURE

ERIC
UTNE

RANDOM HOUSE | NEW YORK

Published in the United States by Random House, an imprint and division of Penguin Random House LLC, New York.

RANDOM HOUSE and the HOUSE colophon are registered trademarks of Penguin Random House LLC.

Brenda Ueland's comments in Chapter Three, "Closer Than Kin," adapted from her essay, "On Making Choices," Brenda Ueland Papers, the Minnesota Historical Society. Parts of the dialogue in Chapter 20, "Meeting the Shadow," adapted from "A Gathering of Men with Robert Bly," *Bill Moyers Journal,* January 8, 1990; *A Little Book on the Human Shadow,* Robert Bly (pp. 42–43); and *Seven Sources of Shame,* Robert Bly (pp. 23–24).

Photo credits are located on page 337.

Cartoon on page viii by Noel Ford ©Punch/Rothco, published in Nov./Dec. 1988 *Utne Reader.*

Library of Congress Cataloging-in-Publication Data
Names: Utne, Eric, author.
Title: Far out man: tales of life in the counterculture / Eric Utne.
Description: First edition. | New York: Random House, 2020.
Identifiers: LCCN 2019033630 (print) | LCCN 2019033631 (ebook) |
ISBN 9780812995282 (hardcover) | ISBN 9780812995299 (ebook)
Subjects: LCSH: Utne, Eric. | Editors—United States—Biography. |
Journalists—United States—Biography. | Publishers and
publishing—United States—Biography. | Utne reader.
Classification: LCC PN4874.U895 A3 2020 (print) | LCC PN4874.U895 (ebook)
| DDC 070.92 [B]—dc23
LC record available at https://lccn.loc.gov/2019033630
LC ebook record available at https://lccn.loc.gov/2019033631

Printed in the United States of America on acid-free paper

randomhousebooks.com

2 4 6 8 9 7 5 3 1

First Edition

Book design by Susan Turner

Dedicated to my sister, Mary, and brother Tom,
both of whom are over yonder.
Thanks for your continuing love and support.
I couldn't have done it without you.

Life is trouble. Only death is not.
To be alive is to undo your belt and look for trouble.

—NIKOS KAZANTZAKIS,
Zorba the Greek

Is it possible to observe the unfolding human attack on nature with horror, be determined to do whatever you can to stop it, and at the same time know that much of it cannot be stopped, whatever you do? Is it possible to see the future as dark and darkening further; to reject false hope and desperate pseudo-optimism without collapsing into despair? It's going to have to be, because it's where I am right now.

—PAUL KINGSNORTH,
Confessions of a Recovering Environmentalist

"Weep! Weep!" calls a toad from the water's edge. And I do. If grief can be a doorway to love, then let us all weep for the world we are breaking apart so we can love it back to wholeness again.

—ROBIN WALL KIMMERER,
Braiding Sweetgrass

How monotonous our speaking becomes when we speak only to ourselves! . . . If we no longer call out to the moon slipping between the clouds, or whisper to the spider setting the silken struts of her web, well, then the numerous powers of this world will no longer address us—and if they still try, we will not likely hear them.

—DAVID ABRAM,
Becoming Animal: An Earthly Cosmology

Listening is a magnetic and strange thing, a creative force. . . . When we are listened to, it creates us, makes us unfold and expand. . . . A creative fountain inside us begins to spring and cast up new thoughts and unexpected laughter and wisdom. . . . This little creative fountain is in all. It is the spirit, or the intelligence, or the imagination— whatever you want to call it.

—Brenda Ueland,
from her essay "Tell Me More"

There is a land of the living and a land of the dead
and the bridge is love, the only survival, the only meaning.
—The Abbess of the Convent of Santa Maria de las Rosas,
from Thornton Wilder's *The Bridge of San Luis Rey*

Could it be that one of the main reasons we are on this earth is to remember who we are? The song that sings in our blood, the song of our sacred ancestors, transcends the boundaries of a lifetime.

—Steven Foster,
We Who Have Gone Before

CONTENTS

FAR OUT

Dear Reader,

I'm probably the least likely person in the world to write a memoir, let alone publish a magazine, especially one with the word *reader* in its name. Why? Because I'm the slowest reader I know.

I couldn't read at the beginning of first grade and was terrified that the whole class would find out. When called on by the teacher for any reason—to answer a question or read a passage from a book—I'd simply lower my head, break into a hot flush, and wait for the teacher to pick on someone else.

As a child I gravitated to magazines. They were more visual than most books, and I could dip into and out of them at my own pace. When I started *Utne Reader*, a kind of *Reader's Digest* of the alternative press, I told the readers I was doing it to make a difference in the world, to advance both "personal growth and social change," to help make the world "a little greener and a little kinder."

But that was only part of the truth. I also started *Utne Reader* because I'd become addicted to magazines, and publishing my own allowed me to hang around my office day after day reading everything from *Vanity Fair* to *Centrifugal Bumble-Puppy*. *Utne Reader* was my way to get free subscriptions to more than two thousand of my favorite publications, maintain my magazine-reading habit, and, I hoped, get paid for it.

So . . . why was I such a slow reader? My super-high-IQ sister, who skipped her last year of high school and got full scholarships to Radcliffe and Wellesley, was a fast reader. Why the difference?

Though I've never been diagnosed, I suspect I'm dyslexic. Malcolm Gladwell wrote about dyslexia in his book *David and Goliath: Underdogs, Misfits, and the Art of Battling Giants.* He called dyslexia a *desirable difficulty* because "what is learned out of necessity is inevitably more powerful than the learning that comes easily."

Was my scrambled reading a "desirable difficulty" that helped me found, publish, and edit a magazine ironically named *Utne Reader*?

My favorite compliment about the magazine, which I heard countless times, went something like this: "*Utne Reader* is so tuned in to what's going on in my life just at the time it arrives that I look forward to its arrival to find out what's going on in my life." We anticipated the 1987 stock market crash, the mythopoetic men's movement, the HIV/AIDS epidemic, media concentration, the pressures on the family farm, the neighborhood salon movement, online dating and community building, cyber-spying by the government, and dozens of other mainstream and countercultural phenomena. Futurists, trend watchers, and the rest of the media monitored the magazine closely.

How did we do it? How did we tap into the zeitgeist (in German, "the spirit of the times")? I believe my struggle with reading led me to develop ways to sense or "read" the zeitgeist. *Far Out Man* is the story of how I learned to read the spirit of the times, and what I saw. It's also the story of how I lost that gift, what happened when I did, and how I found it again. I hope you enjoy it.

Sincerely,
Eric Utne

P.S. *Utne* rhymes with *chutney* and means "far out" in Norwegian.

SEARCHING FOR HOPE BEYOND HOPE

Do you know what it feels like to give up hope? I do.

I started *Utne Reader* in 1984 to change the world, to help bring on what I called "the emerging culture." But now, as I write these words thirty-five years later, things are only getting worse.

My sense of hope had its roots in the sixties. I was an idealist back then. Like many baby boomers, I rejected the Vietnam War and the establishment's materialistic values. I believed that we were living at the dawn of a new age, and that the world was getting more democratic, more just, and more free through the power of love.

When I got my hands on the first *Whole Earth Catalog,* in early 1969, I knew I'd found my bible. It was massive—a thick black tabloid-sized paperback. Its cover featured a NASA photograph of planet Earth taken from outer space. There it was, our celestial home—a shimmering orb pulsing with life, floating in space, laced with eddies of wispy white clouds. Oceans, grasslands, and forests glistened in blues and greens. Deserts, too hot for cloud cover, sat sunbaked and blood red. There were no borders.

The catalog was an eclectic field guide and operating manual for building the new culture, with reviews and excerpts of such "essential tools" as the works of Buckminster Fuller and Carlos Castaneda, the *I Ching,* the *Dome Cookbook,* and *Survival Arts of the Primitive Paiutes;*

how-to guides on keeping bees, making tepees, and building solar panels; tips on where to get the best calculators, desert moccasins, kerosene lamps, and baby carriers; and much more.

Editor Stewart Brand proclaimed his publication's purpose on the first page: "We are as gods and might as well get good at it." I took that statement to mean that humans, among all of God's creatures, have extraordinary, awesome, and perhaps inordinate powers to affect the rest of life on earth, for good or for ill. Having so much power, Brand seemed to be saying, we really ought to learn to use it wisely. I thought it was a statement of humility, not hubris.

By some estimates as many as one million young people moved from the cities to the countryside in the late sixties and early seventies—by far the largest mass urban exodus in U.S. history. Many more began living communally in the cities. I turned on (to LSD and magic mushrooms), tuned in (mostly to the Beatles, Ravi Shankar, and the Jefferson Airplane), and dropped out (of architecture school). I moved to Boston, joined a commune, and began learning to cook natural foods and studying Chinese medicine. Some historians call this period of political, cultural, and religious ferment America's Third Great Awakening. Student radicals and hippie dropouts were united in our rejection of techno-industrial society. The old rules no longer applied. We would build a new world—more egalitarian, more peaceful, and more free—with love.

By the mid- to late seventies, many boomers, including me, had married, taken jobs, and begun families. Many of us lacked the practical skills needed to live on the land or the social graces necessary to thrive communally. Soon some of us grew despairing or cynical about politics and civic engagement. Were we thwarted by the system, or had we simply been distracted by the dailiness of life? Some of us forgot our original vision, forgot our purpose, forgot our revolution of love.

In the early eighties, despite Ronald Reagan's union busting and trickle-down economics, I began seeing signs of hope. I felt I was glimpsing an emerging culture, one that continued and extended the countercultural vision of the sixties and seventies. I believed that the love revolution was alive and well, and growing. I could see its tendrils reaching to the margins of the mainstream media on the pages of my favorite alternative press periodicals. I wanted to introduce its disparate denizens to each other, to help make this culture conscious of itself and accessible to the rest of the world.

For months I cast about, trying to determine what kind of magazine the world needed and wanted. It would need to bridge the New Left and the New Age, I decided, and would aspire to be, like the Greens in Germany, "neither left nor right, but in front." It would be a general-interest magazine in an era of specialization, giving readers perspective and connecting them with others who were actively engaged in building a new world. Each issue would profile and appraise the people and ideas behind America's movements for personal growth and social change. The articles would be "by, for, and about people who are making a difference" and would "help readers stay informed and get involved in the emerging culture."

In February 1984, I launched *Utne Reader*. By November 1986 the word *yuppie* had entered the vernacular, to describe self-absorbed young urban professionals who had sold out their sixties and seventies concerns in favor of good pay, hip fashion, and "green" consumerism. But I had hope. I wanted to believe the love revolution was impervious to co-optation.

I began asking *Utne Reader* readers, "Have you given up?" Did they still care about what was going on in the world? Did they still believe they could make a difference? To what extent did they act on their concerns?

We conducted a survey of our readers in 1986 with the help of experts from the Stanford Research Institute and *American Demographics* magazine. We learned that they were among America's most civically active and influential citizens, and that they had most definitely not given up. In fact, the generosity with which they gave their time and money to the causes and issues that concerned them appeared to be almost boundless.

We ran the same "Have You Given Up?" survey again in July 2013, twenty-seven years later, this time inviting Gen X-ers and millennials to respond as well as boomers.

In the introduction to the 2013 survey, we asked: "Did you march in Selma in the '60s, or serve with the Special Forces in Vietnam? Did you door-knock for McGovern, or hang out on a hippie commune in the '70s? Or both? Did you work for the PIRGs in the '80s, Greenpeace in the '90s, and against the invasion of Iraq in the '00s? Or did you spend that time trading junk bonds on Wall Street? No matter what your age, even if you weren't a glimmer in your parents' imagination until the turn of the millennium, if you're old enough to read this, let us know what you're thinking about today."

Again, the research showed that *Utne Reader* respondents hadn't given up. But the *motivation* for their social and environmental activism had changed. Achieving a more just, peaceful, and sustainable world, which most boomers believed was possible and even likely back in the sixties and seventies, seemed naïve by 2013. The very idea of progress was in retreat. Most activists felt like they had their fingers in the dike. They were working to delay imminent climate collapse, slow the spread of handguns, and rein in Wall Street. They were trying to forestall the spread of GMOs, narrow the gap between the rich and poor, and avert the collapse of civilization caused by climate chaos, aka "the Great Disruption." They went about their community activism not so much to achieve a vision of a better world, but simply because what they were doing felt like the right thing to do. They were no longer trying to build a new age. They'd joined a bucket brigade.

"I have no illusions that life is getting better anymore," said seventy-year-old Bryce Hamilton, who was a Peace Corps volunteer in the sixties and a founder of Earth Day in 1970. "In fact I'm pretty sure things are going downhill fast. But I'm not giving up. My children and grandchildren and future generations are my motivation now."

That was in 2013. Since then things have only gotten worse. Consider the evidence:

Since the first Earth Day in 1970, human beings have killed off between a quarter and a third of all the world's nonhuman life, including 25 percent of all land-based species, 28 percent of marine species, and over 25 percent of Arctic wildlife. That's in less than fifty years.

Meanwhile, humans have cut down half of the world's forests, destroyed half of the planet's topsoil, and acidified *all* of the world's oceans. Ice sheets in Greenland and the Antarctic are melting at accelerating rates, far faster than predicted even last year. Sixty percent of the world's insects have disappeared. Extinction rates of all species are currently between a hundred and a thousand times higher than they would likely be were humans not around.

Add to these depressing environmental statistics the growth of the human population, which has doubled since 1970, to over 7.5 billion people. Of these 7.5 billion, eighty individuals own half the world's wealth, while the bottom 80 percent currently hold just 5.5 percent of the world's wealth. And the three richest people in the United States—Jeff Bezos, Bill Gates, and Warren Buffett—own as much wealth as the bottom half of the U.S. population, or 160 million people.

We have changed the world irrevocably, and we ourselves are changing in ways I could not have imagined in 1970. The breakdown of civic discourse, the intolerance on all sides of the political spectrum, xenophobia, the attack on civil liberties, the rolling back of social and environmental protections, the invasion of our privacy by corporations and government via digital technology—these and other outrages pushed me over some invisible edge into genuine despair. Not long after Donald Trump's election I realized that if Hillary Clinton had been elected, even if Bernie Sanders had, we'd still be rushing headlong over a cliff. That's when I gave up.

But author Derrick Jensen says that giving up hope is a good thing. "Hope is what keeps us chained to the system . . . that is causing the destruction of the Earth . . . ," he writes. "To hope for some result means you have given up any agency concerning it."

Once I'd given up hope, despair sometimes overtook me. At such times I could not locate myself. Nothing held. Long-denied, painful feelings insisted on being noticed. I searched for something, anything, with which to distract and busy myself—a goal, some direction, the promise of a worthy accomplishment (or at least a diverting amusement). Anything to avoid the cognitive dissonance.

Author Joanna Macy describes what she calls despair and empowerment work. "Just as grief work is a process by which bereaved persons unblock their numbed energies by acknowledging and grieving the loss of a loved one, so do we all need to unblock our feelings of despair about our threatened planet and the possible demise of our species. Until we do, our power of creative response will be crippled." Or, as Jensen writes, "When hope dies, action begins."

In my state of hopelessness, I was surprised to occasionally find myself feeling feelings that seemed very much like hope. Hope when I met young people learning to use their hands to plant, cook, build, make art, and heal. Hope at the birth of my grandchildren, and the children of strangers and friends. Hope when I met young writers who were searching for words that serve life.

Now I know that these feelings were not hope at all. They were something else entirely. This book is the story of my lifelong search for hope, how I lost it, and what I found on the other side that keeps me going and sustains me in my darkest moments. Perhaps I can help you get to the other side of hope too. I hope so.

HIPPIE
DROPOUT

1

ALL YOU NEED IS LOVE

I was born on August 6, 1946, the first anniversary of the dropping of the atomic bomb on Hiroshima. The Bomb detonated the Baby Boom, the largest and most privileged of American generations. I grew up in an era of unprecedented affluence and security made possible by America's unprecedented economic and military might. Our

Utne family (*left to right*): Bob Jr., Mom, Mary, Dad, Tom, and me (Rick)

privilege and safety were products of things we could not see, or chose not to.

Every year, when the new car models came out, my parents assembled our family for a photo in the driveway of our suburban ranch home, one of about fifty houses on Ridgewood Lane, all of them built just after World War II. We gathered in front of our new Buick station wagon. My older brother, Bob, younger brother, Tom, and baby sister, Mary, and I, along with our parents, all beamed for the camera. We looked like a happy, successful, all-American family. We were well-dressed, well-scrubbed, and healthy. We had a three-bedroom ranch house with attached garage, memberships in St. Michael's Lutheran Church, the St. Paul Athletic Club, and the Town & Country Golf Club. We recorded family holidays on reel-to-reel audiotape and said grace over dinner and our prayers at bedtime. We were living the postwar American Dream.

Our neighbors did the same. Everyone smiled and said nice things. They all appeared to be happy tending their new homes along the lanes and cul-de-sacs of suburbia.

Our home was in Roseville, Minnesota, a suburb of Minneapolis and Saint Paul, located exactly halfway between the equator and the North Pole. A boulder with a plaque marking the forty-fifth parallel sits not far from our front door. The terrain in this part of the world is called *oak savanna*—broad expanses of rolling grassland and teeming wetlands, flecked with wildflowers, ribboned with meandering rivers and streams, and studded with clusters of oak, birch, and maple. It's an "in between" zone, a liminal space between the moist broadleaf forests of the eastern United States, which end in Minnesota, and the drier great prairies of the west, which begin here.

Water comes right up out of the ground in most parts of Minnesota. Springs flow into creeks that converge into streams that grow into mighty rivers. The state is the headwaters of North America, the source of rivers that flow in three directions to three separate oceans. The place where the state's two largest rivers, the Mississippi and the Minnesota, come together is known to the indigenous Dakota Indians as Bdote. Some Dakota consider it the center of the universe, the place where the first humans emerged from their underwater realm.

In one of my earliest memories I'm standing alone in our front yard. It's a soft midsummer evening. The sun has just set and everything glows in the shadowless twilight. Surveying my realm, I raise my arms high, hands splayed up and out, and declare out loud, "I'm Rickey Utne. I'm seven years old. And I'm ALIVE!"

My friends and I spent every moment we could on, in, and around the swamp that lay beside our neighborhood. This was where we floated on our makeshift raft, setting off through cattails and milkweed to cross what we called "the Western Sea." The swamp was where we caught and released painted turtles and garter snakes, dodged fluty red-winged blackbirds, plugged our noses when the green algae turned fetid in the dog days of August, built tree forts and sank knee-deep in the gooey black mud. We told each other to watch out for drop-offs and quicksand. One false step and we might disappear forever. We gazed into those dark waters and glimpsed the mysterious underworld that lay just beneath the surface of our lives.

One hot August day when I was ten years old Butch Seymour made a butterfly net. Soon all the kids made butterfly nets. As if on cue, a massive migration of monarch butterflies descended on our neighborhood. Thousands of shimmering orange and black mariposas alighted on our three backyard apple trees. We screamed and howled as we ran from tree to tree, swinging wildly. I must have caught a dozen butterflies with a single swipe.

A few weeks later, a gigantic swarm of green darner dragonflies filled the sky in every direction as high as the clouds. Unlike the regal, silent monarchs, this zigzagging horde made a loud droning buzz—like fast-moving, now-hovering, now-darting, four-winged berserkers.

My bedroom was in the basement, and the only light came in through what we called a window well, which looked like a backlit terrarium at ceiling level. One day my friend Jeff and I were playing in my room when we thought we noticed something moving in the sand of the window well, so we went outside to investigate. That was when

I met my first salamander. There must have been four or five of them. We were both excited and scared, and we dared each other to pick one up. I went first, digging my fingers into the cool sand. The little dragons with their darting tongues and smooth skin moved slowly and were easy to catch.

But, of course, these salamanders were out of place. Their home was under attack. They were refugees escaping from the giant dump trucks and the earth grader that had come to fill in our swamp, covering it with truckload after truckload of gravel and dirt until it simply wasn't there anymore.

Later that day, around sundown Jeff and I went to the construction site. We were noble knights. Our duty was to defend the realm. The earth grader, with its fiery, smoke-belching exhaust pipe rising above the cab, was an invading dragon. We threw mud balls into the dragon's black maw until it was filled to the top. We rode home on our steeds, our deed accomplished.

The next morning I was in my classroom at summer Bible camp when the police arrived, lights flashing. Everyone looked out the window, excited to see what had happened. But the policemen came to our classroom door. They said they were looking for Rickey Utne and Jeff Hilger. We were apprehended like criminals and put into the back of the squad car. I was sure we were going to jail, but they drove instead to my house. As soon as we pulled up, my mother came outside, obviously expecting us. She led me by the proverbial ear into the house before what seemed like a throng of gawking neighbors. I was humiliated. Mom made me write "I will never destroy other people's property" a hundred times. But the lesson didn't take. That may have been my first act of protest against the status quo that so mindlessly kills life. Or, to be more accurate, my first attempt to let my life be a "counter friction to stop the Machine," as Henry David Thoreau put it in his essay on civil disobedience. For better or worse, it wouldn't be my last.

By the time I was twelve years old, I thought most humans lived the way my family did, or if they lived differently than us, that we had it better somehow, and we deserved it. We were Americans, after all. We had all the modern conveniences, we believed in progress, we were living the American dream. I didn't know then what I was missing. But I do now.

I was on the baseball team, participated in Boy Scouts, and attended church catechism classes. But the adults leading those activities were just like my parents; they had other priorities—their jobs, their parties, cigarettes and highballs, each other. They wanted to enjoy the postwar perquisites they felt they'd earned. We kids were mostly left to roam our suburban environs on our own. At best, that meant we could discover the world for ourselves, and, at worst, it meant that no one was paying any attention to us, let alone passing down any real wisdom about how to live. Thus began my unease with the American dream.

The Age of the Machine, aka the industrial age, began in the late eighteenth and early nineteenth centuries. William Blake called the Machine "the Beast," and D. H. Lawrence called it "the insentient iron world . . . the Mammon of mechanized greed," declaring it "ready to destroy whatever did not conform." The Machine is anti-life.

By the mid-twentieth century, with the dropping of atomic bombs on Hiroshima and Nagasaki, the techno-industrial edition of the machine age had kicked into high gear. That's when nuclear power plants began to proliferate. The interstate highway system sprawled across the continent, gobbling up entire urban neighborhoods and replacing fertile farmland with suburban developments and "junkspace." Public education was made universal and compulsory. Petrochemicals fueled the generation of energy and the production of food. Plastics and antibiotics became central to our agriculture and healthcare systems. Carbon dioxide filled the atmosphere and began to melt the permafrost in the Far North and glaciers worldwide. Sea levels rose, forests declined, and deserts expanded. Global mass extinction of species at unprecedented levels would soon follow.

In 2012, a team of Stanford University scientists and scholars wrote, "Humanity's impact on the Earth is now so profound that a new geological epoch—the Anthropocene—needs to be declared." The previous epoch, the Holocene, was the twelve-thousand-year period following the last ice age. The new epoch began about 1950, they said, and was likely to be defined by plastic pollution, soot from power stations, concrete, the radioactive elements dispersed across the planet by nuclear bomb tests, and even the bones left by the global proliferation of domestic chickens. "The Holocene must give way to the Anthropocene," the experts declared. "Living as we are through the last years of one Earth epoch, and the birth of another—we belong to 'Generation Anthropocene.'"

At the time, I wasn't aware of any of this. My attention was on more innocent pursuits. I wanted to be a knight in shining armor. *Prince Valiant* was my favorite comic strip in those days. Sunday mornings, while the rest of my family slept, my little brother and I would bring the newspaper in from the front steps and spread out the comic section on the bathroom floor next to the heat vent. We spent hours there, poring over our favorite comics and then drawing together. Tom would draw *Popeye* and *Peanuts* characters while I copied images of towering castles and knights in battle. Eventually I created my own scenes. Arthur was my king, and Guinevere my lady. Sir Lancelot and

Prince Valiant (center) and his charges: Tom and Mary

Gawain were my compatriots, and my guide and teacher with the magic wand was, of course, Merlin.

I see now I was wanting something I could not name, feeling that something was missing. The grown-ups didn't seem happy. My father drank, argued with my mother, and fell asleep under his newspapers. My mother put herself down at every turn. What exactly was the purpose of it all? And so I immersed myself in another world, a world tinged with romance and codes of honor, where knights risked their lives to keep the kingdom safe and didn't spend their days selling insurance and drinking martinis.

I was searching for my Merlin, for someone who would be my guide and counsel, my confidant. Someone who could teach me the chivalrous virtues, like courage, generosity, and courtesy, and how to be a "real man." Someone I could talk to about life, death, and things "over yonder." Someone who would show me how to make a difference in the world.

What was it about America at that time? In another country, or another era of history, kids our age would have been preparing for some kind of initiation—some arduous rite of passage from childhood to adolescence. Many Native American youths must fulfill their vision quests at this age, and Jewish boys and girls still participate in bar and bat mitzvahs. But these are the exceptions in America today, which no longer honors the initiation rites of the past or, in most cases, even remembers them.

In Native American societies, initiation rituals help candidates find and confirm their unique gifts and accomplish essential learning tasks. They are tested—often through fasting in the wilderness. When they complete their initiation, they take, or are given, a new name. Initiation doesn't just help young people become adults, it enables them to become more fully human as they learn what they have to contribute to society and find their place in the world.

But the relentless beat of the techno-industrial system has made traditional forms of initiation an endangered cultural relic. The twentieth and twenty-first centuries may be the first period in human history in which the majority of the grown-ups in the world have passed into adulthood without the experience of initiation—without any formal guidance from an elder. The Dakota had once camped in the area now occupied by the ranch houses and fenced-in backyards of Ridgewood Lane and may well have conducted their initiation ceremonies on the land that had become my neighborhood. If so, they were now long gone.

Where were the elders in midcentury, Midwestern middle-class America? The adults in my life didn't want to mentor or even supervise us. They were preoccupied with fitting into and advancing the Machine. There was no real community for us to be initiated into anyway—just an expanding suburban sprawl connected by automobiles and television sets.

My father, the grandson of Norwegian farmers, had met my mother, an immigrant from Norway's Far North, in an elevator in St. Paul, Minnesota. They fell in love, got married, and were supposed to live happily ever after. We kids were bit players, part of the entourage, cute and lovable character actors. We had speaking parts, but not many lines. We were there for our parents' greater glory.

I knew Mom and Dad fought from time to time, but their fights weren't knock-down, drag-out battles. More bickering than fighting, I thought. Not something to get divorced over. To me they were the golden couple, the stars of the Hollywood success story that was supposed to be their lives.

In retrospect, there were times that should have been tip-offs. Once I found Dad asleep on the foldout couch in the den, his face bruised and swollen, his mouth and forehead stitched and bandaged. He was a mess, not the dashing club champion and civic leader I was supposed to be proud of. I wanted to shake him awake to find out what happened, to ask him if he was an "alcoholic." But the word was too dangerous to say out loud, and I was too shocked to disturb him.

I spent a lot of time during adolescence pedaling my older brother's three-speed Schwinn as fast as I could. It was green and heavy, with fat white-sidewall tires, and it was stuck in high gear, which was just what I wanted. I needed to feel the resistance. I rode for miles at a time on my own and wouldn't allow my legs to stop churning—no coasting, no sitting fully on the seat, even. I wanted to feel the burn of nonstop pedaling in my muscles. I had to keep moving to escape the looping thoughts inside my brain, which were more agonizing to me than any physical pain.

I ran cross-country in high school, even though I hated it, because running helped me escape those looping thoughts. The movie *The Loneliness of the Long Distance Runner* had come out during my junior year. I loved how the working-class star found peace in running, and how he outran all the upper-class kids in the film's big race only to stop defiantly just short of the finish line, letting the private-school kids win, thus giving his reform-school guards and authorities the "Up yours!" in the end.

By the fall of the next year, I was the only senior on the team, so the coach made me the captain, which meant I had to run every race. I'd fantasize about stumbling into potholes and ending my pain. But I could never let myself be so cowardly.

Eventually, the pain became a kind of solace, the stitch in my side a longed-for marker, something I had to endure to get to the other side of, after which there was a zone of painless, flowing freedom.

Another strategy for escaping my racing brain was denial. I was afraid that if I had bad thoughts they would come true, so I tried not to have any. Allowing a depressing thought into my head increased the likelihood that it would manifest as real. For example, noticing that my father spent more time on the golf course than he did with us, or that my mother would stand at the kitchen sink and cry when she didn't know I was there. This was a dangerous road to go down. What could I do about either? I practiced being hopeful instead and pretended not to notice when anything was amiss.

In time, my nervous system became wired for denial. I knew it in my muscles and bones, down to my very cells. Looking back, I suspect that many Americans were learning to do the same.

The summer I turned thirteen my parents separated, and my father moved to Montana to try to pull his life together. My mother

Before they met: Robert Utne and Anne Hanssen

sold our suburban rambler and found us a cheap apartment in a newly constructed three-story building behind one of the first McDonald's franchises in America.

Had I been raised a Masai, one of the nomadic cattle herders of Kenya and Tanzania, I'd have spent these years preparing for my initiation with the guidance of tribal elders, learning oratorical skills, animal husbandry, a sense of brotherhood, and how to protect the land, cattle, and people of my community.

As it was, in Roseville, Minnesota, I just felt rootless and lost. But I was not alone in those feelings. This was where a lot of the young people of my generation found themselves—abandoned by country, culture, and community. We were faced with lives dictated by the needs and limitations of techno-industrial society . . . the Machine. Could we remake the Machine? Or must we simply find a way to fit ourselves into it? No wonder we would soon turn to the wisdom teachers and gurus of other cultures to make sense of our lives and to give us direction and meaning.

2

THE FUTURE IS IN YOUR HANDS

One day during my senior year of high school, our math teacher didn't show up to class. The bell rang, and the minutes stretched on and on. Finally the door opened, and he walked slowly and deliberately into the classroom. The horsing around had ceased, and everyone was silent now. "I have some terrible news," he said. His face contorted into an expression I couldn't read, as if in his repertoire of expressions there was no look to accompany what he was about to say. Finally he just spat it out. "President Kennedy has been shot."

The shift was so incongruous and unexpected that one of my classmates actually laughed. There was a moment of dead silence after that. Then most of the girls burst into tears. I tumbled into a confounding swirl of numbness; it felt like being sucked down a giant drain.

As soon as high school ended, I decided to join the Marines. I wanted to help save the world, like my father and my older brother, Bob. Dad had skippered a ship in the navy during World War II. Bob had heard President Kennedy's call to "ask not what your country can do for you, ask what you can do for your country," and he'd dropped out of college to join the Peace Corps and serve in Gabon, a territory in the former French Equatorial Africa. Bob wrote me, telling me that he'd met Albert Schweitzer, the Nobel Peace Prize laureate, physician, and author, at his hospital in Lambaréné and that Schweitzer had taken him aside and said to him, "Young man, the future of the world is in your hands." Schweitzer died a year later.

If I wanted my life to matter, if I wanted to make a difference in the world, now was the time to act. I needed to prove myself, to show how much courage I had. Wasn't that why so many young men of my generation had enlisted? It felt like the only rite of passage allowed to us anymore—the only way to become a man.

My friend Ed was going to sign up, too. The recruiter on the University of Minnesota campus had promised we could choose our assignment and serve in the same unit, and that when we got out our college tuition would be paid for. Which meant that joining the military was both the patriotic *and* the practical thing to do.

I wrote to Bob to brag about my plans. Bob wired back, "Don't you dare join the Marines. If you do I'll track you down wherever you are and beat the shit out of you."

Just try! I thought. *I'll be a lean, mean fighting machine by then.* But Bob got my attention. I began wondering if he knew something I didn't about Vietnam.

Building schools in Gabon: Bob Utne, Jr., in T-shirt, front row, center

Apparently Ed did. He had a Plan B, it turned out—an alternative to being my buddy in the U.S. Marines. When his acceptance letter arrived from Harvard, I was cast adrift. I wasn't headed to the Ivies, or any other college for that matter. I hadn't even applied. At the last minute, in late August, just two weeks before school began, I scrambled and got accepted to Gustavus Adolphus, a small Lutheran liberal arts college in a sleepy town in southern Minnesota. They even gave me a decent scholarship, which was important to me because I was proudly (and defiantly) paying the tuition myself. Screw my parents, I thought. Let them fight over money. I would pay my own way.

In an effort to initiate myself into whatever was coming in this next phase of my life (or, in the absence of any initiation, simply to reinvent myself), I began my freshman year at Gustavus as Eric. I no longer wanted to be Rick or Rickey. I started smoking Erik cigars, the ads for which trumpeted, in bold type, "Erik is here!" and featured a glamorous reclining model and the caption "The most interesting idea from Scandinavia since blondes."

Among the required courses at Gustavus was Religion 101, in which I had zero interest. But in that class I found an artsy crowd of Bohemian wannabes just like me. Many were "PKs," and these preachers' kids were by far the most creative, most complicated characters on campus. We spent much of our time trying to get high on morning-glory seeds, acting out scenes from James Bond movies, and breaking into the faculty kitchen at night to steal steaks, which we'd cook and serve to the whole dorm in the wee hours of the morning.

I ended up getting kicked out of Gustavus for participating in an act of protest that turned into vandalism. The college had announced that we could no longer store our sofas and chairs in the dormitories over the summer. Outraged by this terrible injustice, a group of us gathered every piece of old furniture we could find and built a pile twenty feet long, ten feet wide, and ten feet high in the dorm's courtyard. Then we doused it with gasoline and torched it.

As it burned, our act of protest got out of hand. Some onlookers added wooden pop crates, then dormitory lounge furniture. The flames leaped seventy feet high. When the firefighters and police arrived, some of the dorm's residents briefly held them at bay with a barrage of cherry bombs tossed from the dormitory roof. The next day we were all invited, one by one, into the president's office. I admitted that I was one of the instigators and was told I would not be welcome back in the fall.

Perhaps I should have joined the Marines after all. Perhaps all this destructive behavior was just my lame attempt to initiate myself in some way. It seems the closest young people in the West come to initiation these days is self-initiation by engaging in sex, drugs, and high-risk and often death-defying activities like reckless driving, adrenaline sports, and gang-related crime.

And then there's war. Boot camp can be initiatory. So can combat. For many veterans, basic training and war are the most transformative experiences of their lives. There's nothing like facing death to help one realize how precious life is.

Just about every religious tradition and civilization of the past practiced rites that brought initiates face-to-face with their mortality and most indigenous cultures today still do. Initiation is critical for the creation and continuance of culture. Through it, essential knowledge about survival is transmitted from one generation to the next, and one's place in the community is claimed and confirmed. According to author Karen Armstrong, "The tribe cannot afford the luxury of allowing an adolescent to 'find himself' Western-style."

Author Malidoma Somé was initiated in the ancestral traditions of his people, the Dagara tribe of West Africa. He writes, "For me, initiation opened the door to understanding the sacred relationship between children and old people, between fathers and their adolescent sons, between mothers and daughters."

Having abandoned initiation, our society has difficulty leading adolescents to adulthood. Robert Bly asks, "Why do we have so many boys and so few men?"

Looking back on my own uninitiated youth, I see I was clueless about my life's purpose and alienated from "authority." It seemed the only path besides the military was, at age nineteen, losing my virginity. After two years of college waiting for the right girl and the right moment, I was ready. Perhaps if I joined the Peace Corps like Bob, I'd finally find the girl who'd initiate me into manhood.

3

CLOSER THAN KIN

In the spring of 1966, shortly after the furniture fire, a letter arrived in my Gustavus mailbox. This was unusual. I didn't get much mail. It was from my step-grandmother, the writer Brenda Ueland. She was the wise elder I'd been searching for in my adolescence. We had become close in the years after she married my mother's father, the artist Sverre Hanssen, when I was twelve.

Brenda wrote to tell me that she had a special feeling about me, "a sympathy," she said, and that she could see me with her "X-ray eye."

"I sometimes feel you are going through some sad troubles and perplexing questions—as all good, clear and honorable people do," Brenda wrote. "If ever you need affection, let me know."

She signed her letter, "Yours forever, Brenda."

How did Brenda know I was going through some "sad troubles and perplexing questions"? Could she see what was going on in me even when I couldn't?

I was nineteen years old, and Brenda was seventy-five at the time. Sverre and Brenda's "five-year brawl of a marriage," as Brenda called it, had ended a couple years earlier when she threw him out for daring to question her about how much she'd paid for the green beans. The rest of my family said, "Good riddance," but I wasn't about to let the one genuinely wise person I knew in the world slip out of my life. Brenda and I stayed close.

Though I only saw her a couple times a year, Brenda had a way of listening to me that always made me feel seen and heard. Even if she did most of the talking, which was usually the case, I always came away from my sessions with her feeling good about myself, and clearer about whatever issue was at hand. "Be grand, be mighty, be chivalrous," she'd say, as if sending me out to slay dragons or rescue damsels. It was heady stuff for a college kid, but it was strangely empowering, too.

Brenda Ueland, portrait by Sverre Hanssen; Sverre and Brenda

I wrote her back immediately that spring, asking if I could see her. I told her I was considering leaving college to join the Peace Corps and I needed her advice.

I showed up at Brenda's house in Minneapolis at five o'clock the following Saturday night, as we had agreed. The scowling portrait of her father, painted by Sverre, cautioned me as I let myself in through the front door as if to say, "Enter at your own risk."

The television was turned on when I arrived, as it often was, more as dull background noise than as the object of her attention. "Fat tel-evangelists!" she'd say, adjusting her hearing aid. "How can anyone take these people seriously? If you've got a potbelly on your body, you've got a potbelly on your soul. You know that much, don't you, Eric?"

Brenda was wearing dark-blue sailor pants, heavy brogues, a white cotton shirt, a red bow tie, and a white terry-cloth sweatshirt with bright-red vertical stripes, washed so much that there were holes in it and the sleeves were frayed. Her hair, tousled and gray, made her look like an eccentric scientist, or perhaps an Irish poet.

Brenda turned off the TV and asked if I wanted a cup of tea. After she'd put the kettle on, she sat down on her well-worn sofa, and, with a conspiratorial smile, launched the evening's conversation.

"Rickey, sit here, next to me," she said, patting the cushion next to her. "Tell me a-l-l about it."

"I've just gotten my acceptance letter from the Peace Corps," I told Brenda. "They've offered me the position of Physical Education Advisor and Organizer in Bogotá, Colombia. I'm thinking of going. I want to do something with my life, like Bob."

What I didn't say was that I'd just been kicked out of Gustavus for participating in the bonfire "protest" that had gotten so out of hand.

"The Peace Corps is great!" Brenda said. "You could do a lot of good in the Peace Corps. And they'd be lucky to have you." But then she surprised me. "How are things going at Gustavus?"

"OK, I guess." I replied. Then, seeing Brenda's frown, I added, "Well, actually, not so great."

This seemed to brighten Brenda's mood, not because she was happy that I was miserable, but because I was finally getting real. The kettle was whistling, so she got up and made us a pot of tea. When she returned to the living room, she encouraged me to continue. "Yes-s-s . . ."

"My grades are OK, but I hate the Lutheran church, and Gusta-vus is awful. Imagine a catechism that includes the line 'I am by nature sinful and unclean.' What kind of teaching is that?"

"Amen!"

"And the fraternity I joined makes its pledges memorize and recite in one breath 'Sir, I am a vile, cankerous hulk of pus-infected eruption, putridly odiferous, fiercely mucid, hatefully lymphatic, hopelessly dull, thick-skulled, muddleheaded, and generally considered brainless. A scum is a man that has been deprived of the name *man* and thereby is classified along with the gangrenous gorp, leprous half-breeds, and blubbering idiotic waterheads. . . . I am a scum, sir!' "

Brenda was horrified. "Get out of there right now!" she exclaimed, leaping up and sloshing her tea as she spoke. "That's no place for anyone. I can't imagine . . ."

I had been waiting for someone to say this. Even if I had taken the matter into my own hands and gotten myself expelled—out was out, however it happened. Gustavus would soon be a thing of my past.

"Rickey," she said, "you have some decisions to make. Let me give you some advice." She told me she was about to give a speech at her church, the First Unitarian Society of Minneapolis, then she recited it, almost verbatim. I opened the sketchbook I carried with me and began taking notes. I'd never done this before—the sketchbook was for sketches—but this felt like a lesson that really mattered, and I didn't want to miss a word.

This was the first of many notes I would take in Brenda's presence. Sometimes the writing helped me listen more intently. Other times it seemed to get in the way of being fully present to the meaning behind her words. That day it was the latter. The advice she gave would prove invaluable later, but I wasn't necessarily ready to take it all in then.

"This making of choices I have mulled over all my life," Brenda began. "The choices turn up every few minutes, every hour. 'To be or not to be.' To choose bravery or flight. To choose your natural carefree, rollicking self or your cautious, pussyfooting self."

I was writing as fast as I could.

"We must try to make wonderful choices," Brenda continued, pausing for a moment to allow my pen to catch up with her words.

She was standing now, looking across the room as if she were in a lecture hall, her voice raised so those in the back row could hear her.

"Now, no one said this was easy. For one thing, we don't know who we are."

Brenda stepped forward a few paces, then turned to face me.

"I often feel that I am about seventeen different people. So the question becomes: How to single out the true Brenda? I seem to be sometimes my mother, sometimes my father. Sometimes I'm a whiner, and sometimes a queen—or a slob, a simpering old lady, or a minister. A weasel or a lion."

Brenda was still holding her cup of tea. I realized now that she was rehearsing her speech. I was a willing audience. She took a sip and set it down on the TV tray in front of me.

"The point is, Rickey, we must try to find our true self, our true conscience. We must find our very center!" She pointed to her heart.

She stopped and I looked up. She was staring at me. My true self. That part had gotten through to me.

"Now, when you get to know this center, or as you approach it, it is much easier to make choices. But how to find it? That part is very hard in our cacophonous times, fractured with yelling activity, feeding, drinking, galloping, of frantic uncertainties that lead to psychiatry and booze. But you must try to find it. It is the old stuff—know thyself."

"Yes, to know myself," I said. "That's what I want." Or, I thought, maybe I want to lose myself, and my racing thoughts, in the world.

"But it takes solitude," Brenda added after a final sip of tea. "And there is none."

Brenda let that last thought hang in the air like a challenge.

I knew how to be alone. It was easy when I was a kid. My mother limited our TV time to a couple hours a week, and there were no laptops or smartphones. No social media. I could hang out for hours just daydreaming, or shooting baskets, or drawing pictures, or reading the *Encyclopedia Britannica*.

But the place I had felt most fully in solitude and yet still connected to the world around me had always been the swamp. That is where I felt closest to the thrum of life. I missed it and the way I felt when I was there.

Brenda was staring at me. Satisfied, apparently, that I was taking some of this in and not just setting it down in my notebook, finally she nodded her head.

"Gandhi's rule for himself, like so many of the saints, was to be silent for twenty-four hours one day a week—not to utter one word. That way, one is bound to look inward eventually, at which point the center begins to appear."

"These days I'm almost never alone," I blurted out. "And yet, I sometimes feel alone even when I'm with other people."

The funny thing was, I'd arrived at Brenda's that day with a plan to join the Peace Corps, but now, suddenly, I didn't trust it.

"Know that you will make dreadful mistakes with almost every choice," she was saying, seeming to read my mind. "*Hurrah!* Congratulate yourself for daring, honorable, ridiculous mistakes. Children are hampered most when their parents try to prevent them from making their most important mistakes."

I know I was. My father, mostly absent from our family even before my parents divorced, was neutral about whether I should join the Peace Corps. But my mother wanted me to study architecture at the University of Minnesota, starting the coming fall. I was interested in architecture—it combined my love of art and my aptitude for math. But I wasn't as excited about becoming an architect as Mom was in having me become one. The more she pushed me to go, the less interested I became.

Brenda continued, anticipating my thoughts.

"There are tests to submit your choices to. The original great test was the Ten Commandments. Still very good."

Brenda sat down on the couch and slung one knee up on the cushion between us so she could look me in the eye.

"I have my own two commandments to propose to the world, and curiously enough they are not stressed in the Bible. They aren't even included in the seven deadly sins."

She paused to let me ponder what they could be.

"No cruelty. And no lying," she said, then added, "That would take care of everything—ignorance-inducing newspapers, advertising, war, stealing, murder, vivisection, adultery."

Could I really come to know myself, find my true self, by simply not lying and not being cruel? It sounded too easy.

"The true viciousness of adultery is not the romantic love—who would object to Tristan and Isolde? But it's the cruelty and the lying, for lying is bad for the liar and an injustice and a cruelty to the person lied to."

"I will never lie and never be cruel—ever," I vowed to myself, ready to follow Brenda's Two Commandments if it meant I wouldn't become my father.

"And if my commandments prevailed, there would emerge a world without psychiatrists, salesmen, or nervous breakdowns."

That would eliminate half of my parents' friends, I thought, and immediately began wondering how committed I was to telling the truth. I often lied simply to avoid making people feel uncomfortable. Could I be brave enough to tell the truth? I hadn't told Brenda about being expelled or shared my fantasies involving the Peace Corps and finally meeting the girl of my dreams.

"So, in conclusion, Rickey, remember this: Avoid in your choices all cruelty and lying. After that I say, 'Be bad or good, whichever is best for you.'"

Brenda stood up. "Here endeth the first lesson," she said, as she gave me a firm handshake goodbye. A minute later, sketchbook in hand, I was standing outside the door.

I left feeling buoyant and resolute—or, rather, thinking that I should feel buoyant and resolute. The truth was, I was confused. Brenda had made choosing the right next step seem so simple, but I was still juggling the pros and cons of each path. I decided then and there, on Brenda's front steps, to take a leap, even if it turned out to be one of Brenda's ridiculous total mistakes. I would decline the offer from the Peace Corps. I would go to the University of Minnesota School of Architecture after all.

But the truth was, although I was certain of my decision, I hadn't a clue why I had made it. Joining the Peace Corps seemed like a great adventure, whereas going to architecture school was, on its surface at least, simply doing what my mother wanted me to do.

Only much later did I realize I'd overlooked a crucial consideration, although a part of me—maybe the deepest part—was aware of it at the time. Staying in America meant I could keep seeing Brenda.

4

THE SUMMER OF LOVE

In the fall of 1966 I enrolled in the University of Minnesota's School of Architecture. By the following summer, fellow architecture student Toby and I shared a hippie crash pad. The ramshackle three-bedroom cottage was the last house on a dead-end street that ran straight uphill and ended just below the Witch's Hat water tower, in a neighborhood called Prospect Park. It sat smack dab on the border between St. Paul and Minneapolis. The walls of the living room were covered with Grateful Dead posters, along with big swatches of paisley-printed cloth. The furniture was late provincial Goodwill—worn couches and pillows tossed about the floor.

There was no escaping the loud music banging off the walls and heavy breathing reverberating behind our bedroom doors. The music tended toward Toby's tastes: Frank Zappa and the Mothers of Invention, Velvet Underground, and Jefferson Airplane's Grace Slick singing "Feed your head." I preferred more exotic fare, like Ravi Shankar on the sitar and Leo Kottke playing the twelve-string guitar.

One day Toby and his girlfriend, Cindy, and a girl we called "Crazy Harriet" and I decided to take LSD together before we went to one of Minneapolis's first love-ins. Toby procured the acid, which, according to his supplier, was none other than Purple Owsley, the very best LSD in the world, made by San Francisco's legendary trip master Owsley Stanley himself.

We dropped the acid as *Sgt. Pepper* played on Toby's record player, and by the last cut of the album, "A Day in the Life," I was atop a high plateau, flanked by all of humanity on either side and behind me. We were, all of us, kings and queens. We kneeled together, as if in prayer, looking down from the precipitous ledge at a vast panorama, a great river wending through the valley below us, dotted with towns and villages on either side, surrounded by small farms and vast forests and framed by wild prairies and deserts, with cities and mountains in the distance and oceans beyond them. We were at one with all creation. And we always had been and always would be. This was the natural state. It just took a little help from my friends, and the LSD, to be conscious and aware of it, to be lifted out of our mundane, everyday thinking. This is what we mean when we say higher consciousness. The energy that coursed through our bodies and that animates and illuminates all things is life itself.

I had not felt this deeply alive since an unexpected moment in church when I was thirteen years old. Our pastor was a creepy guy with puckered lips and a waxy sheen. During his sermon on Easter Sunday, when he was talking about Christ's sacrifice, how he died for our sins, I realized that I knew what he was going to say before he said it. This boggled my mind. I'd never imagined that such a thing could happen.

He wasn't reciting Scripture, which I might have memorized, nor was he saying anything I'd ever heard him say before. But I knew which words were coming as—or even a half beat before—he said them. I couldn't believe it at first, so I tested it. I whispered the words to myself, under my breath, so no one could hear me. Sure enough, Pastor Lawrence and I spoke the same words in unison. It was as if I had tapped into another reality beyond the one I normally experienced. I was in the zone. In the flow of life. It lasted about a minute, but it really shook me up. I didn't know what to make of it, but I knew that it was the point of everything.

As the final chord of "A Day in the Life" sounded, we on the cliff all rose together, lifting our arms and reaching toward the heavens.

The chord, which seemed to last an eternity, was a sound for which the only lyric could be "Ta-da." It was the sound of universal peace, harmony, and oneness with all creation.

It was a gloriously sunny day, and somehow I was chosen to drive, if you could call it that. We *flowed* through the streets of Minneapolis in slow motion, everything clear as crystal. I was surprised to see light radiating from everyone and everything. Passersby were iridescent. Everyone smiled. They knew we were high, and they were too, and it was all OK. Life was more than OK, it was transcendent. All was light and love.

We found over a thousand people grooving to the music when we got to Loring Park. About half of them wore love beads, their faces beaming with a luminescence only slightly amplified by Day-Glo paint. Soap bubbles wafted through the air. People were passing joints to each other. To think I could have passed all this up for coaching soccer in Bogotá, I thought. Was it possible I didn't need to leave home to change the world? Was it possible that I only needed to change my mind, to open it, expand it, and be Love?

But before we could find a place on the grass to sit down, a man with a fancy camera approached our blissful foursome and asked if he could take our picture for the local daily newspaper. Toby said, "Sure!" But I was hesitant. I felt an unexpected stab of paranoia. Who is this guy, I wondered, really? He must be FBI. I turned my back to him, and as I did, I saw a middle-aged woman a little ways off, standing in a knot of hippies. It was my mother. This was no hallucination. She was really there.

She was wearing a strapless tank top, Bermuda shorts, and gigantic Jackie Kennedy sunglasses. The only thing missing was the highball.

"Surprise!" she said, stepping toward us. "I just had to see what all the excitement was about."

All I could manage to say was "Not now, Mom, not now," as I slipped into the teeming crowd to try and get away from her.

Talk about a downer. I felt invaded. I needed psychic space and there wasn't any.

Mom (Anne H. Utne), highball in hand

Two weeks later my mother was hospitalized with a "nervous breakdown." When she told me that learning I'd taken LSD was the cause of her breakdown, I felt falsely accused, as though I'd been pushed over some invisible edge. How did she know I'd been tripping? Was I that obvious?

I hated her for putting the blame on me. She had plenty of other stresses in her life besides me—after all, she was a single mother trying to raise my younger siblings on just five hundred dollars a month. And she'd just ended a long-term love affair. At the same time, though, I couldn't help but think it might be true that I was to blame.

I hitchhiked to San Francisco in August 1967, at the tail end of what had already been dubbed the "Summer of Love." The cover story in the July 7 issue of *Time* magazine summarized the hippie philosophy as follows:

Do your own thing, wherever you have to do it and whenever you want.

Drop out. Leave society as you have known it. Leave it utterly.

Blow the mind of every straight person you can reach. Turn them on, if not to drugs, then to beauty, love, honesty, fun.

Sounded good to me.

My road mate was a bashful guitarist and Donovan look-alike. Mark and I wanted to join forces with the thousands of free-spirited souls who, like us, were questioning every political and social convention, celebrating radical honesty and creativity, and imbibing copious amounts of psychedelic substances—though not necessarily in that order. People our age wanted to remake the world from the ground up, and they wanted to start in California.

By the time we got to Montana, however, Mark and I were sick of hitchhiking. We tried to jump a freight train but were chased off by Pinkerton marshals. Outside of Seattle we caught a ride with a mortician who regaled us with stories about the gruesome things he did to cadavers. He dropped us off at three in the morning in San Francisco's Golden Gate Park. A few hours later a wild-eyed hippie woke us with an urgent "Ditch it! The *Man* is coming!" Who's "the Man"? I wondered.

We spent the next day wandering up and down Haight and Ashbury streets, getting panhandled by speed freaks, junkies, and long-skirted young women from Blue Earth, Minnesota, and Orange County, California, wearing flowers in their hair. There were burned-out hippies and winos on every corner begging for something—cigarettes, spare change, acid.

By the end of the day Mark and I had had it with Haight-Ashbury. The glazed eyes, the monosyllabic lingo, the grunginess of it all had gotten to us. "If San Francisco is the mecca of love," I told Mark, feeling disoriented and disappointed, "then I'm an infidel." The movement had become a groovy caricature of itself, I decided, hyped to death by the Machine's propaganda arm—*Time* magazine and the rest of the mainstream media. A few weeks later, neighborhood residents, led by the Diggers, would stage the Death of Hippie event, a mock funeral mourning the death of their beloved social movement, now co-opted, they said, by the "mass media."

The Diggers were a group of radical community activists who'd joined forces with members of the San Francisco Mime Troupe. They provided free food and overnight shelter to anyone who needed it and organized free concerts in Golden Gate Park. The San Francisco Diggers advocated a society as far outside of the Machine as possible, free from buying and selling and all forms of private property.

Mark and I hated San Francisco, but we were inspired by the Digger idea. Soon after getting back to Minneapolis, we started our own Digger house across Cedar Avenue from the Scholar Coffeehouse. Both the *Minneapolis Tribune* and the *St. Paul Pioneer Press* wrote stories about the place.

"We realize this is a pretty lonely world," Mark told the *Tribune*. "We want a place open to anyone who needs help in any way. We don't profess to be counselors or Ann Landers, but we'll listen.

"We feel Christ and Thoreau could have been hippies," Mark added sagely. "A hippie is not the way a person dresses, but how he *feels*. There are hippies going to work in downtown offices in pinstriped suits. They're searching for a good life, and they have enough faith in themselves and their brothers to feel they're going to make it through love."

Even with the free publicity, our Digger house lasted all of two months. When we could no longer cover the rent and food costs out of our own pockets and donations failed to materialize, we had no choice but to shut it down.

I found it hard to concentrate on my architecture studies in our hippie crash pad that autumn. I began attending meetings of the Students for a Democratic Society to learn about what was going on behind the scenes politically. Young men of all races were being sent to their deaths in Vietnam by older white men like Lyndon Johnson, Robert McNamara, and William Westmoreland. The nation's adults had abdicated all responsibility as elders, and the insatiable Machine was devouring my generation.

Many of my friends messed themselves up to avoid the draft. One showed up for his draft physical high on LSD, stripped himself naked, and did backflips all around the draft center. That was the mayor's son—he was the Minnesota state gymnastics champion—and it worked. He was hauled off to a psychiatric ward (that was the downside), but he didn't have to go to Vietnam.

Others fasted for days, and then took speed—methedrine or Dexedrine—just before showing up for their physical. The combination of amphetamines and fasting would cause the liver to leak protein into their urine, which they hoped would help them fail their physical. It worked for some, but not for others.

I considered registering as a conscientious objector because I opposed the war on moral grounds, but the one person I knew who applied for conscientious objector status got conscripted anyway and came home in a body bag. Unless you'd been raised a Quaker, belief in the sanctity of life and declarations of lifelong pacifist convictions held no weight with the draft board.

I worried incessantly about the draft. I worried about having to go through boot camp with drill sergeants shouting in my face. I worried about getting shipped to Vietnam, hauling heavy gear through jungles and swamps while getting shot at. I worried about becoming a person trained to kill. I worried about having to kill someone even more than I worried about getting killed.

I visited Dr. Louis Flynn, a psychiatrist and friend of my parents, in hopes that he would help me obtain a deferment. This seemed less self-destructive than the measures some of my friends had taken, if no less desperate.

Dr. Flynn slept through our several appointments. I couldn't tell whether this was a therapeutic technique ("Get over yourself already! Your troubles don't interest me!"), or if it was just that he was getting on in years—that he'd done a favor for my parents and squeezed me into the last available spot, the hour of his usual late-afternoon nap.

Dr. Flynn had me take the Minnesota Multiphasic Personality Inventory (MMPI). Who knew ferreting out psychopathology was even a thing our state was famous for? The test consisted of six-hundred-plus true or false questions, ranging from "I have nightmares every few nights" and "I find it hard to keep my mind on a task or job" to "I have had very peculiar and strange experiences" and "At times I feel like smashing things." The survey asked me a dozen times, in many different ways, whether God spoke to me directly ("Of course he did!") and whether I had black, tarry bowel movements ("Never noticed").

I gave up trying to be consistent and finally just answered each question as honestly as I could. The test was crazy-making, and I felt crazy taking it. In the end, I forgot about dodging the draft and just wanted to know if I might, just possibly, be truly bonkers. I was growing increasingly fearful about getting busted for drugs or drafted and sent to Vietnam.

It took forever to receive the results of my psychological evaluation. After six weeks, I decided I couldn't wait any longer. I had to flee the country. I would go to Norway. I told my family I needed to see Europe, to experience firsthand the architecture, the ancient cathedrals, the great cities and rustic villages. I'd be back in a few months, I assured them. But I really had no idea when I'd be back, or if I'd ever come back at all.

5

DROPPING OUT, TUNING IN

I flew to New York City immediately after Christmas, hoping to work my way across the Atlantic on a Norwegian freighter. When that proved impossible, I spent more than I could afford of my meager savings on an Icelandic Airlines ticket to Norway.

I rang in 1968 at the tip of Norway's Far North where I spent a month with my mother's relatives largely in the dark. From there I hitchhiked toward light—to the Rock of Gibraltar in southern Spain—and then for the next six months trekked around Europe. I wasn't alone. I had a Swedish girlfriend. She was beautiful, wild. And for a while we had a lot of fun. My expectations for Europe had probably been shaped by my earlier reading of *The Last Temptation of Christ* and *Tropic of Cancer*. Sometimes I fancied myself a devil-may-care expat, other times I feared I was an ugly American. At that stage I wasn't sure I'd ever go back. The summer of '68 was shocking. First the assassination of Martin Luther King, Jr., and then that of Robert Kennedy, during a Democratic presidential primary campaign. What kind of country would I be going back to?

When summer came, I moved to London and found a job working as an architect's draftsman. I joined a street theater group to protest the war and hung out in the legendary Watkins bookstore reading every spiritual and psychological book I could get my hands on. One day I stumbled across a copy of P. D. Ouspensky's *In Search of the Miraculous*. I devoured it, reading it from cover to cover several times over the next two weeks. I drove myself crazy trying to practice the book's central teaching, "self-remembering"—paying attention to what's going on around you and to what's going on within you at the same time.

I tried to watch myself while walking down the street, or eating a meal, as if standing a few feet outside myself, while at the same time being aware of my thoughts as I thought them. Attending a Hyde Park rock concert/love-in high on pot while trying to self-remember was both mad and maddening. Imagine listening to Jethro Tull sing "That Sunday Feeling" ("Got to clear my head so I can see . . . that old feeling won't let me be"), followed by Pink Floyd's "Intergalactic Overdrive," while trying to self-remember. I could barely think, let alone *watch* myself think. Self-remembering made me feel schizophrenic, or perhaps it revealed just how schizoid, or split, I really was.

Ouspensky's spiritual teacher was G. I. Gurdjieff. In Gurdjieff's memoir, *Meetings with Remarkable Men*, he described his own journey through far-off lands in search of enlightenment. He was aided in his quest for spiritual awakening by a number of wise teachers, whom he called "seekers of truth." I decided I needed a wise teacher, a seeker of truth.

Walking through the streets of London late one night, while trying to self-remember, I thought of the inscription at the entrance to the Temple of Apollo at Delphi: "Know Thyself."

I realized then that this was my quest. I must learn to know myself. But to know myself, I reasoned, I would need to know every conceivable self. Why? Because I felt like a blank slate—I could become anything. I needed to know the full range of possible selves, what it's like to be any and every person who has ever lived—aristocrat and beggar, dissolute rocker and religious zealot, drug addict and faith healer. I decided that my personal mantra would henceforth be "Know all possible selves."

At the end of August I finally found out that I'd been declared "unacceptable for military service," classified 4-F by my draft board, and given a psychological discharge. Had Dr. Flynn intervened on my behalf, or was I certifiably crazy? It wasn't clear. I returned to Minnesota and moved in with my mother until I could figure out what to do with my life.

After so much time on my own, it was strange being at home again. While Mom cooked delicious meals—Swedish meatballs, roasted chicken, tuna casserole, meatloaf, lamb chops, broiled halibut, homemade bread—she also tortured my younger brother and sister with criticisms.

"Mary, I'm worried about you," she said on my first night back, as she began doing the dishes while we ate. "Why do you wear those awful miniskirts? They make your legs look like sausages. You should wear long dresses that go down to your ankles, like Mama Cass. Here, have another piece of garlic bread."

Then it was Tom's turn. "Tom, I just wish you'd get your hair cut." Tom hunched over his plate, shoveling his mashed potatoes in as fast as he could while giving Mom a sideways glance.

"It makes you look like a bum," she added. "I'm embarrassed to be seen with you." She stepped to the fridge, grabbed a half-gallon bottle of milk, and turned back to Tom. "And sit up straight, for God sakes. Where's your backbone? Have some dignity!"

"More milk, Eric?" she said, turning to me and topping off my glass without waiting for a reply.

Oh boy, I thought. Here it comes. I felt a familiar tingling sensation, one I hadn't felt for months. It was like I'd bumped the crazy bone in my knee, except that the feeling engulfed my whole body. I was on high alert, yet frozen in place.

Returning the bottle to the fridge, Mom stepped back to the table so she could run her fingers through my longish hair. "You're such a fine, handsome Norwegian," she said, reaching toward me. I deflected her hand with the back of my wrist. It was a practiced move that anticipated what was coming next. "I'd be so proud of you, if only you'd finish architecture school."

I felt shredded and yet somehow complicit, caught in the familiar conundrum that Mom invariably set up: Stay put, eat her delicious food, and endure her attacks . . . or leap up and run out of the house with what was left of my self-respect still intact. I wanted to please her, to do what she wanted me to do. After all, she'd sacrificed so much to raise the four of us, mostly on her own. But the future she wanted for me and my siblings was all about fitting in and succeeding in the Machine, a system I never wanted to be a part of.

"Anything else, Eric," she added, "would be a waste of your God-given talent."

Mom was skillful. She knew how to get a rise out of each of us as surely as she could bake perfect bread. It was like a toll she expected us to pay for the meal. Listen to her or leave. If we were going to eat her food, she was entitled to extract her critical tax.

I pushed my chair back from the table and stood up.

"Cut it out!" I shouted. "I can't stand this bullshit anymore!"

I'd surprised everyone, including myself. Tom and Mary looked on in disbelief. I hated myself for falling into a trap I knew was coming. Why couldn't I just distract her or ignore her, or tune her out?

"You point out what we're doing wrong—always! How we're disappointing you," I added, filling the shocked silence. "And that's such bullshit," I added, repeating myself, a little lamely, I admit.

Mom had a pleased look on her face.

"But you're wrong, Rick," she said, not missing a beat. "I'm a mother eagle. My job is to make you strong, so you can soar to the highest heights. That's all I'm doing."

Mom lived her life through us kids. Dad lived his life as if we didn't exist.

I acquiesced to the inevitable in the end and enrolled again in architecture school, moving in with my old roommates. Soon I began to sell pot, and then mushrooms.

My source for the magic mushrooms got the stuff from "some crazy professor at Harvard." The professor turned out to be one Richard Alpert, who, along with Timothy Leary, became a pioneer in LSD research until the two of them got kicked out of Harvard. Alpert would later become famous as Baba Ram Dass.

I sold psilocybin to hundreds of people, many of whom said it gave them "the most profound spiritual experience" of their lives. For me mushrooms were every bit as powerful as LSD, but in a different way. As the "shrooms" came on, I felt myself descend into a swirling kaleidoscope of color and sound. Soon I was hurtling down an undulating slippery slide as a succession of otherworldly beings raced by, some of them beautiful, some grotesque. There was no going back. Everything was alive, intelligent, organic, and connected. But I had to surrender. This must be what it's like to die, I thought, to go into the light at the end of the tunnel and come out the other side.

I became the Johnny Appleseed of magic mushrooms. I wasn't dealing contraband. As I saw it, I was on a mission, helping people transform their lives. This was how I was going to bring peace to the world. Within a few months I had a congregation of clients who'd "seen God," aided by the miraculous properties of psilocybin.

Meanwhile, my experiences taking LSD and speed were not nearly so transcendent. When I tripped, I became desperate to turn off my increasingly fearful mind, plagued by herky-jerky, spinning

The Johnny Appleseed of magic mushrooms in his Stashmobile

thoughts and filled with doubts about the motives of others and judgments about myself. Could I trust my customers? Could I trust my roommates? Could I even trust myself?

I got three speeding tickets in a month, though I swear I never drove more than five miles an hour over the speed limit. Were the drugs making me paranoid, or were the cops finally closing in on me? On several occasions, I feared I might never come back from the hallucinatory whirlwind I was about to enter, but I swallowed the capsules anyway. I'd rather risk becoming permanently deranged, I told myself, or even dying, than continue playing host to my painfully discombobulating thoughts.

That's when I discovered a walnut-sized growth in my neck. How had I missed it? I didn't want to say the word *cancer*, even to myself, but it hovered there, unspoken, in my mind, like a verdict ready to be handed down. I'd avoided the draft, but now my time was up. Eric Utne was going to die.

The doctors at the university's health service didn't know what to make of it. I overheard them discussing my X-rays from the next room. "This reminds me of that twelve-year-old girl from San Diego back in '52 when we were in med school," one of them said. "But this growth isn't on any lymph node." They prescribed antibiotics—first penicillin, then tetracycline—but neither led to any improvement.

I was increasingly agitated and fearful. My life was spinning out of control.

Finally, one doctor broached the possibility of cancer and suggested a biopsy. I soon found myself in the hospital facing Dr. Henry B, a slight, dark-haired man with a heavy German accent and one thick eyebrow stretched clear across his forehead. He was standing at the foot of my bed with a half dozen white-smocked medical students flanking him. My mother was there, standing by my side.

Dr. B hunched over as he spoke, rubbing his hands slowly, and said with apparent eagerness, "Ya, vee vil haf to go een und look at zat."

My mother's response to Dr. B's comment was completely out of character. She usually took whatever doctors said as gospel, but in that moment she nearly threw herself across my bed, arms outstretched, and exclaimed, "Stop this instant! Don't you dare cut my boy!"

Dr. B and the residents all looked at my mother, dumbfounded by her outburst. This wasn't an ordinary hospital, after all. It was a medical school. The esteemed doctor wasn't just an expert but a professor—a specialist whose word was to be trusted and rarely questioned.

I'm sure the students were wondering if this rude woman would be dismissed from the floor and waiting to see what Dr. B would do next. I was with them in that. I didn't know whether to be proud of my mother for trying to protect me or embarrassed for her audacity. But Mom had found her opening, as she always did, and she plowed right on through it.

"Just stop giving him the medicine!" she said, now using a calmer, more level voice. By the look on Dr. B's face I could see she'd won, and she knew it. I knew it. I'd seen it a hundred times before.

It was as if my execution under klieg lights in an operating theater had been stayed by a last-minute reprieve. And my mother was right. The antibiotics were stopped and miraculously, without any further treatment, the growth began to shrink a few days later.

As soon as I was released from the hospital I went to see Brenda. I needed to talk with someone other than my family or my fellow psychonauts about what had happened, and the only person I knew who would give it to me straight was Brenda.

"I'm thinking of giving up college . . . again," I blurted as she made us a pot of tea. College seemed pointless to me now. Martin Luther King, Jr., was gone. Bobby Kennedy was gone. U.S. troop levels in Vietnam had soared to over half a million, the highest of the war, with more than three hundred Americans being killed every week. Antiwar protests at the Democratic National Convention in Chicago had been met with police violence. The world was in chaos. I couldn't get out of bed for my morning classes and was failing at least two of them. But I didn't tell Brenda that.

"I just don't like my classes," I finally said. It was a few months before the end of my fourth year of college, but only my second year of architecture studies. I had another year to go. "The professors only care about modern designs by modern designers. They're not teaching me the things I really need to learn."

I could tell by the pained look on her face that Brenda thought I was wrong about quitting school, but she listened as I continued my lament.

"It's all prestressed concrete, plate glass, and corrugated aluminum. What about wood? What about brick and stone?"

"Eric, I hope you don't quit school just because you don't like it," she said, giving my balloon a puncture that didn't completely pop it, but let out a slow, steady stream of hot air.

Brenda said she wanted to offer me a bit of advice.

"First of all," she began, "you can't be sane unless you are healthy."

Where's she going with this? I wondered. I hadn't told her how nuts I'd been feeling. Could she tell I was worried about going crazy?

"You're descended from a thousand years of Norwegian farmers," she said, "and you've chosen the path of weakness and passivity. You're not on fire, Eric. You've got no daring, no outpouring of constructive passion."

She didn't wait for a reply. She wasn't looking for one anyway.

"Nothing but complaints and protests. Your generation doesn't seem to want to do a lick of work. That's not the way!"

She wasn't looking at me. Her arm was outstretched, index finger stabbing the air.

"While you are alive," she said, "be *alive!*"

She paused to let her words sink in, then took a sip of tea.

"Plato said that the purpose of life on earth is 'the tendence of the soul,'" Brenda continued. "That is to say, we are all learning, and the world is our school. Like Plato, I believe in reincarnation, and that at the end of life our soul is waiting to talk with us and hopes we've passed with good marks and have learned something—through striving, mistakes, suffering, and the like."

Brenda held me fixed in her gaze. I felt torn between jumping up and running out and staying put to hear more. I didn't like being called lazy, but something in me knew that Brenda's words were good medicine. She was standing now, facing me.

As if sensing she'd reached the limits of my pride, she spoke instead to my vanity.

"Also, you can't be good-looking unless you are healthy," she said. "You can't have a clear eye or a fresh complexion unless you are really vigorous and strong."

She flexed her bicep like a bodybuilder. "I mean muscular."

That part got through to me. I'd gotten very skinny of late—165 pounds stretched over my six-foot, two-inch frame.

"Without health, there's no courage," she added. "The most you can hope for is grim Nordic stoicism. You won't be cheerful. You won't experience joy."

What she was saying was true. I pulled out my sketchbook and began taking notes.

"Depression, gloom, envy, ill will—these are all due to a lack of vitality. The secret of happiness is energy—a kind of inner élan."

She was on a roll, only pausing now and then in her oration to take another sip of tea.

"This energy is mysterious. It's both physical and spiritual. That's why the words *health* and *holiness* derive from the same root."

Was I making it up, or did the lights in the room surge the moment Brenda said the word *holiness*? I'd had my share of hallucinations, but they had been plant induced. I hadn't had so much as a puff of pot in weeks.

"Marijuana, cigarettes, endless cups of coffee, Cokes, booze." She gave me an exaggerated look of disgust. "Stop it!"

"Your marijuana and LSD and Eastern mysticism—that's all a mistake," she continued. "Be like Michelangelo."

She turned and went to her kitchen to heat some more water for our tea, letting Michelangelo hang in the air. "More tea?"

"I'll pass," I said. "What were you saying about Michelangelo?"

"Michelangelo ate little and worked terribly hard until he was ninety years old, hammering marble and lying on his back on high scaffolding painting the ceiling of the Sistine Chapel."

She turned to pantomime hammering an invisible chisel, then went back to preparing her tea.

"Do you know how you can tell whether you are healthy?"

"How?"

"When you are really well you get up in the morning and experience a sunburst of joy: '*Hurrah!* Give me some toilets to clean!'"

"But what about Sverre?" I asked, remembering my work with him when I was sixteen, high atop scaffolding in the Minnesota state capitol. "You used to say that he was the Michelangelo of the Midwest."

"My marriage to Sverre was a conspiracy of fate," Brenda said with a wave of her hand, as if brushing away a troublesome fly. "To bring the two of us together."

I felt protective of Sverre, but I liked the "conspiracy of fate" part. Brenda extended her teacup, as if toasting. I lifted mine, now empty.

"Because you and I, Eric—we're *closer than kin*."

I loved that. I left Brenda's house resolved to clean up my act and get ready to take on the world. With Brenda in my corner, I felt I could do just about anything.

6

MACROBIOTICS

The day after my conversation with Brenda I ran into a hippie friend named Toad. He was at his usual station on the west end of the bridge over the Mississippi River that connected the university's East and West banks. With his broad forehead, bulbous eyes, and wide mouth, Toad looked like a prime specimen of the species *Bufo americanus*. He'd been one of my best customers when I sold magic mushrooms.

I told him about the mysterious appearance of the growth in my neck and its equally mysterious disappearance. "Hey, man," he croaked in his swampy baritone. "There's this dude in Boston who can teach you to be your own doctor—with food."

Toad told me that macrobiotics master Michio Kushi was in Minneapolis that very night, speaking at the Center for Consciousness. "You gotta meet him, man! He's your guy! It's clearly meant to be."

"Far out!" I said. The dude's presence in my town, and my "chance" encounter with Toad, had to be a cosmic setup. My guardian angels were definitely looking out for me.

A few hours later Toad and I rolled up to "the Center," a crummy little storefront that might have been mistaken for a head shop. It was in a rough neighborhood that has since been demolished by urban renewal and replaced by the Minnesota Vikings football stadium. The sign above the door featured the all-seeing eye from the back of a dollar bill.

The smell of sandalwood incense and patchouli oil permeated the place. Paintings of Egyptian gods and goddesses presided over the inner sanctum. Osiris and Isis hovered from the back wall, each holding an ankh, the key of life, like a scepter. They were flanked on one wall by the falcon-headed Horus and on the other by the jackal-headed Anubis. Native American dream catchers, bronze Tibetan singing bowls, turquoise jewelry, Viking runes, pendulums, tarot decks, and clusters of purple amethyst and pink crystal were scattered all about. Books on astrology, tarot, Wicca, the great pyramids, herbalism, meditation, yoga, alchemy, kabbalah, UFOs, reincarnation, the *I Ching*, the Tibetan Book of the Dead, tantric sex, and chakra healing were displayed face out on the shelves that lined the walls. The center's owner, Larry, was balding, portly, and middle-aged. He wore a tie-dyed T-shirt with psychedelic swirls that pinwheeled from his ample solar plexus.

Whoever picked the center's inventory must have moved on later in life to writing algorithms for Amazon: "If you like books on astrology, you might also be interested in these titles on alien abduction, Egyptian sex magick, and angel spirit guides."

Toad and I sprawled on the floor atop a threadbare Persian rug while some of the older folks sat behind us on metal folding chairs. Michio stood in the front of the room next to a portable blackboard. Dressed in a black suit, white shirt, and dark tie, he was lean and slightly bowed. His black hair was combed straight back, held in place by a hair cream that was no doubt Japanese in origin. He wore functional, black-framed glasses and seemed simultaneously out of place and somehow perfectly at ease in this hippie scene—as if he'd done it a thousand times before.

Mr. Kushi proceeded to blow our midwestern minds with talk of yin and yang and chalk diagrams of the spiral of creation. His lecture, delivered in heavily accented English, was filled with challenges to everything I thought I knew. Evolution, not what you think. Gravity, not so fast. World history, very different. And food? Nothing less than the key to the healthy life and world peace.

Michio Kushi lecturing on macrobiotics and the order of the universe

On the one hand, I asked myself, "Who is this guy trying to kid?" Then, a few minutes later, "Yes, of course, why didn't I think of that?"

During his lecture, Michio chain-smoked Kent cigarettes. When asked why he smoked, he replied with a story about his teacher, George Ohsawa, the founder of macrobiotics. Ohsawa, also a heavy smoker, was asked the same question, Michio said, to which he replied, "Cigarette smoking may not be the only way to cure cancer, but it's one of the most enjoyable."

Michio was serious. He explained that lung cancer generally comes from eating too much sugar and dairy food. It's the chemicals in cigarettes—the sweeteners and burning agents—and not the tobacco itself that cause cancer, he said. Smoking was just people's attempt to balance a yin condition with the warm smoke, which Michio said was yang. If your system is balanced, he said, the chemicals don't have such a harmful effect. You gotta hand it to him, he certainly knew how to be provocative.

Much of what Michio said sounded unscientific to me, but I was ill-equipped to challenge him and only too willing to suspend my disbelief until I better understood what he was talking about. The idea that I was the cause of my own ill health unsettled me. I had learned by smoking pot and ingesting LSD and magic mushrooms that what I put into my body affected my consciousness. It wasn't such a big leap to think that it affected my physical health, too. The longer I listened, the more concerned I became that I would make myself sick again unless I learned what to eat and how to cook.

According to Michio, the true purpose of macrobiotics was more than restoring one's health. It was to "let everyone happily and freely play every day endlessly" in pursuit of an "infinitely growing dream." This wasn't exactly what I was looking for, but it sounded good to me. I knew there had to be more to life than what I'd been taught by my parents and teachers—a bigger, truer reality than the one reflected on TV and in the newspapers. I'd glimpsed it as a child. I'd seen it in my dreams. I'd searched for it in psychedelics. I'd felt it in moments of grace. There was an "order of the universe," as Michio called it— "the way of life in the age of humanity."

There was a right way to do things—a right way to cook, a right way to eat, a right way to sleep, a right way to do everything. But how to choose the right way? Michio clearly knew.

There's no formula, no prescription, Michio said. The right way depends on your level of judgment and your use of the choice-making framework of yin and yang. Yin and yang are the basis of the macrobiotic diet, Taoist cosmology, and all of Oriental medicine, Michio explained. He called it "dualistic monism." Everything in the universe was a combination of these conflicting and complementary forces. Yin was dark, cool, moist, passive, sweet, flowing, feminine. Yang was light, warm, dry, active, salty, solid, masculine.

Michio had answers to questions I hadn't even asked yet. The way of macrobiotics (literally "big life") was attained through "athletic austerity." Living a macrobiotic life, and making decisions according to the principles of yin and yang, was very simple, Michio said, but that didn't mean it was easy. "Macrobiotics will free you and save the world," he promised. "But first it will make you miserable."

After that lecture, I started hearing about macrobiotics everywhere I turned. John Lennon and Yoko Ono were doing it. Bizarrely, so was screen siren Gloria Swanson. Tom the pancake flipper and Mary Lou the waitress at Al's Diner in Dinkytown told me they were trying it, too. Soon Tom and Mary Lou and I, along with three other neophytes, rented a little house on the university's East Bank. We cooked meals and studied Michio's writings together. But after a few weeks, I was losing weight much too quickly, and I had zero energy.

Maybe this was the "miserable" phase Michio promised. I decided I needed to study with him directly. He was clearly a remarkable man, a seeker of truth. I wanted to get to know him, to learn to see the world as he saw it. Within a few weeks I'd dropped out of architecture school for the second time. And a few weeks later I was in Boston.

II

NEW AGE
SEEKER

7

THE BROWN RICE GURU

One of the first people I met when I got to Boston was Peggy Taylor. She was waiting to greet me at the front door of the study house in Brookline that would be my first residence. Peggy radiated a healthy and wholesome charisma, and I was drawn to her energy, but she took absolutely no notice of me. I was clearly just another one of Michio's new recruits. She was cheerful enough, but in a professional, business-like way. She was there to collect the rent, and she moved fast, like a doctor doing rounds in a leper colony. She was clearly a member of the community's inner circle and had little time for an ignorant, question-filled newcomer. After showing me around and introducing me to a few people, she disappeared.

The study house, one of a half dozen or so sprinkled throughout Boston's white-collar neighborhoods, was a three-story brownstone that faced the MBTA streetcar tracks. It housed at least a dozen students, who slept two or three to a room on roll-out futons or Japanese tatami straw mats.

Michio attracted some of the most interesting people I'd ever met. My housemates were all about my age, and included Jeff, an earnest, soft-spoken, cherub-faced Easterner who kept his head bowed and his eyes lowered. I only learned months after meeting him that Jeff had come to macrobiotics hoping to recover from a heroin addiction.

Then there was Nahum, the rabbi's son, studying Shinto religion, and Jim, the diabetic, trying to get off his daily injections of insulin and having the occasional episode that landed him in the emergency room. There was a group of ex-hippies from California whom I thought of as the Merry Pranksters. They talked often about the light shows and rock concerts they had produced at San Francisco's Fillmore auditorium. Several of them became pioneers of the natural foods movement, and wildly successful entrepreneurs.

Some found their way to macrobiotics because they were students of Oriental philosophy, drawn to Michio's teachings about yin and yang, traditional Japanese culture, and the order of the universe. A few were psychedelic tripsters seeking the ultimate high through the austere self-discipline of the macrobiotic diet. Others were sick with cancer or other health challenges. And some were sincere spiritual seekers, trying to raise their consciousness naturally. Some were all of the above. We all had at least one thing in common: We were deeply doubtful about the conventional wisdom of mainstream American science and religion, especially allopathic medicine, and we were searching for alternatives.

Like most study houses in Boston, unless you were part of the cooking crew for that particular meal, the kitchen was off-limits. The Spartan dining room with polished hardwood floors and no curtains was the main gathering place. The long, low table at the center of the room, the altar around which we took "communion," consisted of two hollow-core doors propped on concrete blocks. Most diners sat on their knees atop thin zabuton cushions, the kind used by Zen practitioners for meditation.

A typical dinner included brown rice and miso soup, with sides of wakame seaweed, adzuki beans, and sautéed carrots. I chewed every mouthful one hundred times, following Gandhi's admonition to "chew your drink and drink your food." An entire meal shared by a dozen earnest chewers could pass in silence, the quiet broken only by the sound of chopsticks and chewing. Unable to endure the silence during my first meal, I blurted a compliment to the chef: "Nice rice!" A chorus of heads bobbed silently in agreement as my housemates continued to chomp their rice, trying not to lose track of their chew count.

The All Saints Parish Episcopal Church next door had a small marquee out front with a quote from the coming Sunday's sermon that spoke directly to me—"The truth shall set you free. But first it will make you miserable." My weight continued to plummet, falling from 165 pounds BBR (Before Brown Rice) to a nadir of 145 pounds.

Michio lectured on Tuesday evenings at the historic Arlington Street Church in downtown Boston, just across from the Public Garden. A clutch of smokers gathered outside the church's side entrance before each talk. Most of the guys wore vests, which made them look even thinner than they already were. Most kept their hair close-cropped, and exuded a martial arts aura. The women tended to wear their hair and skirts long and loose. Unless you knew better, one might assume they were a bunch of down-and-outers having spent their food-stamp money on cigarettes. But a few minutes before seven, everyone stomped out their cigarette butts, which they carefully and conscientiously disposed of in the nearby trash receptacle, and scampered inside.

I was the most eager and earnest student imaginable. But so was everyone else. The first time I attended, I took a seat in the front row, then turned around and surveyed the fifty or so people sitting in the pews. Every person there was on a quest. I wondered what their stories were. What had brought them to this place tonight? Had they turned their lives upside down to get here, as I had? Who and what had they left behind? Would any of them become my friend? What might we do together to help change the world?

Much to my alarm, it was soon apparent that Michio began each lecture by having people in the front row read letters from some of his students who were traveling and studying abroad, in Japan or France or Brazil. For the most part, the letters were thoughtful, well written, and interesting. But I was too self-conscious to stand in front of a group of strangers for any reason, especially to read. I wasn't ready for that much attention. I didn't know the people, and I hadn't learned my cues. What if I messed up? So I moved to the back.

After one or two lectures, I decided that I was being a coward. After all, I was now a man of the world. Surely I could read a letter in front of these kindred souls. So eventually, at my fourth meeting, I forced myself to sit in the front row.

Sure enough, Michio called on me. Oh God, I thought, here we go. I was terrified. I swallowed hard, screwed up my courage, and stood up. Michio handed me the letter. It was seven pages long, typed single-spaced on thin onionskin paper. I began reading, and my voice quaked. I burst into a sweat after just two sentences. The letter was about the Japanese macrobiotic community in Brazil and their recipes for miso. I was completely botching it. I didn't know the difference between soybean, barley, and rice miso, let alone how to pronounce their names in Japanese.

I remember feeling like I was flooding the floor with my sweat, so overwhelming was my embarrassment. Michio patted me on the back and thanked me as he peeled the letter from my hands. I rushed down the center aisle and into the church basement, removed my shirt, and wrung it out in the men's-room sink. My sweat filled the bottom of the basin. What's the matter with me? I wondered. Why had I melted down like that?

Why did a situation that brought attention to me, a circumstance that part of me craved, cause me to blush, stammer, and come undone? It was a mystery that would take me many years to solve, but this fear would also be, strangely, an asset in my life. I became adept at listening and asking questions, anything to avoid speaking in front of a group.

In a typical lecture Michio covered a dozen diverse subjects. He'd touch on astrophysics, biochemistry, psychology, Chinese medicine, prehistoric Europe, and, one of my personal favorites, the "Seven Levels of Judgment." Michio listed the seven levels on his blackboard and said that modern workers and businessmen, "ruled by time," typified the lower rungs, whereas "creators of doctrine and dogma" like Lao Tzu, the Buddha, Socrates, Moses, Goethe, Emerson, Shakespeare, and Johann Sebastian Bach had attained the sixth level of judgment. Only the seventeenth-century Japanese haiku master

Basho, according to Michio, had achieved the seventh level. That is, he was the only truly free man.

Yes, I thought, I want to be a free man like Basho, not held back by so many inner restraints, thought loops, judgments, sympathies, and antipathies.

In order to grow to the higher levels of judgment, Michio said, one needed poverty, difficulty, and hardship. "Man must struggle through each level, one by one."

I will thank God, or karma, or the order of the universe, for present and future difficulties, I told myself. Boston was my boot camp. Bring on the austerity. Bring on the difficulties. Give me toilets to clean!

But not everything Michio said made sense to me. Could Jesus and Gandhi really be so low on the judgment totem pole? Michio had consigned both to level three—"Sentimental Man," who is "ruled by likes and dislikes." I wondered about Gandhi's teachings on nonviolent resistance, and Jesus's mission of love. Both seemed well beyond simple sentimental "likes and dislikes" to me.

And where were women in Michio's hierarchy? He once said it was much easier for women to develop higher levels of judgment because "their lives are so much more difficult." Men, on the other hand, he said, are just "tilting at windmills." Still, he rarely mentioned any actual women in his lectures.

In my notes from one of his lectures, I wrote, quoting Michio:

We are infinity.

The body is always creating balance with environmental influences. As above, so below.

To raise your level of judgment you must have: 1. Difficulties; and, 2. Good food (quality, volume, proportion [mix of grains, root vegetables, leafy greens, fruits, animal products, etc.], and chewing).

I'm glad I got to witness so many of Michio's performances. That's really what they were—intellectual improvisational jazz. Michio's

Michio Kushi in costume for a macrobiotic community celebration

lectures were ad-lib riffs on material that he knew well and was continually expanding. Each lecture was a house concert, think Miles Davis crossed with Neil deGrasse Tyson. And Michio's audience, including me, lapped it up.

Though he rarely talked about himself, over the course of my studies I gleaned that Michio had been a young soldier in the Imperial Japanese Army, stationed near Nagasaki when the atomic bomb was dropped on the city and its inhabitants. Afterward, Michio took a train through Hiroshima, where he saw the effects of the bomb and its radioactive aftermath. He decided then to devote his life to achieving world peace.

After graduating from Tokyo University he came to the United States with his wife, Aveline, for graduate studies in political science at Columbia University, but he gradually became disillusioned with the possibility of achieving any kind of global harmony through political means.

Eventually he embraced the teachings of George Ohsawa, whose lectures he had attended in Japan. Ohsawa taught that food is the key to health because only truly healthy people can be peaceful. Peace had to begin within one's own body. Michio changed his diet and began to teach macrobiotics.

After a few weeks in Boston, I knew I had found my teacher, and I was in it for the long haul. That summer Neil Armstrong landed on the moon, and the Woodstock Music Festival marked the full-throated, blissed-out arrival of the counterculture. But what I was learning from Michio was more compelling to me, and, I believed, more likely to make a real difference in the world than any kind of technological innovation or rock-and-roll revolution.

I needed to support myself during my studies with Michio, so I got a job at the Erewhon Trading Company's natural foods store on Newbury Street in Boston's Back Bay. Started by Michio and Aveline out of their garage, Erewhon was named for Samuel Butler's utopian novel *Erewhon* (*nowhere* spelled backward, kind of). It was one of the first natural foods stores in the country, and it became the pioneer natural foods distribution company in North America.

The floor had wide wooden planks, the walls were natural barn board, and the shelving stained and varnished pine. Grains and beans were sold out of big wooden barrels. The fresh fruit and veggie displays were kept well stocked, an overflowing cornucopia. Packaging was kept to a minimum. Sales were so good that would-be imitators photographed every inch of the shop to replicate the store's design and layout in other cities across the country and the world.

Roger, the store manager, dressed like a California cowboy—boots, jeans, and shirts with snap buttons. He was worldly-wise and a bit skeptical about my gosh-almighty enthusiasm. He told me he didn't want to hire me, but that Michio had made him do it.

"Michio says you're going to be a world leader someday," Roger told me, both of us laughing at the absurdity of the idea. "Someday," he repeated.

I was as surprised as Roger. I'd gotten no indication from Michio that he even knew my name. "World leader?" I wondered. "What does Michio see in me?" Surely not someone who can read a letter or speak before a group.

Here I was, a college dropout and grocery store clerk living in a study house with a dozen other people, many of whom were sick. What would a "world leader" even look like? Would I ever practice architecture? Could teaching others to eat natural foods and live according to the order of the universe really lead to world peace, as Michio claimed?

My first duties at Erewhon included packing items like brown rice, rolled oats, and adzuki beans in five- and ten-pound bags. I got so good at estimating weights and quantities that I almost didn't need to use the scale. Stocking the shelves became my art form. My favorite task was unloading forty-thousand-pound shipments of brown rice in hundred-pound bags. Ten or twelve of us, all skinny macros, accomplished the feat in about two hours. One or two guys would climb on the back of the semitrailer with the driver and tip bags off the end of the truck so they landed gently on your shoulder. Those of us hauling bags took quick, tiny steps, scampering through the front door to the back of the store, gaining speed as we approached the growing hill of stacked bags, then tossing our bags neatly into position on the top of the pile.

Housemates: Michio with some of his student devotees, circa 1969

About a year after I arrived in Boston, a room opened in Michio's home, and I asked if I could take it. I wanted to be as close to my teacher as possible, to learn as much as I could, and to see if he was living what he was teaching. Michio said OK.

The house was an old New England colonial with yellow clapboard siding, wooden shutters on all the windows, and white trim. It was enormous, like all the other homes in the neighborhood, and unobtrusive. The household included Michio and Aveline and their five children, plus about eight other students, mostly women. There was Judy, a former Orthodox Jew from Philadelphia who tiptoed through the house wearing Japanese kimonos and flip-flops. Jane, from "Oklahoma oil money," was the community gossip. She had the ability to make a second helping of fried rice seem absolutely sinful. Rosemary was a fresh-faced twenty-five-year-old Irish schoolgirl who was so good I was sure she'd someday be a nun, or a saint. Anne, it was whispered, was Michio's favorite. She was as dark and exotic as a Hindu temple goddess. She was artistic and refined, with a vaguely tragic air about her. Then there was Adele, who was small and shy and introspective. I got the feeling Michio and Aveline had decided that Adele and I were supposed to be a couple, but I had no idea how to connect with Adele, and never did. From time to time I thought of Peggy, the remarkable woman I had met when I first arrived in Boston, but when I asked around about her, I discovered that she had gone to study in Japan.

I shared a big room in the basement with Bill, a thoughtful man who was a PhD candidate at Harvard Divinity School, writing his thesis on transcendentalism. Bill and I each commandeered a corner of the room for our own, rolling out sleeping bags on the house tatami mats.

In contrast to the study houses, all the action in Michio's home was in the kitchen, on comfortable chairs, around a real table. One night I sat through three rounds of dinner. The first group was Michio's students who lived in the house. We ate a big pot of brown rice mixed with Japanese adzuki beans and lots of hijiki seaweed sautéed in sesame oil with carrots cut matchstick style and sprinkled with toasted sesame seeds.

Next came the Kushi kids, who ate egg-drop soup with buckwheat soba noodles in a tamari broth flavored with kombu seaweed and topped off with tempura shrimp, a much more substantial meal than our high-carb, low-protein fare. Finally, I sat with Michio as he ate, last and alone, a bowl of fried rice with egg and mixed veggies.

As Michio was finishing his meal, Norio, the Kushis' oldest son, a senior in high school, burst through the swinging door from the dining room on his way to some other part of the house. Michio stopped him, saying, "Norio, please sit down." Obviously surprised, Norio got a look on his face that said sitting down there and then was the last thing he wanted to do. He kept moving, but Michio repeated, "Norio, please . . . Sit down. . . . We need to talk." Norio reluctantly complied.

For the next fifteen minutes I had the rare privilege of witnessing my teacher, who was like a parent to me, parent his son.

"Norio," Michio said again, "Norio. You must go to school."

No response.

"Norio . . . please . . . Please go to school."

Still no response. It went on like this interminably. Norio smiled throughout, but I don't recall him ever saying one word. It was painful and awful, and yet strangely inspiring to watch. I felt for Norio. Michio was not letting him off the hook. And I envied him. I wished that my father had cared enough to talk to me the way Michio was talking to Norio.

Although I tried to make myself unobtrusive, I worried that my presence was making Norio mute. I felt it was wrong that I was there. I don't know if Norio ever went back to school.

By this time I was managing Erewhon's retail store, but I was a terrible manager. I couldn't ask anybody to do anything, for fear they'd resist, or simply say "No!" Then what would I do? It was much easier for me to just do it myself.

It was exhausting work. When I got home I'd remove my shoes at the bottom of the stairway inside the front door. Before I could untie my laces I'd fall asleep in a heap at the foot of the stairs. My house-mates needed to step over me to climb the stairs to the second-floor living quarters. This was embarrassing, but I reminded myself, "The truth shall free you, but first it will make you miserable."

Once I started working the cash register, I got to know the customers. One of my regulars was a German woman who ordered a twenty-five-pound bag of organic carrots every week. Her skin was bright orange. We called her "Goldie." Another customer was Victor Kulvinskas, the director of Ann Wigmore's Hippocrates Health Institute, just down the street. Victor and Ann were passionate advocates of raw foods, especially sprouted wheatgrass. Every time Victor rushed into the store, I mistook him for a bicycle messenger. He wore a helmet, close-fitting inclement weather gear, and running shoes. He was skinny, always in a hurry, and flushed bright red.

One day he lurched across the store to the fresh fruit section, grabbed an apple, and started chomping on it, as if he were having a diabetic attack and desperate to raise his blood sugar. He then strode to the cash register and shouted, "How much?" holding up the core.

Apples were priced by their weight. "Make me an offer," I replied.

"Ten cents!" Victor barked, bits of apple flying from his mouth.

"Twenty-five!" I said. The apples were worth at least that.

"Deal!" answered Victor, avoiding a scene.

Around this time my mother, sister Mary, and brother Bob came to visit me, staying in guest rooms in Michio's house. Mom downplayed her concern, but I knew she was worried that I'd joined a Manson-like cult. She wanted to see for herself the scene I'd gotten myself into. They stayed for a couple days, met Michio and Aveline, and had several meals at the house. I gave them a tour of the macro scene around town, including the Erewhon warehouse and retail stores, the Red Wing Bookstore, and Sanae, the macrobiotic restaurant on Newbury Street, all owned by the Kushis.

Mom and Mary left feeling reassured, but Bob wrote to me and said, "Those are some of the plainest-looking women I've ever seen. They look positively Amish in their long dresses. If you put different clothes on them, and some makeup, they'd all be beautiful. If I was Michio," he said, "I'd be sleeping with every one of them."

I was shocked and horrified that Bob could even think such a thought, let alone speak it. Michio was my teacher, guide, and mentor. I dismissed Bob's suspicions as crass cynicism, and perhaps envy. Later, though, I learned that one of the young women had indeed been Michio's lover.

During the hot summer of 1970 my ankles swelled to almost double their normal thickness. I must be too yang, I thought.

I was working very hard, drinking very little water, and definitely eating too much salt, all very "yang-izing." Then again, maybe my problem was that I was still too yin. Michio said that tall Nordic types were constitutionally yin from generations of eating too much dairy food. "Cow's milk is for cows," he said, "not people." Perhaps I was still consuming too many liquids and needed to make myself more yang. Eating by yin and yang could be very confusing.

My body was my laboratory, my daily diet an ongoing experiment that felt like a crapshoot. Could it be that I was eating too much salt? Salt makes you retain water, and too much salt can lead to edema. But only my feet and ankles were bloated. Perhaps I was standing too much at the cash register and moving too little. Maybe I simply needed to move around more. Could the swelling be related to my lymphatic system? Maybe my liver was damaged when I had hepatitis in my summer traveling around Europe, and that was affecting my ability to digest fats, which was leading to blood clots in my lower limbs, another cause of edema.

After trying to sort things out on my own for several weeks, I finally sought an audience with Michio. He was a very busy man, and I didn't want to bother him with my stupid problems, but I was unable to solve the puzzle of my enormous ankles. They had ballooned to gargantuan proportions, and I was desperate.

It was late in the evening. Michio was sitting alone at the kitchen table. He sat facing the wall with his back to the kitchen, writing notes, perhaps for his next lecture. I approached him from the side and asked if I could have a few minutes of his time.

Michio and me, 1970: Is anybody having any fun around here?

"Hmmm!" he grunted softly, almost inaudibly, with a slight nod of his head. He lit a Kent cigarette, cocked his head to one side, raised his eyebrows, and gave me a hint of a smile. "Yes. What is it?"

"Michio-san," I started, using the traditional Japanese honorific. Most people didn't address him so formally, but I was trying to ingratiate myself with him. Maybe he'd think kindly of me if I was more polite than most Americans. Maybe he'd remember me.

"I hate to bother you," I said. "But I've got a question for you."

I lifted one foot onto the seat of the chair next to Michio and raised my pant leg. "I've got swollen ankles and I've tried everything I can think of, but they just keep getting bigger and bigger."

"Hmmm," he grunted again, looking at my elephantine ankles. "Very interesting, don't you think?"

Interesting? I wasn't so dispassionate. I was scared.

He squeezed my ankle between his thumb and forefinger, took a long draw on his cigarette, and let the smoke hover around his face as he closed his eyes in contemplation. The pressure left deep pits where he had squeezed that gradually subsided.

At last he spoke. "Take five umeboshi plums every day for five days. See if that helps." Then he turned back to his notes without another word. Audience over.

That's it!? I thought. Five salted plums! Every day! Is he crazy? That's like eating five tablespoons of salt every day. That'll kill me.

Did Michio really not know what I should do to heal myself? Or did he not care? Whichever it was, that was the first moment I began to doubt my teacher. I had put Michio on a pedestal, and he was climbing back down. But I decided to give him the benefit of the doubt. Michio must be trying to show me how to be my own teacher, I thought, how to trust my own experience. Perhaps what he was really saying was "Trust your own judgment (you idiot). Figure it out for yourself." How brilliant. How wise.

"Thank you, Michio-san."

I made a half bow and backed away. I turned and went right to the refrigerator, found a large white daikon radish, scrubbed it, cut it into carrot-stick-sized pieces, and ate the whole thing raw. Daikon is a diuretic. Within hours I began to pee profusely. I did the same thing each day for the next three days. Within a week my ankles were back to normal.

8

DIET NUMBER SEVEN

Late in the autumn of 1970 I attended a performance of the Japanese tea ceremony for Michio's students that changed the entire direction of my life. I was skeptical about seeing a Westerner demonstrate a traditional Japanese cultural art form. I didn't have the words for it at the time, but it smacked of cultural appropriation to me. I felt the same way about so many of Michio's male students taking up the traditional Japanese martial art of kendo, literally "the way of the sword." They'd dress in Japanese quilted cotton pajamas, with protective gloves and helmets that made them look like samurai, and bash each other with bamboo swords.

My interest in studying macrobiotics with Michio was less about learning traditional Japanese culture than it was about discovering universal principles that apply to every human being. What would it mean to eat a balanced diet in the North American Midwest, with its hot summers, cold winters, short growing season, and great distance from both coasts? It wouldn't include brown rice, miso soup, and seaweed, would it? Might it be more like what the indigenous people of the region ate—corn, squash, and beans, sourced locally and in season? Or wild rice, roots, and berries, and the occasional meat dish?

I know kendo and the tea ceremony are profound activities that teach practitioners discipline, respect, and other salutary virtues, but a demonstration like this one just seemed wrong to me.

But all of my critical thoughts vanished when I saw the woman performing the tea ceremony.

It was Peggy Taylor, my long-ago rent collector. Peggy had spent the intervening year in Japan, teaching English, studying Japanese, and learning some of the traditional arts, like flower arranging, calligraphy, and the tea ceremony. She had returned to Boston when she and her boyfriend, also studying in Japan, ended their relationship.

Wearing an indigo kimono, Peggy was delicate and captivating as she glided through the tea ceremony. Could this really be the same woman who sped through my Beacon Street study house so officiously? She moved quietly, deliberately, taking tiny steps. She kept her eyes focused on the task at hand, which appeared to interest and delight her. She was the living embodiment of artful presence. At the end of her performance, Peggy looked up and out for the first time, smiling broadly, and then she bowed. That did it. I was smitten. When she then announced that she'd been hired to manage a restaurant in London and needed help, to my surprise I raised my hand and blurted out, "Sign me up!"

Within weeks I was the vegetable cutter and tempura chef at the Seed, a macrobiotic restaurant located in a quiet terrace house in the Notting Hill section of London. I was ready for a change. Michio's prescription for my swollen ankles had shaken my faith in his omniscience. Maybe he didn't know everything. Or, maybe I'd learned all I could from my teacher. Now I needed to learn to trust my own judgment.

The restaurant was owned by Craig and Greg Sams, two Americans who'd founded a natural foods store on nearby Portobello Road. Peggy had been in charge of the renovations of the garden-level establishment. It was up and running, if shorthanded, by the time I arrived.

The restaurant had only been open for a month and was already turning people away. Sean Connery, star of the James Bond movies, and three of the four Rolling Stones were regular customers. I'm told they sat on the Japanese zabuton floor cushions and tatami mats like everyone else in our Zen-minimalist establishment. I never saw them because I was confined to the kitchen and never peeked through the beaded bamboo curtain that separated the "back of the house" from the "front of the house."

Peggy and I spent a lot of time in the restaurant kitchen alone together, she cooking and me serving as her sous chef, cutting vegetables Japanese country style according to her instructions, washing the pots and pans, scrubbing the counters, and mopping the floor. After closing, while we cleaned up, we sang folk songs, show tunes, lullabies, the Beatles, anything, often in two-part harmony. Peggy was a gifted musician—she'd left Skidmore College to study piano with Madame Margaret Stedman Chaloff, the legendary teacher of Leonard Bernstein, Keith Jarrett, Chick Corea, and Herbie Hancock. And she brought out the music in me.

There was something about Peggy. She had vitality, presence, and a wholesome innocence. Her laugh was infectious. If she was butting heads with someone about something, say one of the carpenters about how to place the tatami mats in the most auspicious arrangement, or with me about how much to heat the cooking oil in the Frialator for the perfect watercress and lotus root tempura, she'd win you over to her point of view by kidding and poking and laughing with you until you complied. If that didn't work, she'd just bulldoze you, informing you that she'd made up her mind and that was the way it was going to be. She always got her way.

After about a month Peggy and I realized the restaurant was generating a lot of interest in macrobiotics. We decided we needed to start a study house with about a dozen residents. Peggy would teach cooking classes, and I would lecture, Michio-like, about shiatsu massage, Eastern philosophy, yin and yang, and the order of the universe. We scoured London looking for a place. We told prospective landlords that Peggy and I were married, but we were looking for much more space than the two of us could possibly need. We weren't very convincing and it wasn't working. After searching for weeks, Paul, one of two carpenters from Boston who'd come to help Peggy build the restaurant, said to me, "You know you'll never find a place until you do Diet Number Seven." Diet Number Seven consisted of eating nothing but brown rice. That was it. Brown rice and nothing else.

Like most of Michio's Boston students, I was an extremist. If a simple diet was healthful, I reasoned, then the most simple diet—just brown rice—must be best. I decided Paul was right and began what became a twenty-day rice fast. I got very focused, very determined, and very thin. About ten days into my fast, feeling amazingly clear and lightheaded, I decided to tell the truth to potential landlords. Somehow I found my way to the chief planning officer of the Kensington Borough Council. I told him that Peggy and I wanted to set up a study house and that we planned to have up to twenty people in the house once or twice a week for Peggy's cooking classes and my lectures. I freely admitted that we were not married.

Without a word, he got up from his desk, retrieved a large rolled-up map, and unraveled it across a nearby tabletop. He pointed to a house on Lancaster Road, a block or two from the famous flea market on Portobello Road. "I hope this will suffice," he said. It was a four-story walk-up, spacious and light, and he gave it to us rent-free. He explained that he was trying to keep squatters out of the house until the borough could complete an urban renewal project for the blighted neighborhood. What he didn't tell us, but we learned from the few remaining neighbors, was that in the 1940s and '50s a serial killer had buried his victims in his nearby backyard garden.

As soon as we'd moved in, though we were both still working in the restaurant, Peggy started giving weekly cooking classes and I taught macrobiotic theory. I was not a very good mini-Michio. I was still self-conscious in front of a group, but I had very thorough notes from his lectures and my audiences tended to be eager learners and very forgiving.

By this time Peggy and I were falling in love. At least I was falling in love with her. I had been enthralled with her since seeing her perform the tea ceremony. I loved working with her and imagined us raising children and growing old together. Maybe we would even be "world leaders" someday, we joked.

We took a trip to Paris. On a bridge over the Seine, while considering whether to ride to the top of the Eiffel Tower, Peggy told me that she was feeling nauseous. My first thought was that she might be pregnant, and I began to compose an on-the-spot marriage proposal as I guided her to a nearby bench. Of course I had no ring, but I couldn't let the moment pass. I got down on one knee.

"Peggy," I said, trying to pull myself together. "This only accelerates what I already planned to do. I've been certain of this since the moment I met you. Will you marry me?"

I don't think she believed the part about being certain since the moment we'd met. I'm not sure I believed it myself. But I knew that, if she was willing, we'd have the baby and get married.

Peggy looked me straight in the eye, as if searching for the real me, the future me. Then she lowered her eyes, grinning like she did at the end of her tea ceremony performance, and said, "OK, let's do it."

Suddenly life quickened, and I felt myself losing control. We were only twenty-four years old. Were we really ready to do this? Could I be a loving husband and good father? I could think of very few marriages that I wanted to emulate, certainly not my parents'. Brenda and Sverre had divorced. Michio and Aveline's marriage wasn't much help either. Aveline had moved to L.A. to set up a macrobiotic center there. It was whispered that their marriage was in trouble. What the hell, I thought, we'll just have to figure it out for ourselves. Damn the torpedoes, full speed ahead!

We decided to return to the States as soon as possible, get married at her home in upstate New York, and then move to Minnesota, where I would complete my architecture studies. It was as if everything we'd gone through together—studying with Michio, cooking in the restaurant, and teaching together—had been part of our student days. Now it was time to graduate and enter the real world. Peggy would return ahead of me to prepare for our wedding, while I wrapped up our lives in London.

Peggy's and my wedding day, June 26, 1971

Peggy and I were wed under the spreading arms of the giant Japanese heartnut tree in her backyard in upstate New York. She was three months pregnant and already showing. We wrote our own vows and had a local Unitarian minister perform the ceremony. Lots of macrobiotic friends from Boston came, as did my mother and father, my brothers, Bob and Tom, and my sister, Mary. Loudon Wainwright III, a friend of a friend in the macrobiotic community, performed at the reception, singing "Dead skunk in the middle of the road . . ."

The next day we set off to Minneapolis with Mom and Mary in Mom's big old Buick sedan. I was at the wheel, Mom rode shotgun, and Peggy and Mary shared the backseat. Peggy had morning sickness, the air-conditioning didn't work, it was one hundred degrees, and my mother and my sister bickered the entire eight-hundred-mile journey. When we arrived in Minneapolis, the city was blanketed in smog.

I turned to Peggy, who was nauseous again. "Welcome to our new life."

Peggy and I found a place near the University of Minnesota in Prospect Park, not far from my old drug-dealing den of iniquity. We had the entire upper floor to ourselves, above the elderly couple who owned the house. I enrolled in architecture school at the university for the third time while Peggy gave cooking classes and I taught acupuncture massage in our home.

We started a business called Heavenly Dreams, selling buckwheat hull pillows that Peggy sewed and I attempted to market. Our first label featured my drawing of a tiny cottage, illuminated by candlelight, under a starry midnight sky. It read, "Throughout history the poor and the wise have enjoyed deep sleep and sweet dreams by resting on pillows filled with grain husks. In the Far East the people use buckwheat husks because they are firm, durable, and stay cool all night long. Heavenly Dreams buckwheat pillows are natural and homemade." I also sold vacuum cleaners to try to make a living, but neither venture was particularly profitable.

My flyer for Peggy's and my "people's self-reliance class," 1972

Our son, Leif, was born at home with the help of a very round, very competent midwife who had been catching babies for over forty years. Though midwifery had been banned in Minnesota for more than a decade, she had been "grandmothered in." She wore a white nurse's uniform, white hosiery, and white orthopedic shoes, and drove a big white Cadillac that she called "the Stork."

Throughout the entire birth process, Peggy and I were in it together. We took Lamaze classes, and I coached her breathing during the delivery: "Easy there, that's it, you're doing great. Now pant, keep going, a little more, you're awesome. Now blow. . . ."

Leif's delivery went beautifully. He was big and pink, with a clutch of red hair. Right from the get-go he was a happy baby and wore an impish smile that made him look just like his mother, or maybe his grandfather, or maybe Winston Churchill.

With Leif sleeping on my chest, feeling his heartbeat and inhaling his sweet puppy breath, I was a proud papa, happier than I'd ever been in my life.

Soon women friends started showing up to cook and help around the house, and to sit with Peggy and swoon over and cuddle Leif. I was thrilled to hold Leif and felt more tender and loving and protective toward him and Peggy than I had toward anyone in my life. But I didn't know what to do to make myself useful. The women who descended on our place made me feel like I was in the way, that caregiving was women's work, not men's. I decided that the folk tradition of leaving childbirth to the women made a lot of sense. I should be in a pub, I thought, distributing cigars, or in the woods splitting firewood, or hunting a woolly mammoth with my tribesmen, or some other, more primordial "male" pursuit.

In the spring of 1972, when the ground had thawed, Peggy and I buried the frozen placenta in the garden and planted a rosebush on top of it. I had a wonderful wife and a beautiful son. Architecture seemed like the perfect profession for a dreamer like me—I was learning how to communicate my visions, and the process by which to make them real. I worked part-time as a draftsman in an architect's office, I was nearing the completion of my studies, and my professors

I loved designing buildings, but would they stand up?

rewarded my efforts with top grades. Peggy and I had very little money, but our needs and wants were few, and we never felt like we had to go without anything that we desired.

I wrote to Michio from time to time to let him know how Peggy and I were doing and to report on the macrobiotic scene in Minneapolis, and he always wrote back. Yin and yang and macrobiotics still made sense to me, but our friends in Boston seemed a long ways away. We missed them.

I was happy to be in school again. I loved architecture, especially design. I loved imagining that my ideas might someday become reality. But I was beginning to realize that the practice of architecture in real life was very different from what I had hoped it would be. I'd worked part-time during the first few years of my studies, in Minneapolis, Boston, and London, and had seen for myself that no one working in any of those offices seemed happy. None of them were doing much design. They were spending too much of their time appeasing current clients and trying to find new ones, dealing with greedy contractors and sloppy builders, and trying to get local governments to bend zoning requirements or grant variances. For every Frank Lloyd Wright or Louis Sullivan in the profession, there were thousands of guys (they were mostly guys) bent over and dying on their drawing boards, putting their names to working drawings for office parks and shopping malls that shouldn't be built. And every one of them was nursing a hopeless dream of someday building their very own Fallingwater or Xanadu. That was not the life I wanted.

I decided that learning about life needed to start with learning how to heal, both myself and my society. I enrolled in a two-year distance-learning course in "five-element" acupuncture and Chinese medicine offered by a teacher in London. I also helped some friends start the Whole Foods macrobiotic restaurant on the University of Minnesota campus. Though still enrolled in architecture school, I took a job managing the People's Warehouse, a fledgling food distribution center created to serve the needs of Minnesota's growing food co-op movement. The People's Warehouse dealt directly with local producers who practiced ecologically sound farming principles, paying them more than they could get from commercial buyers. We distributed the goods to about ten inner-city food co-ops in Minneapolis and St. Paul, and another twenty co-ops around Minnesota, selling the products for much less than the conventional agribusiness food system, with all its middlemen, could afford to do.

Although the co-op movement was a national phenomenon, according to co-op historian Craig Cox, the Twin Cities co-op network was the most extensive in the country. It included book, dry goods, and hardware stores, a bakery, a medical clinic, a natural foods cafeteria, day-care centers, free schools, People's carpenters and auto mechanics, and some cultural groups, one of which presented a play about the region's cooperative history, called *The People Are a River*. Most of the co-ops were represented in a biweekly "All Co-op Meeting" where we discussed the policies and practices of the various co-ops. We were zealots for local economies, whole foods, and creating alternatives to capitalism. The co-ops were not about cheap food, they were about community. We advocated for minimal consumption and "voluntary simplicity." We believed that our nascent movement had the potential to change the world.

That spring I interviewed Keith Ruona, one of the founders of the North Country Co-op. I simply turned on a tape recorder, and we had a conversation, then I typed it up. *East West Journal*, the monthly tabloid that Michio and several of his students had founded the year before to promote the study and spread of macrobiotics, ran the article as its cover story. I couldn't believe how easy it was. And fun. To think Keith's ideas and vision might inspire others and help change the world was beyond my wildest imaginings. I wanted more.

9

THE EYES OF A CHILD

It was the spring of 1972 and "Earth Week" at the University of Minnesota. I was sitting in the midst of a thousand people, jammed into the Great Hall of Coffman Memorial Union. I'd dropped out of architecture school twice since my conversation with Brenda six years before, in which she gave me her lecture about making choices. I was thinking of leaving school for a third time, this time for good.

We were there to hear Buckminster Fuller, the philosopher, architect, and inventor of the geodesic dome. Outside on the plaza a student bazaar was abuzz with activity. A partially assembled geodesic dome stood surrounded by a jumble of tables covered with posters and flyers for various student activities and causes, everything from the Students for a Democratic Society's campaign to end the war in Vietnam to the Pollution Report Center, an environmental group that collected tips and complaints about the dumping of toxic chemicals and the dissemination of "mind pollution by newspapers."

The University of Minnesota, with the largest student body on one campus in America, was still recovering from the tumultuous events of two years before, and it was about to explode again. In 1970 nearly half of the university's thirty-seven thousand students participated in demonstrations triggered by the revelation that President Nixon had ordered the secret bombing of Cambodia. The nationwide student strike shut down more than two hundred college and university campuses, including ours. During the strike four student protesters at Kent State were killed by the National Guard in what came to be known as the May 4 massacre.

In 1972 the protests would turn violent once agian. On April 16 news stories revealed that Nixon had ordered the bombing of the North Vietnamese city of Haiphong. Students were simmering with outrage. Tension was in the air.

Earth Day, 1972, on the University of Minnesota campus

But today, April 30, 1972, was a gorgeous spring day. We'd come to hear Bucky, as he was affectionately known, talk about "Spaceship Earth." The campus had been plastered for weeks with posters quoting the tiny, bow-tied, Mr. Magoo look-alike: "Young people today want to learn the principles by which the universe operates. I've discovered some of those principles. That's why they come to hear me."

Over the course of his remarks, Bucky laid out a number of principles he had discovered.

"I live on Earth at present, and I don't know what I am," he began. "I know that I am not a category. I am not a thing—a noun.

I seem to be a verb, an evolutionary process—an integral function of the universe."

Bucky said the youth of today were absolutely right in recognizing this nonsense of earning a living. "We keep inventing jobs because of this false idea that everybody has to be employed at some kind of drudgery because," he said, "according to Malthusian-Darwinian theory, we must justify our right to exist."

"So we have inspectors of inspectors and people making instruments for inspectors to inspect inspectors. The true business of people should be to think about whatever it was they were thinking about before somebody came along and told them they had to earn a living."

Was he telling us to forget about getting a job and earning a living? Yes, he was indeed.

"The things to do are the things that need doing," he said, "that you see need to be done, and that no one else seems to see need to be done. This will bring out the *real* you."

I liked what I was hearing. I wanted to be the real me. But how?

Concluding his talk, Bucky invited questions from the audience.

"Happy to answer questions," he said, "but I think that the main ideas really are out in the open. . . . I could give you lots of details. . . ."

I raised my hand. This was not like me. I rarely asked a question in any of my classes, but in this moment I couldn't restrain myself.

"May I—" I broke in. "May I ask one question?"

"Yes, sir," Bucky replied, pointing to me. "Go."

"You're teaching various principles that you've discovered over your life." I paused, trying to find the right words.

"History has shown us that man finds it very difficult to apply his teachings unless he can *experience* them for himself," I stammered.

Then I asked if he could teach us *how to discover* the principles that he'd discovered *for ourselves* rather than having to come to him to learn the principles.

Fuller had cupped both ears as he listened to my question, looking directly at me. When I finished he adjusted his Coke-bottle glasses. Then looking up at the ceiling as if he were looking right through it, into deep outer space, he spoke.

Bucky Fuller listens to my question: How can I discover the principles by which the universe operates?

"Oh, I would tell you . . . I didn't make the beautiful discoveries that Newton did . . . But I have made some discoveries. I'll tell you how I did, as far as I can be conscious. What I did deliberately, was to try to go back and be as sensitive as I recall being when I was a little child . . . before people said to me, 'Life is very hard, you've got to get over that sensitivity,' and so forth. So I tried to go back and be as simple as I know how. I'll give a little bit of an example of how. . . ."

Fuller then went on for the next sixteen minutes giving examples of how he had seen the world as a child. Then he concluded his answer.

"In other words . . . You asked me to disclose to you what I do with myself [to discover the principles]. Mainly, just be simple, simple, simple, and certainly not kid yourself. There's a terrific amount of self-kidding. Just try to get back to where you were as a little child, utterly naïve and sensitive. Thank you."

That was his answer. I left the lecture roiling. He didn't answer my question, I thought. He just gave me another principle. How, I wondered, can I discover universal principles myself? How can I learn to see without preconceptions? How can I learn to see, naïvely and sensitively, with the eyes of a child?

While working at the People's Warehouse I met a young Ojibwe woman who was teaching traditional cooking methods at the

American Indian Center on Franklin Avenue in Minneapolis. Once, when we were talking about medicinal foods, she told me she thought I should meet her grandfather, Ojibwe medicine man Dan Raincloud. I was game.

To prepare for my audience I visited the Minnesota Historical Society every day for two weeks, reading everything I could about Ojibwe culture and beliefs, especially the mystical Midewiwin Grand Medicine Society, also known as the Secret Medicine Society. I was struck by the Ojibwe belief that everything is alive. I read an article by anthropologist Mary Black Rogers, who had spent a great deal of time with Dan Raincloud. In it she described the way in which the Ojibwe see the world around them as "animate, including trees, plants, rocks, and other natural features that other cultures see as mute, lifeless, and inanimate."

She wrote, "There seems to be a continuous spectrum of powers, going down to the most mundane, which are receivable from some non-human source and which are not inherent in human beings." Human beings received these powers from spirits, she said, to which the Ojibwe believed they needed to show gratitude.

Peggy and baby Leif and I made the five-and-a-half-hour pilgrimage to Red Lake Reservation in northern Minnesota in our VW Beetle. The moment we crossed the border into the reservation forest I began to feel anxious. I was so estranged from wild nature I thought I would die in those woods if I had to survive on my own.

The village of Ponemah seemed desolate and empty to me. Rundown homes with corrugated metal roofs dotted the bare earth. There was not a soul to be seen, though I imagined a number of eyes on me. Once we'd identified Dan Raincloud's home, I knocked on the door. A large middle-aged man drew back the window curtain and peered out, then slowly and wordlessly opened the door. After I announced myself he motioned for us to come in. I offered him a carton of Pall Mall nonfiltered cigarettes and a can of Cherry Blend pipe tobacco, but he declined with a wave of his hand, then he said, "Just a minute." He reappeared followed by an older man, upright and thin. This was Dan Raincloud.

He had horizons in his eyes. He shook my hand in the old way, the way many indigenous people do, with a soft, gentle grip. His palms were dry and weathered, yet they had energy in them. I would have considered his handshake a "dead fish" if there hadn't been so much energy in it. Dan Raincloud graciously introduced his son, the man who had met us at the door, then invited us to sit with him in his tiny living room. His son made his exit as we settled in.

Horizons in his eyes: Ojibwe medicine man Dan Raincloud

Of course I immediately bombarded Dan Raincloud with my impertinent questions about Ojibwe history and culture, but he was much more interested in flirting with my pretty wife and playing with our red-haired baby boy than dealing with me. When I missed a few of the things he said, I asked him if he could speak a little louder. Dan Raincloud gave me a look that told me his tolerance was being tested, saying, "The Indian only speaks loud enough to be heard." Then he turned back to Peggy and Leif.

After patiently enduring my questions for what seemed like hours, Dan told us his life story. Much of it had been spent "between cultures," he said, dealing with white government officials, bureaucrats, and academics on behalf of his people. This put him in an awkward position vis-à-vis both cultures. At times, he told me, he was trusted by neither.

At one point I asked about the Ojibwe Grand Medicine Society and "Red Medicine." I had seen Red Medicine referred to by nineteenth-century Christian missionaries in several of the materials that I had read at the Historical Society, but it was usually discussed rather dismissively, as an example of the Ojibwe's "superstitious" belief system.

"Can you tell me about Red Medicine?" I asked. "From the little I could find, it sounds like the power to heal or hurt from a distance, like voodoo."

"What do you know about Red Medicine?" he asked me incredulously.

"Nothing," I replied. "But I've just started studying Chinese medicine. When I read between the lines in these old books by the missionaries, I sense there's something similar between Chinese medicine and Red Medicine. They're both all about energy. Spirit."

Apparently, that was the right answer. Dan Raincloud then confided that just two weeks before our visit he had buried the Red Medicine amulet, which had been passed down to him from a long line of initiates, stretching back centuries. To complete the amulet, to make it his own, he said, he had to kill a bear. He told us that medicine men from all over the eastern forest tribes and across Canada had come to him for many years trying to get him to teach them Red Medicine, but he never would. He said this ancient knowledge would come to an end with his death.

"Why?" I asked, sensing that I was witnessing a tragedy—an ancient wisdom tradition going extinct.

"Because there's no one fit to hold the power anymore," he said. "This power will die with me."

"Isn't there anyone?" I pleaded.

Dan Raincloud shook his head. "There was a white guy once who could really dance. He could 'shake the wigwam,' as we say. But no, he wasn't fit to hold the power either. Red Medicine will end with me."

Nixon announced that spring that Haiphong's port would be blockaded and explosive mines would be planted by the U.S. Navy. Within days the University of Minnesota turned from peaceful candlelight vigils and teach-ins to occupations of university buildings and riots, provoked by police wielding bullhorns, mace, and billy clubs. National Guard troops were called in. Helicopters sprayed tear gas on crowds of frightened and angry students. Hundreds of heads were beaten.

Then, in June 1972, the Watergate scandal broke. My world and the world around me were in chaos. Over the next few weeks I became convinced that we were living in the end times, at the end of history, and, I hoped, at the dawn of a new age. I was convinced that the old order was over, had reached its end point, and that a new order, a new age, would need to be brought into being. I decided that academic credentials counted for nothing. Why finish school when degrees don't mean anything anymore anyway? I reasoned. Peggy agreed. It was time for us to move on. We would raise our son with our eyes on the future, not the past.

I wrote a "Declaration of Independence" to my professors and fellow students, telling them I was leaving architecture school. I wasn't trying to lead an uprising. I just wanted them to know why I was leaving. And, I think, writing my manifesto helped me explain it to myself.

"I need to learn more about life before I can design spaces for people to live in," I wrote. "The real teacher is life experience." I concluded my manifesto with a quote from Brenda: "While you are alive, be *alive!*"

10

ACUPUNCTURE STUDENT

Peggy, Leif, and I moved back to Boston and began running one of Michio's study houses in Brookline. We had almost no money and lived on less than three thousand dollars a year, but that was plenty when you lived communally. We always had enough and never felt like we were doing without. We knew we could survive by teaching cooking classes and giving lectures, if nothing else.

Shortly after getting back to Boston I got a job at the New England Acupuncture Clinic in Kenmore Square, serving as a liaison between the Chinese-speaking practitioners and their patients, which was odd, because I didn't speak a word of Chinese. One of the doctors, John Shen, who came from a long line of Shanghai traditional Chinese medicine practitioners, told me the secret to his good health and longevity: "Never carry your own baggage."

I continued my correspondence course in acupuncture and Chinese medicine. Graduates would earn a license from the school to practice acupuncture. Acupuncture was still exotic and mostly unheard of at the time. Nixon hadn't visited China yet, and the *New York Times* columnist James Reston hadn't yet had his appendix removed using only acupuncture for anesthesia. I felt like a pioneer, part of the vanguard, the cutting (or needle-poking) edge.

I loved my acupuncture studies. I learned anatomy and

Family portrait, Boston, 1973

physiology, the relationship of the five elements to the twelve meridians, and how to read the twelve pulses. We studied the two-thousand-year-old *Yellow Emperor's Classic of Internal Medicine,* the Chinese calendar, the mother-son cycle, the destructive cycle, the twelve ministers and officials, systems of correspondence, and more. At last, I felt I was discovering some of the principles by which the universe operates.

Toward the end of the two-year program our class met in Oxford for the final two weeks of our studies. It was taught by the school's founder, J. R. Worsley. Dr. Worsley presided like a circus ringmaster. He wore flashy suits, pastel shirts, and paisley ties and loved to put on a good show. He diagnosed each of us in front of the whole group, claiming he could sense if someone had taken as little as one puff of pot in the previous two weeks by reading their liver and kidney pulses. He insisted his students abstain from mind-altering substances during their studies, which wasn't an issue for me, since I had quit all drugs

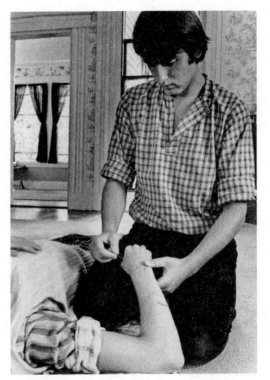

Colon point four: practicing acupuncture on my brother Tom

when I took up macrobiotics. Cigarettes and coffee didn't count, of course.

Worsley had us palpating each other's pulses to read our partner's constitutional energy as well as their current condition. I got rather good at it, as did many of my colleagues, and we could tell more about our partners than seemed possible given the little time we'd spent together. I knew that one friend from Boston must be feeling a great deal of anxiety and fear because his kidney fire was weak, and that another classmate was prone to explosive anger because of a "brittle" feeling of his liver pulse. Was I making it all up, or was I really learning to read another's chi energy as Chinese healers had done for thousands of years?

While in Oxford I had a falling-out with Worsley. I asked too many questions, he said, the answers to which I was "not ready for yet." I thought they were perfectly ordinary questions, like why use of certain points on pregnant women was "forbidden," whereas other points were considered "rescue points" for particular emergencies. I'm sure Worsley was right, that I wasn't ready for some of these discussions, and that if I'd just kept quiet and listened, in time all would have become clear to me. But I had the feeling he was either holding out on me and my classmates, or that he didn't know the answers.

I left feeling indignant, and no doubt a little petulant, and found my way to Worsley's former colleague and partner, a Dr. Bennett, who let me observe his practice. I assisted him as he worked on an Israeli soldier who had just come from the Sinai Peninsula, where he fought in the Yom Kippur War of October 1973. The man shivered and twitched with posttraumatic shock. The doctor's gentle presence and professional demeanor calmed the soldier's nerves, even before he applied the needles.

Around this time a friend sent Peggy and me an article in *East West Journal* about Findhorn, a spiritual community in northern Scotland. Findhorn had become famous because of its spectacular gardens, which produced ten-pound cabbages and waist-high broccoli on sandy soil that couldn't possibly support such abundance. Community members explained that they did it by communicating with the nature spirits—the devas and fawns, the elves and faeries, and even the great god Pan.

Peggy and I were thrilled by the article and decided we had to see Findhorn for ourselves. As it happened, we had ten days left on our Icelandic Airlines twenty-two-to-forty-five-day excursion fares, so we called the Findhorn office to see if we could come for a brief visit on short notice. The office manager informed us that the BBC had just aired their third TV special in as many months on Findhorn's miraculous gardens. He said, "So many people want to come here that there's a waiting list two to three months long."

Just then, while we were still on the phone, two Findhorn residents walked into the manager's office and told him that they were leaving the very next day for a week, and that their mobile home/caravan would be available. The manager said, "Looks like the devas are looking out for you." We jumped on the overnight train with Leif in a snuggie, and a dozen cloth diapers, and arrived the next morning.

Findhorn was an unlikely travel destination, and even less likely to become one of the preeminent new age spiritual communities in the world. It was really just an acre or two of trailer homes and tiny houses surrounded by abundant vegetable and flower gardens and connected by meandering footpaths. A large common house for various performances and events stood at the center.

At the time of our visit, Findhorn was home to about 120 people. Leadership positions tended to be held by middle-aged or older community members. Peter and Eileen Caddy and Dorothy Maclean were Findhorn's founders. Eileen was a spiritual teacher and psychic who channeled "God's guidance" and "the Christ within." Dorothy received gardening and building directives from the nature spirits and relayed them to Eileen's husband, Peter, the handsome, white-haired, sometimes kilt-wearing ex-innkeeper, whose job was to put Eileen and Dorothy's directives into action. They believed that "every need could be met" and encouraged followers to "expect abundance on every level."

From the moment Peggy, Leif, and I arrived, we were treated like visiting royalty, which I found off-putting. Like any good Minnesota Lutheran of Norwegian descent, I was highly suspicious of any kowtowing, toward me or anyone else. But after a while I realized the community members were treating themselves like royalty too. They explained that what made Findhorn special was not so much the huge vegetables and lush flowers. What they were really about, they said, was growing *people*. Findhorn was a hothouse where human beings flourished.

A couple of days into our weeklong stay I decided to get into the spirit of the place and simply be myself. I would be as "magnificent or as corny as I really am." I wouldn't try to be cool or hip. Sometimes I'd be earnest, sometimes irreverent, sometimes playful, whatever felt right in the moment.

Soon I was asked to give a lecture to the entire community about acupuncture and Chinese medicine. I was terrified. I'd been studying Chinese medicine for nearly two years, and there was plenty I could talk about, but images of stammering in front of my class in grade school and bursting into a sweat while attempting to read the letter in front of Michio's students came flooding back to me.

I needn't have worried. The Findhorn community members were so interested and encouraging that I soon felt strangely emboldened. We assembled in the common house, and the entire community turned out. I began my talk by teaching everyone Chinese facial diagnosis the way Michio had taught me. Lines between your eyebrows mean your liver is shot, I told them. Dark circles or puffiness under your eyes mean your kidneys are out of balance. A swollen upper lip means your stomach is "too yin." I went on.

In the middle of my talk I realized that I was teaching my listeners how to notice what was *wrong* with people, themselves and others, whereas the whole premise of Findhorn, the reason people blossomed there, was because they'd learned to notice what was *right* with people. I paused and almost stopped my presentation midstream. How could I go on? An intuition told me to shift my talk to a discussion of the body as a community of ministers and officials working together in efficient harmony, a concept I'd learned in my acupuncture studies, and so I did. The Findhorn folks appeared to love it.

Afterward, I pondered my epiphany. What a concept, I thought—to notice what's *right* with people. My mother never did that. Neither did my father.

When I got back to Boston I had about a dozen people waiting for acupuncture treatments. These appointments had been set up before I went to England, in anticipation of me finishing my studies. But after my epiphany at Findhorn I decided I didn't know enough about Chinese medicine to be poking people with needles. Acupuncture suddenly seemed too invasive, so I set my needles aside. Still, since the appointments were already set up, I decided to see the people, without charging a fee. After all, they wouldn't have come to me, a twenty-eight-year-old novice, unless they were desperate. They must have tried every other conventional and alternative therapy, I reasoned. I felt I owed it to them to at least see them.

Over the course of three weeks I saw people seeking treatment for everything from pain caused by a spinal fusion to chronic menstrual pain and continuous bleeding, to severe migraines, obesity, nicotine addiction, general lack of energy, and other conditions.

I decided to simply "be" with each person. I talked with them, asking the usual inventory of lifestyle questions used in the traditional Chinese medical diagnosis, but that was it. I didn't poke them with needles. I didn't prescribe any lifestyle changes. I would just *be* with them.

Each patient arrived thoroughly identified with their presenting symptoms, but I found that I couldn't help but see them as I'd learned to do at Findhorn: as their best, brightest, healthiest selves. I didn't pretend their pain wasn't there—this was not about the power of positive thinking. Instead, I acknowledged the reality of their symptoms but saw those symptoms as just a partial, incomplete view of a much larger, truer picture. It was this bigger picture that I found myself searching for and relating to.

One young woman who came to me was trying to quit smoking. I felt her pulses and, following an intuition, asked her if her father was living.

"No," she said, "he died when I was sixteen."

I then asked, "When did you start smoking?"

"At sixteen," she replied, breaking into deep, moaning sobs. We had opened a reservoir of dammed-up grief. I held her as she cried. Her healing had begun.

During those three weeks all twelve patients reported back to me that their symptoms had disappeared. They wanted to attribute their healing to me, or to chi energy, or traditional Chinese medicine, but I didn't think any of those was the answer.

What's going on? I wondered. This was just like the mysterious disappearance of the growth in my neck seven years earlier. My patients were somehow healing themselves. I knew that I was involved in some way, perhaps as a catalyst, but I felt I was more witness than cause. I could not explain what it was I was doing that they wanted to pay me for. What kind of shingle could I possibly hang out for myself? All I was doing was being a witness for my patients, someone who listened deeply to them, someone who shone a light on more than their presenting symptoms. Could it be that this kind of witnessing was in itself healing?

11

CRACKING THE KARMIC EGG

Studying acupuncture and Chinese medicine had been deeply satisfying. I loved seeing people heal themselves and feeling that I was participating in their recovery in some way. But I could not imagine practicing acupuncture, or whatever it was that I was doing, for the rest of my life. Instead of spending my days with people who thought of themselves as sick, I wanted to be with people who thought of themselves as *well* and wanted to create something beautiful with others. I began to consider going to work for *East West Journal,* wondering whether it was possible to do what I began to think of as "healing journalism."

I sought the advice of Kalu Rinpoche, a high lama of the Shangpa Kagyu lineage who was one of the first Tibetan masters to teach in the West. He was staying in the Cambridge home of David McClelland, a professor of psychology at Harvard University who later became known as the world's foremost authority on motivation in general and entrepreneurship in particular. McClelland's home was a kind of way station for itinerant consciousness explorers and spiritual types, including the psychedelic pioneers Ram Dass and Timothy Leary.

From my readings about Buddhism I had learned that to "serve the dharma" meant to alleviate people's suffering and to aid in the liberation and enlightenment of all sentient beings. I wanted to ask the lama if he thought journalism could be a force for serving the dharma and for social healing.

I arrived at the appointed hour for my audience with the Rinpoche and was shown to a large, overstuffed living room that looked like the study of a nineteenth-century explorer or a sixteenth-century alchemist. There were piles of books everywhere; curvaceous wood, bronze, and stone statues of Hindu deities; brightly colored Tibetan thangkas; and Mayan masks staring down from the walls. His Eminence, the tiny, rail-thin Rinpoche, dressed in a saffron tunic overlaid with a maroon robe, one bare shoulder poking out, waited for me on a big upholstered chair. We had the room to ourselves.

The Rinpoche offered me hot buttered Tibetan tea. I was unschooled in the social niceties of small talk with a holy man and skeptical of hot buttered tea. But I accepted the drink and then got right to business. I asked him, "Is it possible to serve the dharma through journalism?"

Kalu Rinpoche considered my question for a moment, and then he burst out laughing. He laughed and laughed, and laughed some more. What could I have said to set him off so?

After an uncomfortably long time, which was probably only a minute but seemed like an eternity, he answered, "In the Tibetan language the word for news is also the word for illusion. As long as you remember that anything new is an illusion, then yes, you can serve the dharma through journalism."

Kalu Rinpoche's advice to remember that there's nothing really new under the sun was helpful, but it wasn't sufficient. I considered it a precondition to practicing healing journalism. I wanted to know if my healing experiences following my visit to Findhorn were somehow related to the way I'd learned to see the bigger picture of my patients rather than just the partial, symptomatic view they had of themselves. And if they *were* related, then what would be the equivalent way, the healing way, of reporting in journalism?

East West Journal was founded in 1971. Originally intended as a vehicle to spread the ideas of macrobiotics—and to keep its staff gainfully employed, off the streets, and out of the pool halls—it had grown into something else. It had become a thriving business. The editor was a twenty-eight-year-old, harmonica-playing wild man named Robert Hargrove. Robert was loaded with boyish charm and highfalutin rhetoric. I started selling ads for the magazine because nobody else wanted to.

The magazine had published the article that so intrigued Peggy and me about Findhorn. New age author and New Troubadour David Spangler, spiritual raconteur Ram Dass, *Secret Life of Plants* co-author Christopher Bird, and William Irwin Thompson, author of *At the Edge of History*, all became regular contributors. I wrote several articles for EWJ. One, published in September 1973, was titled "Acupuncture in America." It included these lines:

> Despite constant exposure on radio, TV, and in the newspapers, acupuncture remains as mysterious and inscrutable as ever to the American public. This situation concerns me, for in America we tend to place those things that we don't understand into the hands of experts. If left to the scientific community acupuncture will be treated as a curious relic of the past. . . . If we permit this to happen we will lose the most important aspect of acupuncture, its philosophical base. This base is the common heritage of everyone in the Orient, a view of life that sees no separation between body and mind, that sees nature as a benefactor to be harmonized with rather than exploited, that sees cooperation rather than competition as the way to relate to one another, and that sees the invisible aspect of life as being as real as the visible.

My next article was an elaboration of my speech at Findhorn. It described traditional Chinese medicine's concept of the body's twelve main organs as a community of cooperating ministers and officials. Another article was titled "Toward a New Definition of Health." In it I wrote,

> Many people meditate to get in conscious touch with the creative source within. Meditation is essentially turning one's attention to

what is real. Looking for the divine in everything brings one into a state of awareness akin to deep meditation. Treating everyone like angels lets them become angels.

Some of my happiest memories from working at EWJ are the staff lunches we shared—all of them standard macrobiotic fare. Visitors were always welcome to join us. Yogi Bhajan, the founder of 3HO, a Sikh sect that advertised in the magazine, came to our offices with an entourage of turban-wearing followers. The yogi, a large and lusty omnivore, took one look at the soba noodles and fried tofu and courteously declined.

Robert Hargrove was a gifted and instinctive provocateur. One day he brought me to a popular diner in Cambridge, a couple blocks from Harvard Square, where he ordered me turkey and bacon on a bulky roll for lunch. This was way off the macrobiotic diet. I hadn't had bacon in years, and I was reluctant to try it. I felt like a teetotaler coming off years of abstinence. "Well . . . maybe just this once. . . ." I savored each bite, and remembered that food could be a source of immense *pleasure*. The sandwich was sublime! Why had I denied myself the pleasure of bacon for so many years? Had I become so fearful of making myself sick that I couldn't embrace life? That's when I began to question my commitment to my strict macrobiotic regimen.

By this time, I had come to see Michio—the mentor to whom I had been so devoted, who had taken me into his home and taught me how to live every aspect of my life—as a dark specter. He focused on illness rather than health. And, of course, there were rumors of infidelities with some of his female students. And one of my friends had claimed to have seen him in a diner eating chicken! I told myself that Michio was exploiting his naïve supplicants by teaching them the order of the universe but living very differently himself. *He is worse than evil*, I thought. *He's a hypocrite.*

I have come to see this phenomenon as typical guru-devotee behavior. The student/disciple builds the teacher/guru up into someone or something larger than life, capable of doing no wrong, possibly

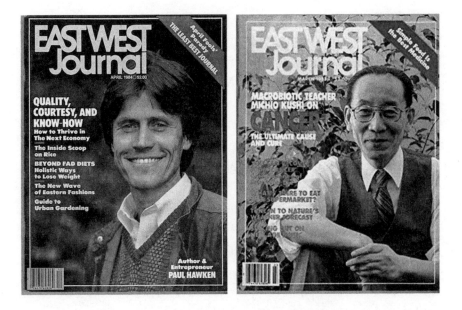

with the encouragement of the teacher. The Hindus call this "bhakti yoga," or devotional yoga, "love for love's sake," and "union through love and devotion." Bhakti yoga, like any other form of yoga, is a path to self-realization, to having an experience of oneness with everything. By worshipping the divine in the teacher, the student is locating, and learning to identify with, the divine in him- or herself. Inevitably, if the student is to "graduate" from the teacher, there must be a break. And often, the bigger the buildup, the bigger the falling-out.

One never knew what to expect at EWJ. One day Robert was notified that his presence was desired for an interview with the Spanish surrealist painter Salvador Dali. The interview would happen in a dark salon in New York's St. Regis Hotel. Dali had assembled an entourage for the event; Robert was their entertainment. Dali transformed the interview into grand performance art, by turns ridiculing Robert for his too-conventional thinking, then riffing on art, holography, DNA, and God. The proceedings were confounding, surreal, and thrilling. Listening to the recap afterward in the office, I was envious. I wished I had been there, and I began to realize that publishing could be a passport to just about anywhere I wanted to go, an entrée to anyone I wanted to meet.

Michio's ideas and community now felt too narrow and constrict-ing to me. My interests and enthusiasms were carrying me in other directions, into other worlds. Several of us on the EWJ staff no longer considered ourselves students of Michio. We were married and had young children. We were not busting our asses to produce the maga-zine just for the learning experience, or to spread the macrobiotic gospel. The magazine had become our vocation and our mission, and we wanted to keep doing it, possibly for the rest of our lives.

Michio, however, was the sole owner—albeit an absentee owner—of the magazine. But he never came into the offices, he didn't try to have any influence on the editorial content, and he had nothing to do with the finances, even though the name "Tomoko Kushi," an invented name that both Michio and Aveline used to sign checks, was on the bank account, and our paychecks. Without his input, we came to think of the magazine as ours.

At one point we asked Michio to allow the staff to own part of the company. Michio said no: "If the staff owns the journal," he said, "someday you will have a conflict that will divide you. It will be brother against brother. It's better that I own the magazine one hundred percent."

Michio was standing in the way of what we wanted to do, or so I believed. Robert and I found this unacceptable and decided to leave the magazine. We would start a new one, we decided, one that the staff could own collectively. We would make our decisions by consensus.

A dozen of us formed the founding group of the new magazine. Only a handful of the people were from EWJ. Two others were *Boston Globe* alums. A guy by the name of Guru Das would handle newsstand sales. Peggy, who hadn't worked for EWJ, joined us as managing edi-tor. We pooled a total of three thousand dollars among us to launch the magazine.

We sent a message to all the EWJ subscribers announcing that we were leaving to start *The New Journal*. Frequent EWJ contributors like David Spangler, Ram Dass, and Chris Bird would join us. Robert wrote in the introduction that we were resigning from EWJ to found a "truly New Age publication, cooperatively owned and community based." He said we wanted to give the publication the "spiritual underbelly" it needed if we were going to evolve as a communications vehicle, and as people. "If a publication talks about the liberation of the spirit," he wrote, "it must simultaneously provide for the liberation of the people who put it together. It's as simple as that."

Sending that message to the subscribers was tantamount to stealing the EWJ subscriber list. Readers were confused. Was the old EWJ ceasing publication? What would happen to their subscriptions to EWJ, for which they had already paid? Who among the staff was going and who was staying? Michio was silent on the matter of *The New Journal*, and the stolen mailing list. Robert avoided talking with him. The EWJ staff was divided—some had decided to stay with EWJ, while others were leaving.

My brother Tom had followed me to Boston a few years earlier. He wanted to see if he could cure his lifelong struggle with severe allergies and asthma through the macrobiotic diet. His symptoms seemed to get better with macrobiotics, but he still had to carry an inhaler with him wherever he went, just in case he had an asthma attack. Tom chose to stay with the Michio loyalists, which was very difficult for both of us. Michio was right—our insistence on ownership was pitting brother against brother.

I decided I needed to talk with Michio myself, so I set up a meeting and went to see him, hat in hand. Though I felt that we were entitled to the subscriber list because we had created it without Michio's help, the fact of the matter was that he owned the company, so it was legally his. I felt both remorseful and self-righteous. Robert and I had betrayed him, and he had every right to tell us to go to hell, or worse, to sue us. I expected explosions, fireworks, legal threats, or at least the suggestion that we were ungrateful, self-deluded, and shortsighted SOBs.

Michio met me for tea in the library of his new residence, a huge old Gothic estate in Brookline. I was struck by the baronial, medieval furnishings and decor—the only Japanese items in sight were a couple of large scrolls and an antique samurai sword. I asked Michio to sign a letter I had drafted giving us his formal permission, retroactively, to use the EWJ mailing list to launch *The New Journal*. He read the letter in silence and gave no indication of his feelings. To my surprise, he pulled out a fountain pen and graciously and magnanimously signed the letter and promised not to sue. Instead of a vengeful devil, Michio was being an angel. I was in shock and disbelief as he ushered me to the front door, shaking my hand with both of his, wishing me and the rest of the staff all the best in our new venture, and bowing as I departed.

The first issue of *The New Journal*, which came out on Halloween 1974, featured an excerpt from Joseph Chilton Pearce's book *The Crack in the Cosmic Egg*. Our cover line, "Cracking the Karmic Egg," alluded to Pearce's book while coyly referring to our own karmic break with Michio. The cover bore a photo collage of the entire staff bursting out of an eggshell.

Within a few days of our launch, Sam Bercholz, founder of Shambhala Books and a regular advertiser in EWJ, walked into the magazine's Cambridge warehouse offices and bellowed, "What the hell is *The New Journal*? That's a terrible name." He said, "Make a statement with your name. Tell people who you are and what you stand for, right in the title!"

Sam was a longtime student of Tibetan Buddhist teacher Chögyam Trungpa. He looked like a Jewish version of Hotei, the rotund and jolly Laughing Buddha. He then told us about a journal of ideas published in the 1920s in Paris by a man named Alfred Richard Orage. Orage was a friend of P. D. Ouspensky, the student of Gurdjieff and author of *In Search of the Miraculous*, the book that had changed my life so many years before. Orage's magazine was called *The New Age*.

"Call yourself *New Age Journal*," Sam said. "It's a name with a noble lineage and tradition."

The term *New Age* hadn't really entered the vernacular yet. It carried vague connotations of Edgar Cayce, the clairvoyant "sleeping prophet," and the new agey actress Shirley MacLaine. I couldn't help picturing drawing-room matrons bent over Ouija boards discussing past lives and the ascended masters every time I heard the term. Nevertheless, we decided to claim the term *New Age* and make it our own. The magazine would be an ongoing definition of the New Age, one that examined every aspect of society: politics, religion, business, health, science, the arts, sports, you name it. We would look at how institutions were changing from without and within, with alternatives springing up on the margins as well as large institutions reforming themselves from the inside.

As we worked on the second issue, whose cover section would explore the subject of money, Bill S., a devotee of Swami Muktananda, walked into the office. He was hoping to persuade us to do a story on his guru, but I was more interested in turning him into an advertiser. Hundreds of pilgrims were flocking every weekend to his ashram in the Catskill Mountains to be blessed by the guru, or rather zapped with spiritual energy, a transmission called "shaktipat," with the touch of his hand, the wave of a peacock feather, even just a glancing look. Why not spread the word in an ad? Before he left, Bill wrote out a check for ten thousand dollars, enough for us to print the next issue.

The third issue was all about sex. At least one key staff member was having an extramarital affair throughout production of the issue, and everyone knew. We wrung our hands and worried, but we didn't know what to do about it. Should we tell the wife, who was a close friend of Peggy's and mine? If we did, would the magazine implode? We said nothing, and, as far as we knew, the affair ended without incident.

Our fourth issue was all about power. By this point, everyone had a spiritual teacher or tradition or workshop to advocate for and sometimes argue about. There was no greater cause or mission or vision about which we all agreed. Were we already losing our sense of shared mission? What was our purpose? Who should decide the theme for the next issue—the editor, all the editors, or the entire staff? How much should each person be paid—according to need or responsibility? Should those with children be paid more? As we tried to hash out these issues, our landlord, a skinny tech entrepreneur with some connection to MIT and/or Harvard, skulked through our offices with a cat on his shoulder. No one was the slightest bit interested in what anyone else had to say. Group consciousness and consensus decision making had turned into group tyranny. Things were looking shaky for the magazine. I decided something had to be done.

I wrote a letter to the entire staff. I told them that for a magazine dedicated to healing society and ourselves, we were doing a pretty shitty job. We had told our readers that we were leaving EWJ to found a "truly New Age publication, cooperatively owned and community based," but we were at each other's throats. We had said we wanted to give the publication the "spiritual underbelly" it needed if we were going to evolve. Had we? I asked. I thought not.

Without having any authority to do so, I asked the entire staff to resign, and to my surprise, everyone did. Peggy and I, and Leslie Smith, the receptionist, then ran the monthly magazine on our own for the next few issues. It was more work than was humanly possible for three people to do, but somehow we did it. A few months later, my brother Tom and several others joined us.

We had some fun and a little bit of success. We grew the publication entirely out of the original three thousand dollars, plus Bill's $10,000 check, without any additional investment. Within a year, we were selling about fifteen thousand copies per issue, and we were well on our way to fulfilling the magazine's original vision. Perhaps we were alleviating some people's suffering and liberating our own spirits. Perhaps, I began to think, we were even serving the dharma through journalism.

I have no idea whether we were aiding in the enlightenment of any sentient beings, most especially our readers, but I do know that I had found my vocation, my calling. This was the work I wanted to do for the rest of my life.

12

THE THIRD GREAT AWAKENING

The card came in the morning mail. The envelope was about the size of a fancy wedding invitation. Square and heavy, it had a rich vanilla-custard color and creamy matte finish, with a handwritten Upper East Side New York City return address, but there was no name on it. I opened the envelope and read the thick, ragged-edged card inside. Written in blue ink, either with a fountain pen or a feather quill, the message was scribed in spectacular, eighteenth-century calligraphy full of fanciful serifs and curlicues.

Dear Eric, Congratulations on your wonderful magazine. It seems you are trying to inform rather than affirm or deny. I think you are destined for a great future.

It was signed "Tom Wolfe."
I was flattered, and flabbergasted.
Tom Wolfe? *The* Tom Wolfe? The same Tom Wolfe who wrote *Radical Chic & Mau-Mauing the Flak Catchers* and *The Electric Kool-Aid Acid Test*? The Tom Wolfe who, with Truman Capote, Gay Talese, William Burroughs, and a few others, had pioneered the "New Journalism" by taking the gentleman journalist out of the grandstand and putting him—that is, himself—into the middle of the stories he covered, in the first person, as a real flesh-and-blood participant? *That* Tom Wolfe?

I knew our readers were interesting. We heard from them frequently, often for some perceived offense on the part of an author, or by one of the magazine's editors. And we got our fair share of notes of encouragement too. But mostly I assumed we were preaching to the choir, that our readers were solidly anti-establishment and countercultural. It hadn't occurred to me that anyone who was famous, or part of the mainstream, let alone a titan of contemporary journalism, would have even heard of *New Age Journal*.

New Age Journal staff photo, 1976. That's my brother Tom on the right.

I raced around the office to share Wolfe's fan note with Peggy, my brother Tom, and the rest of the staff. "Look! We're not invisible!" I crowed. "Tom Wolfe thinks we're doing a great job!"

Everyone was as pleased and puzzled as I was. What did this mean? That we'd arrived? Or that we'd sold out? Lost our edge? Made too many compromises? Or was it a good sign that at least *some-one* in the most elevated echelons of our profession had taken note of us and determined that we were doing something right?

But we came crashing back to earth two weeks later when Wolfe published his earthshaking, decade-dubbing *New York* magazine cover story of August 23, 1976, "The Me Decade and the Third Great Awakening." His article began with a description of an EST (Erhard Seminars Training) session he had attended. The workshop trainer had just admonished the participants lying on the wall-to-wall carpeting to "take your finger off the repress button" and think of "the one thing you would most like to eliminate from your life."

"And so what does one girl blurt over the microphone?" wrote Wolfe. "Hemorrhoids!"

The article went downhill from there. In it, Wolfe made merciless fun of the new age, human potential movement in all its silly, willfully naïve, self-absorbed, navel-gazing excess. He managed to conflate second-century gnosticism, Yale's Skull and Bones society, socialist communes, charismatic Christianity, Esalen, Synanon, Scientology, the Hare Krishnas, nineteenth-century Shaker communes, Edgar Mitchell, Jerry Brown, Uri Geller, Emma Bovary, Erica Jong, Flying Saucer folks, LSD, pot, peyote, group therapy, marriage counseling, group sex, and just about any kind of ecstatic experience. All these and more, he said, were evidence that democracy in America, and a booming economy for the middle class, had created an era of egotism, narcissism, an unwillingness to sacrifice, even for one's own family, and a complete disregard for the social good. He called it "the greatest age of individualism in American history!" It all came down, according to Wolfe, to "Let's talk about Me!"

This time I didn't race around the *New Age Journal* office. I made photocopies of the article and circulated them among the staff. I felt like I was handing out bad reviews to the cast of a Broadway show the morning after opening night. The office felt funereal. Soon we'd be shuttering the place.

Wolfe had dismissed the entire New Age out of hand, which was confusing. Had his praise of the magazine two weeks earlier been sincere, or was it just a sick joke? And yet, when I read between the lines of his article, I was convinced that Wolfe was just as excited as he was appalled by what he called America's "Third Great Awakening."

In his article, he described America's first two Great Awakenings, one in the 1730s and 1740s and the next from 1825 to 1850, as seminal periods of religious cross-pollination, political freethinking, cultural experimentation, and artistic ferment. He seemed to recognize what was happening in America in the early 1970s as a similarly yeasty time, but he was unable, or unwilling, to declare any enthusiasm for it. Was he afraid his fellow New York literati would think him silly and naïve if he admitted to an interest in meditation or yoga or communing with nature?

What *was* clear to me was that Wolfe himself was absent from his article. What did *he* think and feel about the New Age? Was he abandoning the New Journalism that he had done so much to champion? And what was his praise of *New Age Journal* all about? Was it sincere? I needed to know.

I wrote to Wolfe, thanking him for his card and asking if I could meet with him ASAP. He got right back to me, inviting me to visit him in his Upper East Side home for tea, followed by dinner a few doors away at his favorite Chinese restaurant. Soon I was in New York, feeling a flurry of confused emotions. I was indignant about his takedown of the New Age, put off by his dismissals of the human potential movement, and genuinely bewildered that it was so hard to determine what he really thought about the Third Great Awakening. Also, I was curious what he'd be wearing. Would I find him in jeans and a sweatshirt? Or did he wear his trademark white three-piece suits even at home?

Wolfe met me at the door to his four-story brownstone in the East Sixties. He was wearing a brown wool sport coat and tan gabardine pants, with a gold-toned satin ascot that somehow looked casual compared to the getup I'd imagined he'd be in. He introduced me to his fiancée, Sheila, who was working at the kitchen table, and then he gave me a tour of the apartment.

Wolfe's place was exquisite, with comfortably upholstered, carved mahogany banquettes and an assortment of area rugs covered with geometric motifs that reminded me of Klimt or Mondrian, until he told me he'd designed them himself. Warm afternoon light streamed through the windows. After tea and small talk with Sheila, Wolfe and I headed out to Charlie Chan's for dinner.

We were seated at the back of the restaurant, but there were still a couple of tables with customers within earshot. Roiling with my concerns about the article, as soon as we ordered I blurted my question: "Reading between the lines of your 'Me Decade' piece, I could tell that you're both excited and appalled by the Third Great Awakening. What happened to the New Journalism? Why didn't you cop to what you actually think and feel about it?"

It was as though I'd kicked him in the gut. Wolfe pitched forward slightly, then leaned back and took a breath. After a long and uncomfortable silence, he replied, "Let me tell you a story."

Several years before, when he was writing *The Electric Kool-Aid Acid Test*, Wolfe was traveling with Ken Kesey and the Merry Pranksters. They were on a ranch somewhere in California, and someone had welded a huge iron sculpture. Kesey announced that the sculpture needed to be moved to another part of the property and asked for volunteers to help hoist it onto the back of a pickup truck.

Wolfe was obviously reliving the story. His eyes were focused somewhere over my left shoulder as he spoke. I wondered how this could possibly be an answer to my question. The waiter brought us our egg rolls, and Wolfe continued.

"Even then I was wearing a rather natty three-piece suit," Wolfe said, chuckling. "I saw this as an opportunity to be one of the guys, so I joined in, putting my shoulder to the sculpture."

With a great "Heave-ho!" they got the sculpture onto the back of the truck. Wolfe sighed with satisfaction and took a step back to savor the accomplishment and noticed that his suit was covered with fresh paint. He threw a fit, he said. It was hard for me to imagine Tom Wolfe throwing a fit about anything, except maybe a spoiled suit.

Wolfe said that Kesey hadn't seen him show much emotion up until then. He and the others just watched as Wolfe stomped and cursed and blew off steam. When he cooled down, Kesey motioned Wolfe to come over to him.

"As I approached, Kesey glanced around, then looked me in the eye and said, 'Tom, ya gotta realize that when you finally get down into it, some of the shit is bound to rub off.'"

Wolfe then concluded his story. "And you know what? I haven't gotten down into it since."

I couldn't believe that Tom Wolfe would tell such a revealing story about himself. He was telling me that he had abandoned the New Journalism and retreated behind a wall of cynicism and self-protection. He had aligned himself with the New York literary and journalistic establishment, and he was freely admitting it.

Wolfe took pains after his story to assure me that he admired the range and tone of *New Age Journal* and the way we balanced advocacy and objectivity. He also wanted to establish that he was a regular guy. "You may find this hard to believe," he said at one point, "but I tried out for the New York Giants baseball team. I was a decent pitcher in college and the semipros." Tom Wolfe the fop, a major league baseball player? It *was* hard to believe. There must have been something about the uniforms, I thought.

As I rode the train back to Boston, I thought about Wolfe's white suits. His clothing choices seemed distancing and antiseptic, a kind of hazmat coverall suit intended to protect him from contact with contaminating matter. And that was sad to me. He had done so much to define the cause of New Journalism, and now he had abandoned it.

In that moment, I resolved to go the other way. I would *get down into it*, I thought. The whole point of *New Age Journal* was to chronicle, celebrate, and advance the Third Great Awakening, and to hold its leaders and constituents accountable. It was time to stop giving our power away to so-called experts and authorities. My colleagues at the magazine and I would trust our *own* experience, I vowed. Damn the critics and the naysayers. Screw the establishment gatekeepers and the hipster poseurs! We would man the trenches of the Third Great Awakening and champion the New Age.

The previous year I had traveled to San Francisco to meet prospective advertisers (the Sierra Club, Working Assets, Shambhala Books, and many others) and to visit the offices of the *Whole Earth Catalog*, the publication that had started it all.

In his article, Wolfe had likened the counterculture of the 1960s and 1970s to earlier periods of religious experimentation and social tumult in American history. The flames of the First Great Awakening were stoked by charismatic fire-and-brimstone preachers such as Jonathan Edwards and George Whitefield, who challenged the authority of the colonies' religious establishment and of the British Crown. They appealed to people's emotions, treating all listeners, as Edwards put it, as equal "Sinners in the Hands of an Angry God" and emphasizing the authority of one's feelings and individual choices over the dictates of church doctrine and the clergy.

Benjamin Franklin, like most of the Founding Fathers, was a deist who rarely attended church. Like Edwards and Whitefield, he was skeptical and critical of organized religion, yet he did not subscribe to Whitefield's theology either. But Franklin admired Whitefield for urging people to perform good works. He published Whitefield's sermons on the front page of the *Philadelphia Gazette* for several years and helped promote the evangelical movement in America.

According to Wolfe, the Second Great Awakening "took the form of a still wilder hoe-down camp-meeting revivalism, of ceremonies in which people barked, bayed, fell down in fits and swoons, rolled on the ground, talked in tongues, and even added a touch of orgy."

Just as Benjamin Franklin had promoted the First Great Awakening, Ralph Waldo Emerson aided and abetted the Second Great Awakening through his essays and lectures and the publication of his magazine *The Dial*. Put off by what he called the "cold and cheerless" formality of Puritan Calvinism and its successor, Unitarianism, Emerson argued that people needed to balance logic and reason with emotion and spirit. Inspired by the Romantic poets and the sacred texts of Hinduism, Buddhism, and Islam, he preached the possibility of direct communion with God and the mystical, intuitive insight of an "inner light" that transcends reason. With Henry David Thoreau he championed transcendentalism, stressing self-reliance, optimism, and individual freedom.

I was excited about the Third Great Awakening, and I believed that Stewart Brand was its Franklin or Emerson. Like Franklin, Brand himself wasn't much of a practitioner of new age doctrines, as far as I knew, but he promoted the ideas and provided access to tools that would enable his readers to live by those ideas. Brand's *Whole Earth Catalog* captured the spirit of the times. His epigraph, "We are as gods

Off to see the Wizard of the Whole Earth (Catalog)

and might as well get good at it," made his catalog the bible of the Third Great Awakening.

My trip to the Bay Area was my first since hitchhiking there in the Summer of Love. Serendipitously, everybody I had wanted to meet was able to see me just at the time I needed to see them in order to see everyone else I wanted to meet. Walking down a sidewalk in Berkeley on my way from one appointment to the next and marveling at how a cosmic scheduler must have intervened, I heard a voice in my head for the first time in my life. It said, "You better get used to it. It's going to be this way from now on."

Stewart Brand cleared his busy schedule to see me. The *Whole Earth Catalog* offices were at Gate Five, a pier filled with houseboats in Sausalito. Stewart's office was in a little gypsy caravan tucked between nondescript outbuildings where the other editors and the business folks did their things. Stewart was welcoming and generous, and he introduced me to most of the staff. But he didn't seem to know what to make of me, or what to make of *New Age Journal.* Perhaps it was the name that confused him, or our focus on people and ideas rather than on tools.

One of the first things Stewart wanted to talk about was advertising. The *Whole Earth Catalog* didn't carry any. They had a policy against it, and Stewart wanted to know why we'd chosen to include ads in our publication. I told him that I didn't think advertising was inherently evil. "If it's the right product or service, handled in the right way, I consider it a service to the reader." He noted that we were running articles by some of the same writers who graced the pages of his catalog. I told him I wished a dozen other magazines would do the same. He marveled at the speed with which *New Age Journal* was growing, and I volunteered to consult with his circulation manager.

At one point Stewart explained his book-reviewing policy. "I never read a book before I review it. If I do, I might confuse my ideas with those of the author," he said. I couldn't believe my ears, but he was serious. "Instead, I write the review first, then read the book, just to make sure I didn't misrepresent the author."

I thanked him for the inspiration, and for his unerring editorial eye, and left with my ardor for him and his work undiminished.

Dick Raymond, a member of the Point Foundation, whose board oversaw the *Whole Earth Catalog*, pulled me aside as I was leaving and told me there was a "wild-ass journalist/entrepreneur" on the East Coast who he thought I should meet. "His name is Bob Schwartz," Raymond said, "and he knows everybody!"

13

THE ENTREPRENEURIAL REVOLUTION

"Slawson, Dawson, Hobson, and Widget, Drop-Forge and Steam-Hammer Company. How may I assist you?" That's what I heard on the other end of the line the first time I called Bob Schwartz.

"What?" I said.

"Slawson, Dawson, Hobson, and Widget, Drop-Forge and Steam-Hammer Company. May I help you?"

"Sorry. I must have the wrong number," I said, about to hang up.

"Wait a second. Who you calling?" came the voice.

"Bob Schwartz," I said. "Is this the Tarrytown Conference Center?"

"This is Bob Schwartz. What can I do for you?"

That's how it went the first time I called Bob Schwartz. He loved to disarm people by answering his phone with a rapid-fire salutation. "Slawson, Dawson . . ." was one of his favorites. It certainly worked on me. When I'd collected myself, I told him my name, my connection to *New Age Journal,* and that Dick Raymond had told me to call.

"I'm a charter subscriber to your magazine," Schwartz told me. "Come down to my humble inn in Tarrytown and let's talk. I'll throw another cup of water in the soup."

As we hung up Schwartz said, "We have important work to do together, you and I."

I was always game to meet an interesting person, especially one who came so intriguingly recommended. If someone was identified with an idea that I found interesting, I felt compelled to meet them. I wanted to see whether, and how, the idea came alive in that person. Were they living it? Did it inform their life? I could have learned macrobiotics from Michio's books, but I needed to meet him, to see for myself how his teachings manifested in his life, and to feel my way into how they might take root in mine. Same with Dan Raincloud, Tom Wolfe, and Stewart Brand. A "wild-ass journalist/entrepreneur" with an interest in the New Age? This I had to see.

Bob's "humble inn" was anything but. Driving up the long, curving driveway was an exercise in intimidation. One was always looking up. Whether on foot or via transport, you were meant to arrive overwhelmed—on your heels and out of breath. Then, when you entered

Bob Schwartz in front of his Tarrytown, New York, estate

the main foyer, you were met by a grand chandelier and a long, curving staircase over which hung a welcome sign listing the day's guests. IBM, CBS, *The New York Times,* Union Carbide, Chase Manhattan Bank, Continental Grain, Xerox, and a few others were all on the campus the day I arrived. This was where the corporate elite came for their retreats, and to enjoy their expense account perquisites.

Bob greeted me in the foyer, looking like a lion in a pin-striped business suit, a great shock of white hair framing his darkly tanned face. Bob was fifty-five years old, and I was twenty-nine. He gave me a big handshake and led me into the dining room, to a vast smorgasbord of food spread over a dozen long tables. He moved as quickly as he talked, as if he were running on pure adrenaline.

After Bob got me to fill my plate, I sat with him at his corner table in the dining room. My back was to the room, and Bob's seat was the classic mafioso's power spot, which allowed him to keep an eye on the entire room while pretending to listen to me. He asked me about the magazine; then, without waiting for my answer, he told me about himself. Bob had spent the first ten years of his working life as a journalist, writing for the army's *Yank* magazine, then for *Time, Life, Harper's,* and other publications. At one point he was the New York bureau chief for *Time,* on the editorial board at *Harper's,* and on the board of directors of *New York* magazine. At *Time* he shared an office with business guru Peter Drucker, and he was called the company's "entrepreneur in residence."

When he was forty-four, Bob bought his "humble inn," the former Mary Duke Biddle estate, with no money of his own. He got IBM and AT&T to go to the bank with him and promise to rent "x" number of rooms per year. On the strength of their endorsement, and Bob's enormous chutzpah, the bank loaned him the money.

Bob told me that the key to his conference center's success was the food. "I give them what they'd never allow themselves to eat at home or order off the menu in a restaurant." The standard fare included smoked salmon, eggs Benedict, sausages, roast beef, rich cheeses, German chocolate cake, every kind of pie you could think of. Who could resist? After nearly ten years of macrobiotic self-denial, not me.

I was intrigued by Bob and decided to get to know him. He had charisma and he *did* know *everybody*, it seemed. He sounded more like the auctioneer at the Minnesota State Fair than any writer I'd ever met, firing words off so fast that I had to concentrate carefully to catch them all. I suspected his quick wit and disarming charm, which seemed so spontaneous, were actually composed and practiced, written in his mind if not on paper long before anything was ever spoken aloud.

Bob was a seeker, for sure, but unlike any seeker I'd ever met. He had an enormous need to know. He was driven to see the big picture and to understand what it all meant. He was compelled to make sense out of what was happening in the world, to identify the key players, the agents of cultural change, the ones who were shaping the emerging culture, and to bring them together and introduce them to one another.

As I departed after that first meeting, Bob invited me to come back in about a month for what he called a conversational "salon." "I bring a bunch of high achievers together," he explained, "and do my best to 'raise the level of their dialogue.'" He affectionately described these cutting-edge scientists, spiritual trailblazers, and visionary businesspeople as "mutants and aberrants with a nagging sense of mission," and "poets and packagers of a new social order." He said the ideas for the French Revolution were seeded in egalitarian salons in Paris in the late eighteenth century. "It's time," he said, "for a new revolution."

A month later, I was back in the library at Tarrytown House. There were a dozen people sitting on leather club chairs and sofas, loosely arranged in a circle. Bob sat on a high barstool, giving him the power position, of course.

Among the guests were such cultural change agents as the mythologist Joseph Campbell, anthropologist Margaret Mead, mind researcher Jean Houston, economists E. F. Schumacher and Hazel Henderson, Nobel Peace Prize winner Muhammad Yunus, and Esalen founder Michael Murphy. I was starstruck and more than a little intimidated.

Perhaps Bob's greatest gift was his unerring instinct for seeing who and what you longed to be, the person you secretly and privately dreamed that you might someday become—your *possible* self. He introduced people, even celebrities, as the person they aspired to be. He introduced Margaret Mead as "Queen Margaret, who has done more to empower women than anyone in the English-speaking world." Joseph Campbell was "the Merlin of the emerging culture." And he called me the "visionary founder of the most important magazine in America today." It was shameless puffery, and everyone knew it, but it worked nonetheless.

Bob told us he was picking up signs of something important. Something was emerging on the cultural horizon that would transform the world—an earthshaking paradigm shift. I could tell he was onto something. I sensed it too. Bob called it "the coming entrepreneurial revolution."

Bob defined *entrepreneur* as "a person who has a vision and makes it real." "Does anyone here besides me sense this shift?" Bob asked, opening up the conversation to the group. He knew damn well everyone present did.

Joseph Campbell spoke first, saying that entrepreneurs, at least as Bob was defining them, were the modern era's version of the hero with a thousand faces.

"The hero leaves the safety of the village and goes off on a quest," said Campbell. Like Odysseus in the *Odyssey*, or Jason in search of the Golden Fleece, or Parzival in search of the Holy Grail, "the hero goes into the labyrinth, gets lost, confronts his or her mortality, and returns to the village with something that transforms the villagers' view of themselves, that enables the village to see itself in a new way."

"At the heart of every entrepreneur is a sense of being an outcast, a dropout from a world not particularly liked in its present form," responded Schwartz.

The entrepreneur as modern-day countercultural hero? This was a whole new way of seeing the world.

Margaret Mead attested that, according to Bob's definition, she considered herself to be an entrepreneur, and that Mother Teresa from Calcutta was the greatest entrepreneur of all. The conversation went on like this for the next two hours.

I sensed a shift in the zeitgeist, and in myself. I finally had a name for who and what I was in the world. I was an entrepreneur. I was not an architect or macrobiotics teacher, or acupuncturist, or even a magazine publisher and editor. I was an "en-tre-pre-neur." And, according to Schwartz, entrepreneurs weren't robber barons or snake-oil salesmen. They were agents of cultural change.

After I got back to Boston I phoned Schwartz and proposed that we do an interview for *New Age Journal*. He loved the idea. I got *Psychology Today* writer Sam Keen to conduct the interview, and I edited it. The result was the March 1976 cover story, with Schwartz sitting behind his mahogany desk in a three-piece business suit, pointing directly at the reader, like Uncle Sam on the army recruiting posters. The cover line read, "American Business Needs You!"

"American Business Needs You!" *New Age Journal*'s March 1976 cover story.

In the interview, Bob said that big industry was more dinosaur-dead than we knew, and that in the dying of every era lies the entrepreneurial opportunity to create a new and better age. Bob said that entrepreneurs were the real agents of cultural change, and that the world needed fewer MBAs. "There ought to be schools for entrepreneurs," he said.

At one point in the interview Bob said, "The counterculture is a hotbed of entrepreneurial potential. Entrepreneurs are more like members of the Peace Corps than graduates of Harvard Business School. Entrepreneurs and members of the counterculture are both essentially inner-directed; they're interested in change and innovation. They don't march to other people's drumbeats. . . . You have to see yourself as a warrior, to see yourself as a risk-taker knowing the fear inherent in risk-taking, understanding it, accepting it, and then proceeding unafraid."

The interview elicited over three hundred letters to the magazine each week for six weeks, more than Bob had seen for any article in all his years of journalism. I urged Bob to launch the school for entrepreneurs that he'd mentioned in the interview. Many of the letters asked when it would start. I then drew up a full-page ad announcing the Tarrytown School for Entrepreneurs for the next issue of the magazine and showed it to Bob. But Bob balked.

"I can't do something so flaky," he said. "What if IBM and AT&T find out? I could lose their business!"

He tried to kill the ad, but I knew in my bones that it was an idea whose time had come, and that Bob was the person to do it. I could also tell he really *wanted* to do it, that his protests were pro forma. "Let's just see who responds," I argued. "We can always decide not to go forward." Bob eventually relented, and we ran the ad. It got such an enthusiastic response, from such a diverse and eccentric cast of characters, that Bob couldn't resist going forward with it.

The Tarrytown School for Entrepreneurs was launched later that year. Its first class was a two-weekend course with what Schwartz called "high-intensity, short-term learning." The first weekend focused on theory and was taught by Bob and a professor from Harvard

Business School. The second weekend featured presentations of each student's business plan and a pitch for funding to venture capitalists. I was a member of that first class, and later of the faculty.

The more I visited Tarrytown, the more bedazzled I became by Schwartz—the pace of his talk and physical movement, the grandiose, larger-than-life scale of his thinking and living. He was a great American personality: a fast-talking, totally charming Robert Preston–style Music Man from Salem, Ohio.

I wanted to be like Bob. He was an outsider from the Midwest, like me. He loved ideas. He was a journalist and magazine person. He'd made it in the big city by any measure of success. And yet he saw himself as a true agent of change. He counted among his friends many in my pantheon of ideological deities, and he was on intimate terms with all of them.

Looking back, I see that I was ready for a change in my life. I was at a turning point. Peggy's and my marriage was on the rocks—living together and working together had gotten to be too much for us. Any conflict or disagreement at home spilled over into the office, and vice versa. We both knew something had to change.

Meanwhile, I was getting increasingly enthralled with New York. The Big Apple was clear and unapologetic about its values—it was all about power, achievement, connections, moving up in the world, meeting fabulous, accomplished, influential people. "If I can make it there, I'll make it anywhere," went the city's weird theme song. Ostensibly, I rejected those values. Nonetheless, I wanted to be there, in the middle of it all.

I wrote a letter to the staff with the headline "What's Happening Here? Power Struggle in the New Age." In the letter, addressed to each of the other seven staff members, I wrote, "Though Peggy publicly claims she does not want me to leave the magazine, privately she admits she wants nothing to do with me. Probably both are true. . . . I've put all my energy, creative thought, and three years of my life into the magazine. I'm not about to be squeezed out in some power-play, nor am I going to try to squeeze Peggy out. . . . That would be unconscionable. So, I'm staying, Peggy's staying, and I hope you all are staying. . . ."

Peggy responded to the letter, saying, "There's no way for both of us to work at the magazine." And she offered to leave. Fearing that her departure would create more turmoil than I could handle, for the good of the magazine, and our son, Leif, I resigned.

The truth is, the New Age had begun to seem too confined to me, a small tide pool on the edge of a vast ocean. The New Age had healed me and fed my family, but I was ready to explore new shores and distant horizons. I decided I'd really rather be living closer to the action in New York City than trying to repair a broken marriage in Boston. Within a few weeks of Peggy's and my back-and-forth letters, and just months after meeting Bob Schwartz, I moved to New York.

14

THE GANDHI/GATSBY SYNDROME

I felt lonely in New York, as lonely as I had ever been, longing for Leif, missing my family in Minnesota and my friends in Boston, remembering the good parts of my marriage with Peggy. My favorite family moments were lying under the baby grand piano that Peggy's grandmother had given her with Leif asleep on my belly, listening to Peggy play Chopin's Sonatas in B Minor. She played them brilliantly. I longed for those moments with my whole body.

I walked the streets at night and looked up at a hundred brightly lit apartment windows in a single building. Somebody up there is feeling lonely, I thought, like me, but I don't know how to meet them.

I was living hand to mouth at the time, literally. I managed to earn a few dollars from several clients who I helped start small businesses, but my monthly income never exceeded one thousand dollars. This covered my rent and most of my other expenses. I lived mostly on buckwheat noodles and broccoli, and became a regular at book launches and charity benefits. One event was held in the two-story Fifth Avenue apartment of the heiress to the Pampers diaper fortune. While the rest of the guests clustered around Andy Warhol, I parked myself at the hors d'oeuvres table, filling both my mouth and my plate with garlic shrimp and sausage-stuffed mushroom caps.

Besides being a social maladroit, I realized that I was afflicted with another problem, what I called the "Gandhi/Gatsby syndrome." I wanted to do good and do *well* at the same time. I wanted to help save the world from social injustice and environmental disaster, and I wanted to make money doing it, possibly lots of it.

I traced the genesis of this malady to the sixties, when I had hitch-hiked to San Francisco. At least I think that was when the Gandhi part of me took hold. LSD, SDS, and peace and love became my priorities. That's when I co-founded a Digger house, distributed magic mush-rooms, and became an apostle of love.

By the late seventies I had grown interested in another set of values—the Gatsby set (or perhaps the *Citizen Kane* set). I wanted to explore the world and, I hoped, get paid for it. I wanted to meet the leading thinkers and visionaries of our time. I wanted to participate in a national conversation about who we were as a people and where we were going. And, to the extent that doing these things required money, I wanted to make money.

At the beginning of the twentieth century, economist and sociolo-gist Thorstein Veblen, a good Norwegian American from Northfield, Minnesota, authored his now classic critique of capitalism, *The Theory of the Leisure Class*. He argued that in industrialized societies the rich establish their good reputation through "conspicuous consumption." My parents' generation showed the world they'd "made it" by buying a new car every year, hiring "summer nannies" and a "cleaning lady," and joining the Town & Country Club.

But by the late seventies the symbols of success had changed. According to the Stanford Research Institute 1978 Values and Life-styles survey, you'd "arrived" when you'd "combined your work and your play, had major societal commitments and free time anytime, and you were independent, loving, and in touch with your feelings." This shift from external to internal measures of wealth, based on Abraham Maslow's hierarchy of needs, had far-reaching implications for every aspect of American life.

Perhaps living in New York City—that mecca of conspicuous consumption—made me want to make money. Perhaps it was Bob

Schwartz's high-rolling lifestyle. Perhaps it was my stage of life—I had a son to provide for and bills to pay. But I wasn't really thinking about spending money—there was nothing in particular that I needed or wanted anyway—I just wanted to *make* it.

I suspect the Gandhi/Gatsby syndrome was epidemic, that other members of the sixties generation were similarly afflicted. We wanted to find a way to change the world and succeed in it simultaneously. But most of us didn't know how.

The beginning of the shift from idealistic values to more materialistic ones can be traced to 1971. That's when Virginia lawyer (and future U.S. Supreme Court justice) Lewis Powell, Jr., wrote what has come to be known as the Powell Memo. After a decade of federal legislative protections for workers, consumers, and the environment, a largely bipartisan effort attributable to the Third Great Awakening and inspired by such brave souls as Rachel Carson and Ralph Nader, the right, and especially corporations, mounted a counterattack. By 1980 the number of firms that had registered lobbyists in Washington had increased from 175 to 2,500. The number of corporate PACs had increased from under 300 in 1976 to over 1,200. These lobbyists and PACs had one purpose: to influence politicians to roll back the regulations.

During this time the clothes, music, and language of the love revolution were co-opted by business. Blue jeans, once the choice of young boomers, as they were of farmers and laborers because of their low cost and durability, became pre-stressed designer jeans and a fashionized weapon of mass consumption. Chicago economist Milton Friedman declared that the sole purpose of publicly held corporations is to maximize profits for their shareholders. By 1980, when Ronald Reagan was elected, the corporate counterrevolution was in full swing. The forces of greed were undermining the forces of love, by design, and paid for with millions of dollars of lobbying, advertising, and celebrity "news."

On August 29, 1978, *Esquire* published my all-time favorite magazine article, "The Dangerous Arrogance of the New Elite," written by

Minnesota attorney David Lebedoff. In the article Lebedoff warned that my generation, the baby boomers, no longer believed in the basic premise of democracy, that is, that the greatest wisdom lies with the majority of the people.

Lebedoff claimed that the various movements for change of the 1960s and '70s—civil rights, the peace movement, women's rights, gay rights, the environmental movement, and others—all championed by college-educated baby boomers, had put that cohort at odds with the majority of Americans. Baby boomers were ahead of the rest of the population on these issues, Lebedoff wrote, and, as a result, they had come to distrust democracy. They had come to believe that highly educated people were more fit to lead than the majority. The fallacy, Lebedoff declared, was the boomers' belief that fitness to lead (i.e., wisdom) comes from education or measurable intelligence. Wisdom, he argued, comes from *life experience,* not from education. And wisdom, not education, is randomly and roughly equally distributed throughout the population.

I believed that Lebedoff was right, that it isn't one's educational degree or wealth or bloodline, or any other credential, that matters in life. It's life experience. I was a college dropout, without portfolio. I was living on less than ten thousand dollars a year. But I was doing my best to amass a mountain of life experience.

Bob Schwartz talked often about writing a book about entrepreneurship, but he hadn't gotten around to actually doing it. He tended to get distracted by his myriad enthusiasms. He was having too much fun to write. Finally, I called his bluff: "It's time to put up or shut up," I told him. I suggested we go to a friend's cottage on Cape Cod to write a proposal that I could use to sell the book to publishers. We hauled six cardboard boxes, five briefcases, and the backs of five hundred envelopes to the island, all filled with notes for the book. I sorted through the lot, arranging them into piles representing chapters, and wrote a page and a half summarizing each.

Bob read what I wrote and said, "Eric, this is brilliant! It's perfect." I knew he was lying. I didn't have his gift. But I also knew that once he was faced with having my words represent his thinking, he would sit down and bang out his own brilliant prose, which he did.

Within three days we had our proposal for *The Coming Entrepreneurial Revolution*. I created an auction, sending the proposal to fifteen publishers, with a cover letter telling them we wanted to hear from them within the month. I attached a faux review that I'd written and typeset as if it were photocopied from *Publishers Weekly*, announcing that the book had secured a huge advance, was a Book of the Month Club selection, and other hyperbole. It got the publishers' attention. They read the proposal, and within a week Bob had accepted a six-figure advance from Random House.

At one point, I got my father and Bob Schwartz together for lunch at the legendary Mortimer's. It felt strangely satisfying to introduce these two men who were so important to me. One Bob was my role model, someone I wanted to emulate. The other was the person I was afraid I might turn out to be, the person my wife would point to during an argument when she said, "You're just like your father!" For much of my life, he was the last person in the world I wanted to be like.

At the end of the meal my father leaned over the table toward Schwartz and said, "It must be nice to know Eric as a friend."

Very nice indeed, I thought, *for me*. I wished that all young people could have a mentor like Bob, and that all fathers and sons could know each other deeply. Bob Schwartz was both my mentor and my friend.

I attended a memorial gathering for Margaret Mead shortly after her death in November 1978. During his eulogy, Bob spoke the following words, attributing them to Mead, "Never doubt that a small group of committed citizens can change the world, indeed it's the only thing that ever has." After Bob spoke, Mead's partner, Rhoda

Métraux, exclaimed, "She never said that!" to which Bob replied, "Yes she did . . . and if she didn't, she should have."

The words were actually written by Bob. They perfectly encapsulate Bob's two great passions in life: people and ideas, and the power that comes from bringing them together to make a difference in the world. They were my passions as well.

15

BETTY FROM MINNESOTA

In late January 1979, the seventh class of the Tarrytown School for Entrepreneurs was being offered. I wasn't teaching that session, but I went up to Tarrytown on opening night to check out the class, and to eat some of Bob's fabulous food.

As usual, participants were instructed on arrival to assume a new identity—not to tell anyone their real name, where they were really from, or what they did. This tended to drive entrepreneurs mad because all they ever want to talk about is who they are, where they're from, and what they do. But I loved it. The rules created a charged and playfully theatrical atmosphere where anything, even magic, might happen. For some reason, I decided that night I would be "Nelson from Tarrytown."

As I entered the dining room with my plate piled high, I looked for a seat and saw that all the tables were full, except for one where a woman had just sat down with her plate all by herself. I saw a man walk over to her. He was wearing a name tag that identified him as someone from the IBM group also using the conference center that weekend. He was clearly hitting on her and I decided to intervene.

I walked up and asked, "Is this seat taken?" Without waiting for an answer, I sat next to the woman, wedging myself between her and the still-standing man. I introduced myself as "Nelson from

"Betty" was clearly *not* from Minnesota.

Tarrytown." The woman, who had a ringlet of dark curls across her forehead and dazzling blue eyes, gave me a warm smile and said, "I'm Betty from Minnesota." The IBM guy shrugged and left.

Some enchantment was at play. "Betty" was clearly *not* from Minnesota. I guessed she was a native New Yorker, and I, the rube from Minnesota, had taken the name of the forty-ninth governor of New York and forty-first vice president of the United States, Nelson Rockefeller, who in an even weirder bit of kismet, would die that very night, January 26, 1979.

The next weekend I showed up again in Tarrytown, this time for the class graduation party. When a slow tune came on, I invited "Betty" to dance. As we twirled and bumped around the crowded dance floor, I pulled her close and asked if she was married. She threw her head back and, as if in a West End play, tossed off, "Yes . . . unfortunately."

But the "unfortunately" landed with a thud, and we both knew how unfortunate her marriage really was. Before the night was over, Betty told me her real name was Nina, and that she'd come to the

Tarrytown School for Entrepreneurs because she'd started a greeting card business with a friend and it wasn't going so well. "My friend designs the cards and I sell them, which is fine," Nina explained. "But the production keeps getting interrupted because my friend keeps joining spiritual cults."

A few weeks later a friend brought Nina to a party I was having in my apartment. At the party, I found myself having libidinous thoughts about her. I could tell my thoughts were reciprocated.

After the party ended and everyone had gone, Nina helped me clean up, then sat with me on my couch. Something I said reminded her of a song. I asked her to sing it for me, but she demurred.

"I can't sing," she said.

I tried to encourage her. "Just a few bars."

"No really, I can't sing."

"Anyone can sing," I persisted. "How about humming a few notes then?"

She started to cry. "When I was a little girl I was told that I'm tone-deaf," she said. "I was told to lip-sync when others sing."

"Someday we'll sing together," I promised, giving her a hug, "in two-part harmony."

Nina called me a few days later and offered to host a small gathering at her place to introduce me to a few of her friends in Manhattan. She and her husband lived across the park from my place, in a corner apartment on Park Avenue. She told me the last owner was the fashion designer Diane von Fürstenberg. I could tell I was supposed to be impressed, but I was not. I had no idea who Diane von Fürstenberg was. During that conversation she also told me her last name was Rothschild. I said, "As in the European banking Rothschilds?"

"Unfortunately not," she said, and laughed. "We're distant cousins. Our family is the Brooklyn branch." This, I learned later, was Nina's standard line, meant to obfuscate rather than enlighten and to discourage gold diggers while maintaining the patina of old money and good breeding. The truth is, Nina's family had money, at one time gobs of it, but it came from Nina's grandmother on her father's side, not the Rothschilds.

At Nina's soirée I instinctively sat in her husband's favorite chair. He spent the evening in the kitchen, fuming and slugging down whiskey. Things were getting complicated. By this time I was completely smitten with Nina. She was a great beauty, but she didn't seem to know it. And she claimed to be socially awkward. "I can't stand up and have a conversation at the same time," she'd say. But she was the most adroit and skillful schmoozer I'd ever met. She was genuinely warm and seemingly comfortable with and able to make small talk with anyone—doormen, club kids, panhandlers, and political big shots alike. She knew how to put people at ease, in any situation, even if she wasn't feeling at ease herself. She was by turns thoughtful, glib, or demure, as the situation warranted, and she could make anyone feel that she was interested in them, because she sincerely was.

This was probably what intimidated me most about Nina and her family. And also what attracted me to her. I felt awkward around Nina's crowd, as if I'd stumbled onstage in the middle of a comedy of manners, Oscar Wilde's *The Importance of Being Earnest*, say. I didn't know my lines. Perhaps I could learn from Nina to be more at ease, I hoped, not so self-conscious and tongue-tied.

A few weeks later Nina told me she and her husband were separating. Whoa! This made me very nervous. I was horrified at the thought that I might be the cause of their separation. I had no steady work. I was a "consultant," trying to help people "get paid for being themselves," as I put it. I decided to back off until Nina was finished dealing with her marriage, and we could see where we were after that. Nina got her own place on Washington Square, filed for her divorce, and then we began dating.

A few months later, I met Nina's family for the first time. I was totally intimidated. Surely they will see me for the Midwest rube I am, I thought, even if Nina could not.

They lived on the north shore of Long Island. The house, a red-brick colonial, sat on about five acres of broad lawns, with spreading elms and well-tended gardens. I felt like Minnesotan Nick Carraway visiting Jay Gatsby's mansion in East Egg, which was just across the bay. The only difference was that Nina's family home was the domain of *old* wealth. Though they had servants, everything was understated and discreet, nothing ostentatious or garish about it. Nina's father drove a Chevy II, not a Mercedes or a Rolls-Royce, because, as Nina explained, he was "an anti-snob snob."

Nina showed me a photo of herself with "Mrs. Gus," her Norwegian nanny, taken when Nina was five. Both were dressed in *bunad*s, the traditional Norwegian peasant costumes. "Look," Nina said, "I'm practically Norwegian."

I was overwhelmed by Nina's family. They were the closest thing I'd ever met to aristocracy, and they hobnobbed with British royalty— Nina had spent an entire day with Prince Charles when she was nineteen. What in the world did she see in me?

Yet on that first visit with her family, Nina brought me to meet her neighbor, the Jungian dream analyst and astrologer Alice O. Howell. Alice read our natal charts and told us that even though Nina was a Capricorn and I a Leo, Nina could be "the barmaid" of my soul, "dispensing jiggers of ambrosia." I had no idea what that meant, but I had the impression Alice thought we were a "perfect match."

I was an ambivalent, hot-and-cold, on-again, off-again boyfriend. The more interested Nina seemed to be, the more uncertain I'd become. I suggested we travel overseas together, then changed my mind. We explored several spiritual traditions together, then I backed out. People would sometimes ask us if we were getting married. "We *are* married," we'd reply in unison, "to *other* people." Was I ready for a committed relationship? I didn't know.

While I waffled, Nina got involved in Jerry Brown's campaign for the presidency. She was very good at it, and soon Jerry's principal aide and strategic adviser, the Zen mystery man Jacques Barzaghi, decided Nina would be the perfect first lady for Jerry, or so it seemed to me. Described in the press as Jerry's Svengali, Barzaghi kept putting Jerry and Nina together on the campaign trail, seating them next to each other on flights, and placing them in adjacent hotel rooms. I could tell Nina was growing increasingly devoted to Jerry and everything he stood for. And I imagined her feeling right at home in the White House. I decided I needed to declare myself. I hoped I wasn't too late. I went with Nina to Manchester, New Hampshire, where Jerry was giving an important campaign speech in a historic old, octagonal town hall.

When Nina and I arrived Jerry was just beginning to speak. Hundreds of reporters filled the seats and lined the walls, TV cameras rolling and flashbulbs popping. Nina and I wedged ourselves into a spot in the back, standing against the wall. Within a couple minutes the pop singer Linda Ronstadt, wearing a full-length winter coat, strode purposefully across the back of the hall directly toward Nina and me. Ronstadt was then known in the press to be Jerry's girlfriend. When she was ten feet from us she thrust her hands into her coat pockets, pulled out a pair of dark socks, and held them out for all to see.

"Here," she said, "I found these at the foot of my bed this morning." Then she threw the socks at Nina's feet. "Maybe you'll find them at the foot of your bed tomorrow!" Wheeling around, she strode back across the floor and out the back of the hall. Jerry saw the whole encounter and quickly brought his speech to a close, then rushed down the center aisle and over to Nina and me, saying, "She doesn't know what's she's talking about. Not a word." Then he raced out of the hall after Ronstadt. From then on, Nina and I were together.

Meanwhile Bob struggled with his book. He went through a number of research assistants and ghostwriters, but they could not live up to his astronomically high expectations. Ultimately, he never finished the book. He was writing for the recognition and to change the culture, not for the money. He didn't need the money. He wanted his book to have impact, like the books by his famous friends. But his standards were impossibly high, and he could not meet them.

In the spring of 1979, Bob asked me to help him turn his salons—his occasional gatherings full of high-minded talk—into a business, which he would call the Tarrytown Group, a sort of ongoing, pre–TED conference meet-up and social club for people who'd scaled their particular mountain peak only to find themselves asking "Is that all there is?" He believed that important initiatives would inevitably emerge from their interactions. I wrote a business plan for the group and designed the newsletter.

By the fall of that year, Bob's huge ego began to drive me crazy. His energy was all-consuming. He sucked everyone around him into his whirlwind. He couldn't resist getting involved in every detail of running the conference center and any other project that came his way, and there were a thousand distractions—and people—who pulled him in as many directions. Worse, I began to notice that he used people the way so many of the social climbers I met in New York seemed to do. The way *I* sometimes did, though I couldn't admit it yet. He traded on his connections to the movers and shakers and the rich and famous.

Agents of cultural change? RLS and me.

Turning the Tarrytown Group into a business bothered me. Charging people money to help them find each other seemed wrong. After all, humans are social beings. We need to be members of a community to feel fully human. If the salons were a business, would we deny membership to those who could not pay? It was the final straw. I decided that I needed to get out of New York and away from Bob Schwartz if I was going to find my own vision.

As it happens, Jerry Brown's campaign was sending Nina to Wisconsin to do advance work. I suggested a visit to Minneapolis so she could meet Brenda and my family. The timing was perfect—the lilacs were in bloom and Nina fell in love with the city. We then decided to sublet our apartments in New York and move to Minneapolis for the summer of 1980. I got a job with the company where my father and brother Tom worked. Nina and I would finally live together.

III

MYTHOPOETIC MAN

16

WHAT DO MEN REALLY WANT?

Soon after returning to Minneapolis, I invited my father to play a round of golf. I wanted to connect with him, and having a four-hour conversation in the great outdoors, doing the thing he loved more than anything in the world, seemed like a good way to do that. We needed to bridge the chasm between us.

The problem was, I never was much of a golfer. To me the game represented a bourgeois way of life that by this time I wanted nothing to do with. Besides, golf courses were environmental disasters. To make matters even worse, pink and lime-green Bermuda shorts simply weren't my style. And then there was the fact that I wasn't very good at golf, and my father was. No wonder I hadn't played for at least ten years.

My father had finally pulled his life together. After living in a hotel room in Helena, Montana, for about a year, he'd moved back to Minnesota, married a woman named Edie, and gotten a job with Wilson Learning Corporation, a management and sales training company where he worked as the company's life insurance industry expert. He'd quit smoking and drinking (for the most part), and by the time Nina and I came to Minnesota, Dad was a new man. He seemed happy with his life and no longer driven to be a big shot. But I still didn't know him, and he didn't know me.

Out on the golf course that day, Dad and I would start out each hole on the tee together, but then our paths would invariably diverge. Dad would hit his tee shot straight and true. I, on the other hand, would try to hit my drive as far as I could, and nine times out of ten I'd slice the ball into the woods on the right or hook it into the rough, or the water, on the left. Then I'd run to where I thought I'd find my ball, clubs bouncing and clanging noisily on my shoulder, while Dad strode calmly down the middle of the fairway to his.

I'd thrash around knee-deep in the tall grass for a minute or two, searching for my errant ball, muttering, "I was sure it was right about here." Eventually Dad would shout something like "It's about ten yards to the left, right in line with that big oak."

And of course that's exactly where the ball would be.

My hoped-for heart-to-heart turned out to be a half-hour chat spread out over four hours on the tees and greens. After our round, instead of feeling more connected to my father, I felt utterly frustrated and defeated by my inability to relate to him.

My dad and brother worked at Wilson Learning, and the company's founder, Larry Wilson, hired me to be the company's first-ever Director of New Ventures, exploring opportunities in everything from cable television production to wellness programming.

The company was good at developing training modules to address the body and mind, but they didn't have a clue about how to talk about the spirit. Since I had edited *New Age Journal*, Larry decided I was the de facto house expert on spirituality, and he conscripted me to develop that module.

My brother Tom, who wrote sections of the wellness program, thought it would be a good idea if everyone working on the project experienced a new form of meditation that he had recently learned from some followers of an Indian guru named Bhagwan Shree Rajneesh. It was called "dynamic" or "chaotic" meditation.

Rajneesh was one of the dozens of Hindu and Buddhist gurus to find their way to America during the 1960s and 1970s. But he was different. He was known as the sex guru. He was brilliant and irreverent where the others were sanctimonious. And he was funny. One of his better-known lectures was about the word *fuck*, which he used two or three times in every sentence, to hilarious, if shocking, effect. And his followers, all of whom wore red or orange to betoken their devotion to the guru, knew how to party.

A friend of Tom's, an orange-clad devotee of Rajneesh, led a dozen of us in a three-part chaotic meditation session. In a large carpeted lunchroom with all the furniture removed, we began with deep, loud, rapid breathing, in sync with pulsing recorded sitar music with a heavy beat. This lasted for at least fifteen minutes, followed by jumping in place with our hands raised over our heads and shouting *"Hoo-hoo-hoo!"* for another fifteen minutes, followed by wild, crazy, manic howling and dancing and spinning for another fifteen minutes.

At the end, we all collapsed on the floor in ecstatic exhaustion. I'd never felt so enlivened and unselfconscious and energized in my life. Hilarious, ridiculous things flowed out of my mouth as soon as they came into my head, if not before. I wasn't the least bit tongue-tied. I loved chaotic meditation.

But I hated working at Wilson Learning. I was struggling for air there. Most of Wilson's employees were refugees from Fortune 500 corporations, and Wilson Learning was Valhalla to them, the promised land, compared to their previous, more bureaucratic workplaces. But I found Wilson Learning terribly bureaucratic and constricting. I realized that if I couldn't be happy at Wilson Learning, then I must be unemployable. I told Brenda how boxed in I felt.

"I've never been able to work in a large office either," she said. "It's my fatal flaw. No herd instinct."

I'd been waiting for several years for my divorce from Peggy to become official, and when it finally did, in May 1981, I drove to the downtown Minneapolis courthouse to sign the papers and get my divorce certificate. While waiting for the paperwork, I noticed a pile of marriage license applications, so I took one to a nearby bar and filled it out. You never know, I thought. The marriage license might come in handy. A guy at the bar asked me what I was doing. When I told him, he said, "I've been married three times. It's crazy! Don't do it!"

I felt like I was stepping off a cliff, taking a "leap of no return." Could I really do this? Had I learned the lessons I needed to learn before marrying again? I didn't know, but I knew the only way for me to find out was to take the leap.

Nina and I were married three days later, with Brenda as our only witness. The ceremony was conducted in a judge's chamber on the seventeenth floor of the Government Center tower in downtown Minneapolis. When the blessedly brief ceremony was over, Brenda, Nina, and I descended to the open-air central lobby. When the elevator door opened, we were greeted by a chorus of about fifty children standing on risers and singing, "May I have this dance for the rest of my life?" followed by, "Mama, don't let your babies grow up to be cowboys."

To this day I have no idea why the kids where there. Did Brenda arrange the choral serenade for us? She was the only person who knew we were getting married. But it was all on very short notice. I think it was a serendipitous cosmic setup.

Nina and me on our wedding day, May 21, 1981

From there we went down into the bowels of the building to the parking garage, where we popped the cork on a bottle of champagne, and Brenda gave a grandiloquent toast that included references to Elizabeth and Robert Browning and Tristan and Isolde. She ended her toast with the words "True love till the end of time!"

Nina and I visited Brenda often, usually when Brenda summoned us by calling at five o'clock and asking, "Watchya doin'?" She was busy training to run to the top of Colorado's 14,115-foot-high Pikes Peak; corresponding with ultra-marathoner Walter Stack; writing her column for *Minnesota Posten* (the Norwegian American newspaper); lecturing and debating around the Twin Cities about animal welfare, human rights, and health and well-being; and editing her diaries, which she would leave to the Minnesota Historical Society. All this at almost ninety years old.

Brenda wanted my help getting her writing published. We made a list of writing projects, including a sequel to her 1939 autobiography, *Me: A Memoir.* The book would be titled *Myself.* A planned third title, you guessed it, would be called *I.* She also worked on her manuscript for a health book, to be titled *Beauty and Bravery,* and another about the life of the Italian hero and statesman Giuseppe Garibaldi.

Helping Brenda with her publishing projects reminded me how much I had enjoyed working at *New Age Journal.* I missed the creative freedom, the access to leading thinkers and visionaries, the chance to explore the world and (hopefully) get paid for it, and a platform to participate in the national conversation. I craved meaningful work, to feel that what I was doing was helping to transform our world. Publishing *New Age Journal* had allowed me to advocate for the Third Great Awakening and what I called the love revolution, in which change would come not through opposition and conflict, but through listening and love. I longed to do that again.

I also missed all the magazines and newsletters that came to the *New Age Journal* offices each day, to which I had become irredeemably addicted. Between us, Nina and I subscribed to more than twenty magazines, everything from *Harper's* and *The Nation* to *CoEvolution Quarterly* and *Brain-Mind Bulletin.* Among our friends, that was not

Nina, Sam, and me, 1982

unusual. Before the Internet, browsing newsstands and visiting libraries' periodical sections was how you surfed the world of ideas.

Current issues and debates surfaced on the pages of magazines before they showed up anywhere else, especially in their news and letters sections. I read them to monitor everything from the antinuclear movement to liberation theology, the New Left, the New Right, and the New Age. While working at Wilson Learning, I whiled away hours in my corporate cubbyhole poring over my favorites.

Being a compulsive proselytizer and pamphleteer, I'd clip and photocopy articles that I considered must-reads and send them to various family members and friends, even though I knew damn well that most of the people I sent them to wouldn't get around to reading them. Still, I figured if a magazine had one article per year that touched my life in some important way—whether it helped me to reframe an issue or led me to contact someone—it was worth the price of a subscription.

In May 1982, the same month that Nina and I had our first child, Peggy published one of those must-read articles in *New Age Journal*. It was an interview with the poet Robert Bly. Quite simply, it changed my life.

Robert first gained notoriety in 1968 when he won the National Book Award for his volume of poems *The Light Around the Body*. At the awards ceremony at Lincoln Center, Robert handed over his cash prize to Resist, a draft-resistance organization, saying: "I am speaking for many, many Americans when I ask this question: Since we are murdering a culture in Vietnam at least as fine as our own, do we have the right to congratulate ourselves on our cultural magnificence? . . . From now on we will have to live with grief and defeat."

The *New Age Journal* interview, by Keith Thompson, was called "What Men Really Want." It launched the men's movement, and it blew my mind. It seemed Bly knew my pain, and what I wanted, better than I did.

In the interview, he described the great gap that separated postwar fathers from their sons when they headed out to the office. Whereas sons had once grown up working side by side with their fathers, now they barely knew them. Robert was describing my life. This was midcentury, middle-class middle America. We were no longer a nation of farmers, as we'd been at the turn of the century. Fathers left the house each day while mothers stayed home, and the kids, once they were school-age or daycare ready, spent the day away from both parents. They raised themselves.

"The strange thing about this is not only the physical separation," he said, "but the fact that the father is not able to explain to the son what he's doing in the world of offices. With the father only home in the evenings, and women's values so strong in the house, the father loses the son five minutes after birth. It's as if he has amnesia and can't remember who his children are. He might as well be in Australia."

Working in my cubicle at Wilson Learning, I might as well have been in Australia as far as Leif was concerned. At *New Age Journal*, when Peggy and I were still married, Leif came to the office regularly, and he was often underfoot. But now he was in Boston, and I was in Eden Prairie, Minnesota. Was I repeating the same crime my father had committed against my siblings and me? Had I abandoned Leif? Would I do the same with my new son, Sam?

In the article, Bly said that during the 1960s and 1970s men began to question what it means to be male and tried to get in touch with their feminine side. They left behind much of their aggressive macho role and discovered feelings, empathy, and nurturing. But, Bly said, men were suffering now. "Every modern male has, lying at the bottom of his psyche, a large, primitive man covered with hair down to his feet."

Had I abandoned Leif? Would I do the same with Sam?

It was time for them to get in touch with the wild man inside themselves, Bly urged, and to put this dormant power to use.

"The kind of energy I'm talking about is not the same as macho, brute strength, which men already know enough about," Bly explained. "It's forceful action undertaken, not without compassion, but with resolve. [It's] positive power accepted by the male in the service of the community. . . . Getting in touch with the wildman means religious life for a man in the broadest sense."

I was thrilled by the interview. Bly was saying that getting in touch with the inner wild man and bringing him into dynamic harmony with one's inner feminine was the aim of men's work. I realized that this search to become a whole human being was essential to becoming a good husband and a loving father. To me, it was nothing less than the quest for the Holy Grail.

But none of these ideas seemed relevant at Wilson Learning. It took me a few months to realize that my job was not to come up with ideas for new ventures (which, by the way, had been the job description) but rather to find a way to make Larry think that *he* had thought of the ideas for the new ventures. Otherwise, new ideas simply would not happen. I also realized I was working for the very beast I had resolved to overthrow a few short years before when I was working at the People's Warehouse. Now I was working for corporate America. Had I sold my soul to Mammon?

17

AMERICAN ALMANAC

On June 14, 1981, a tornado passed right over our home, slicing off the front porch of the house across the street, and carving a path of destruction through the heart of Minneapolis and St. Paul. A fisherman was killed less than a block from our home when he was struck by a flying tree. Beard's Plaisance, a small park just across the street from our house, looked and felt like a battlefield after a massacre. The

Utne Reader's original angel investor: Buff Chace (*left*), with Johnnie Chace

civil defense warning sirens didn't come on until a minute *after* the tornado had passed, adding an eerie wail to the tragic scene.

Later that day my friend Buff Chace, whom I had met at the first Tarrytown School for Entrepreneurs, and with whom I had shared the apartment on Central Park West, arrived with his then girlfriend Johnnie for a visit. They literally flew in on the tail of the tornado, and Buff proceeded to turn my life upside down. Within hours of his arrival, after seeing and hearing how much I was struggling with my job at Wilson Learning, Buff told me, "You were happier when you were publishing *New Age Journal*. Why don't you create another magazine?" He was right. I was withering at Wilson Learning. *I'd love to do another magazine*, I thought. Buff offered to grubstake me, putting up the first twenty-five thousand dollars.

So I began searching for an idea for a magazine that the world both needed and wanted. I read about the history of magazines, how to publish and edit them, what happened to the great and dearly departed ones (think *McClure's, Liberty, The Saturday Evening Post, Life, Look,* and *Saturday Review* for starters), and how to launch a new one. I read the original précis for *Time, Life,* and *People* magazines. I got especially interested in what I came to consider the three progenitors of my magazine: Ben Franklin's *Poor Richard's Almanack, I. F. Stone's Weekly,* and DeWitt Wallace's *Reader's Digest.*

I contacted I. F. Stone and asked him what "alternative" periodicals he recommended. He told me to read *The New York Times, The Washington Post,* and *The Wall Street Journal.* "If you want to offer an alternative," he said, "you have to know intimately what you're trying to be an alternative to."

At one point Nina asked, "Why are you sitting around the house reading magazines and doodling all the time? Why don't you get to work?"

"I *am* working" was my reply.

Nina told me she wanted to work on the magazine with me. It made perfect sense. After all, she was interested in ideas, had a great nose for news, and was a better writer than I was.

"No way," I told her.

"Yes way," she insisted.

"Never," I resisted. "Peggy and I worked together on *New Age Journal,* and it destroyed our marriage. We had no life outside of our work."

"I still think we should give it a try," Nina persisted, to which I replied, "OK, and if it doesn't work out, my next wife will have her own career," to which Nina said, "Screw you. I wouldn't work with you even if you begged me." As it turned out, Nina would contribute frequently to the magazine through her writing, and a thousand other ways, in the years to come.

I considered hundreds of names, including *The Turtle, The Well, Almanac 83, Earth's Almanac, Living Well, The E. J. Utne Fortnightly* (after *I. F. Stone's Weekly*), *Utne's Reading Digest, Utne's Good Life Almanac, Millennium: A Magazine for People Who Want to Make It to the Twenty-first Century, The Utne Report,* and *The Utne Review,* among many others. I filled yellow pads with article ideas, lists of possible names, sketches for logo designs, and treatments of the titles in various typefaces. Finally, I settled on *American Almanac,* in Times Roman, upper- and lowercase, bold italics.

American Almanac would feature what *Harper's Magazine* editor Lewis Lapham called "meaningful generalizations—answers and ideals that hold their shape in the dissolving images of yesterday's news."

I had an ongoing list of magazine articles that I wished someone would write someday, or that maybe I'd write myself. I used them as the basis of a twelve-page précis detailing *American Almanac*'s purpose, audience, and general editorial approach, with a paragraph or two describing twenty sample articles, as well as descriptions of the magazine's departments and format, a wish list of contributors, and thoughts on the publication's mascot/symbol/totem (the turtle).

The précis began with a quote from Alvin Toffler: "Humanity faces the deepest social and creative restructuring of all time. We are engaged in building a remarkable new civilization from the ground up."

By early 1983, I'd finally quit my job at Wilson Learning. I sent the précis to my sister and hand-delivered a copy to Brenda. Mary got right back to me. "Right on, Rickey Roo! Sign me up. I want to be your first subscriber." She sent me pages of comments from her colleagues at the National Opinion Research Center. The feedback was encouraging.

Brenda took a little longer. She covered almost every page with extensive marginalia. Among her scrawled notes she wrote,

"Grand! Splendid!" "Your intelligent warnings vs. the Scienterrific." "Opens the door on the sin of usury—money making money [idleness—hard-heartedness]. Sedentary, uglifying." "This! Great! Gee whiz! The fine, bright, noble explanation to Socialists and Oligarchs and Communists." "And this. Hurrah for the pseudo-scientists. They are all clear-eyed, handsome, and funny."

Brenda wrapped up her comments with the following, dated Friday, January 28, 1983:

Dear Eric:

This is an utterly amazing, learned, and inspired description of a great and successful magazine. And (this is interesting) only you could have done it, with its vision, sensibleness, width, idealism, practical working outline and plan. Its imaginative completeness is astounding. And each thing so interesting—would arouse such craving in readers—craving to read more. I wish you could plan it all—the office, the secretary, the financial backing in the bank. The drive for subscribers (ten thousand), the first 12 numbers [i.e., issues] laid out. I think this syllabus means you can and will do all this—with notable and fairly early success. I draw a star on some of these things. Well, I have scrawled 100 marginalia.

True love, Brenda

Brenda could not have been more supportive. Without her hyperbolic and inflated praise I might not have had the courage to go forward. She acknowledged me for qualities I didn't know I had, and very probably did not have until she claimed to see them in me. Brenda's encouragement made me want to live up to her vision of me, to be better, braver, and more noble—the heroic person she challenged me to be.

I felt like I was finally doing what I was meant to be doing. I didn't think of myself as a magazine publisher or writer or editor. I was a movement organizer, mobilizing a far-flung phalanx of cultural change agents to help realize the love revolution.

I soon realized the world didn't need another magazine—there were thousands on every special interest imaginable, from *Foreign Policy* to *Family Handyman*, *Kite Flying* to *Motorcycle Digest*, *Centrifugal Bumble-Puppy* to *Family Therapy Networker*. People could not digest what was already being published, let alone pay attention to something new. But the word *digest* set off a lightbulb in my head.

How about a digest of the best of what's already out there, I thought, *a* Reader's Digest *for the next generation?*

I began to suspect that *American Almanac* was not the right name. Inspired by *I. F. Stone's Weekly*, I decided it would be better to associate the magazine with a real live human being than some abstract, special-interest concept created by a focus group.

A friend suggested *Utne Reader,* which reminded me that *Utne,* according to my father, means "far out" in Norwegian. What could be more alternative than that? It was simple yet cryptic, which to me was a plus. People would not know how to pronounce it, which meant that the cognoscenti would teach the uninitiated, and thus spread the word by word of mouth, which is the very best form of marketing.

Before following my friend's suggestion, however, I thought I'd better do some fact-checking. I decided to contact Robert Bly.

I didn't know Robert yet, but I had wanted to meet him since I'd read his interview in *New Age Journal.*

I knew that he spoke Norwegian. I also knew his reputation as an acerbic firebrand. He had started his poetry review, *The Fifties,* as he said, "to attack the views of certain older poets. . . . The normal process of human growth from generation to generation involves . . . the new generation attacking the older one. And attacking them strongly, wiping them out as far as possible," he said.

I imagined Robert, who was twenty years older than me, attacking T. S. Eliot and Ezra Pound. I wondered what it would be like to have him try to wipe me out. Raised on a farm in Madison, Minnesota, he was the son of Norwegian immigrant farmers. Big and burly, and famously short-tempered, he seemed like the kind of guy who liked a good fight.

I got his phone number from Peggy and called him.

"Hello, Robert?" I began. "My name's Eric Utne."

"I know who you are," Robert replied. "Your ex just published an interview that I did with Keith Thompson for your old magazine. We're getting a lot of response already."

"That's sort of what I want to talk with you about," I said. "I wanted to thank you for that interview. You described exactly what happened between my father and me. If he wasn't at the office or on the golf course, he was asleep in his easy chair under the newspaper."

Robert laughed as I told him how revelatory I found his insights. Then he surprised me. He told me that our families hailed from the same part of Norway. His ancestors came from Bleie, which is the next village around the bend on the Hardangerfjord from Utne, my family's ancestral home.

"We might be related," Robert said. "Our kin most certainly knew each other."

I had no idea that Robert knew where Utne, Norway, was.

"Perhaps our forefathers rowed Viking longships together," Robert mused, "pillaging and plundering as they went, or cleared boulders from each other's fields, or married a member of the other's family. Perhaps they recited the sagas to each other's kin around candlelight, or leaped over bonfires together on Midsummer Eve."

I was entranced. I felt some disjointed and long-ignored pieces of my life fitting themselves together like a jigsaw puzzle. As a child, I thought my Norwegian heritage was something to be ashamed of. After all, my mother's parents had banned the speaking of Norwegian in their home after they emigrated from Norway to Minnesota when my mother was nine years old. Growing up, I felt my mother's embarrassment over her mother's heavy Norwegian accent. But Robert was actually proud of his Norwegian roots.

And there was more that drew me to Robert during that conversation. I knew I could learn from him. He was a teacher, like Michio, and Bob Schwartz. Robert was a Viking storyteller. A bard. Merlin. Odin on the other line.

"Maybe our ancestors even died in battle together," he said, chuckling, "and are now feasting in Valhalla."

Valhalla is the majestic hall reserved for warriors who've fallen in battle, which is of course the very best way for a Viking to die. Eventually I got around to the reason for my call.

"I'm starting a new magazine, and I'm considering calling it *Utne Reader*," I explained. "Back in the sixties, when I was trying to be a hippie, my father told me that *Utne* means 'far out' in Norwegian. Is that true?"

After a long silence, Bly said, "You could say that." So, with license from the poet himself, I did.

18

UTNE READER

I spent a lot of time imagining the moment the reader would open the premier issue of my new magazine. I pictured an English major at the University of Alabama in Birmingham, a Unitarian minister in Evanston, a biodynamic farmer in Great Barrington, a naturopathic healer in Portland, Oregon. I wanted to reach them all. I wanted each article to be an incendiary device, a packet of energy that would explode in the reader's mind, expanding her perspective, deepening his insight, and maybe changing their lives forevermore. An arsenal of provocative, enlightening, life-changing thought bombs.

I tested the idea for *Utne Reader* in the fall of 1983, using the twenty-five thousand dollars from Buff. The mailing went to about 120,000 people, representing a cross section of subscribers from New Left, new age, and mainstream publications. About 3.5 percent of the people responded. I naïvely thought this was a terrific response. If everyone who'd requested a free sample copy actually paid for their subscription, we'd have a viable business that I could run from my kitchen table. Had I known then what I learned later, I probably would not have proceeded. But I didn't know any better.

Now I had to raise the money to launch the magazine. I told prospective investors, "Here are the terms on which a venture capital firm is prepared to invest [which was true], and they vetted the plan

Dear Reader,

Two hundred fifty years ago Ben Franklin launched *Poor Richard's Almanack* with a confession to his readers, "*I might in this place attempt to gain thy Favour, by declaring that I write Almanacks with no other view than that of the publick good; but in this I should not be sincere ... The plain Truth of the Matter is, I am excessive poor, and my Wife, good Woman, is, I tell her, excessive proud; she cannot bear to sit spinning in her Shift of Tow, while I do nothing but gaze at the Stars; and has threatened more than once to burn all my Books ... if I do not make some profitable use of them for the good of my family ... I have thus begun to comply with my Dame's desire.*"

History has a way of repeating itself. The only difference now is that I'm trying to make some profitable use not of books but of my magazines, to which I am irredeemably addicted.

Magazines and newsletters are important tools for personal growth and social change. They are the best means for gaining and maintaining a working knowledge of a particular arena. I use them to stay informed and feel involved in a variety of fields.

Until a few months ago I planned to publish a great new, general-interest magazine. But the closer I got to having it together, after nearly a year of work (and

continued on back page

The Utne Reader

Prototype   *The best of the alternative press*   1983

The prototype design for *Utne Reader*

thoroughly. But don't invest if you ever want to see a return on your investment: I plan never to sell the company, nor will I take it public. But if you're OK with never seeing your money again, come on in. It'll be fun and we may even change the world."

I loved working with my brother Tom on our new magazine. We could hang out for hours without talking, or have heated arguments about politics, religion, or about how each of us thought the other should be living his life. He was my closest collaborator and friend.

On the night he and I laid out and pasted up the galleys of the prototype for the first *Utne Reader*, it was snowing. I savored the quiet camaraderie of long hours hunched over our drawing boards in focused concentration. We could have been ninth-century monks in a candlelit scriptorium, copying and illuminating calfskin vellum pages in black oak-gall ink with goose-feather quills. I looked over at Tom and recalled the Sunday mornings of our childhood, each of us on our knees on the floor copying panels of our favorite comics characters and then making up our own.

Vapors of Bestine rubber cement thinner and spray fixative nipped at our nostrils. We had decided we wouldn't invest in an Easycoat 9 Waxer until we knew we were in business for the long haul.

Tom and I didn't know that the future was looming with its software to replace our X-Acto knives, rubber cement, and layout boards, our metal T squares, blue lines, and wastepaper baskets overflowing with curling galleys of waxy words. We were still innocent of all that, that separation from the touch and smell and sting of the work.

The prototype was a grab bag of the pieces that I'd clipped, photocopied, and foisted on friends and family for several years. Though the *Reader's Digest* was our inspiration, *Utne Reader* would be different from that amalgam of "condensed" articles. We wouldn't tamper with the authors' language, condensing or altering their vocabulary. We would reprint fully intact excerpts from longer articles and books. The excerpts would stand on their own, unadulterated. And we would introduce each article with an editor's note that explained where we'd found it and why we thought it was significant.

We were laying out columns of words by Paul Hawken and Barbara Ehrenreich, Joanna Macy, Petra Kelly, and a half dozen others. I had written to each of the authors, offering a free subscription in exchange for the right to reprint their work. All had agreed. Our lead article was the interview with Robert Bly from *New Age Journal*. I wrote an introduction describing just how revolutionary I thought Robert's thinking about masculinity was. I knew that "men's work" was an idea whose time had come.

At some point, in the wee hours of the morning, Tom blurted out, "Good enough!" his customary pronouncement that it was time to pack up the issue and send it off to the printer. We looked each other straight in the eye for the first time all night. We knew we'd done a good thing. Snow blanketed everything on the street. Cars parked on both sides were buried in the wake left by the city snowplows.

As I walked the two blocks home, laying down a new trail through the trackless powder, I felt an inner excitement, a quickening. I knew each article was a seed. If we'd done our job well and the reader's mind was fertile, the seed would take root, blossom, bear fruit, and produce new seeds, the entire issue a cornucopia bursting with new life, spreading green tendrils across the country and around the planet.

I could feel it in my bones, and so could Nina. *Utne Reader* was going to change the world.

Within a few weeks I'd found eight people who were willing to invest, including Mary Rower, the daughter of American sculptor Alexander Calder; and Joshua Mailman, an old friend and philanthropist from New York, who explained his investment philosophy: "I back agitators, instigators, and organizers. Those are the people that get stuff done." By the first week of December I'd raised $150,000. I incorporated the company as LENS Publishing Co. (for Leif, Eric, Nina, and Sam), on December 7, 1983.

With the proceeds we did a second mailing of 400,000 pieces the last week of December. This time the response was even greater. Five percent

Founding *Utne Reader* investors Joshua Mailman and Mary Rower

of the recipients accepted our charter offer of a free examination copy. Five percent! This was even more than we'd hoped for. We launched the first issue on Groundhog Day, February 2, 1984. We were in business.

Just before launching *Utne Reader*, I rented a little office above a neighborhood food co-op and hired my first employee, Shoshana Tembeck Alexander, to be the managing editor. Shoshana had recently returned home to Minneapolis after living for several years at Findhorn, the spiritual community in Scotland that Peggy and I had visited ten years earlier. She had edited several books for the community's growing publishing operations, including *The Findhorn Garden*. A free spirit who rejected conventional job descriptions and regular office hours, Shoshana started each meeting with a moment of silence to attune to her higher purpose and the greater good. Her presence was a frequent reminder that we were embarking on a mission to create what I thought of as "healing journalism."

Soon, Julie Ristau showed up at our door. A fourth-generation hog farmer who'd just moved to the city from southern Minnesota, Julie lived next door to Brenda and had heard from her that a magazine was starting up in the neighborhood, so she marched into our office with an article by Daniel Zwerdling she'd clipped from *The Progressive* about the farm crisis. We published it and hired her. She ran the business like an efficient hog farm.

By then Nina had grown frustrated that she couldn't find any women friends who didn't seem "only interested in the next yard sale." We thought about moving the magazine to Whidbey Island, near Seattle. The magazine was small, and Shoshana and Julie were willing to relocate. But could we really publish a national magazine from an island in the Pacific Northwest, especially one that weighed in on cultural issues and tried to influence the national conversation? Was America's Midwest heartland any better?

Minnesotans are sophisticated in a way that only provincials can be. We like to think of ourselves—or we did back then—as well educated, public-spirited, and politically progressive. Like even the most conservative Norwegians, Minnesotans believe in democracy, pay their taxes, and admire Nobel Peace Prize winners. As Garrison Keillor said about Lake Wobegon, "All the women are strong, all the men are good-looking, and all the children are above average."

The word *Minnesota* comes from the Dakota word *Minisotah*, which combines *mini*, meaning "water," with *sotah*, meaning "sky-tinted" or "cloudy." Minnesota is the "Land of Sky-Tinted Waters" and the "Land of Ten Thousand Lakes." Actually, there are more than fifteen thousand lakes. The point where Minnesota's three watersheds meet, known to the Ojibwe as the Hill of Three Waters, is just a stone's throw from Bob Dylan's birthplace in Hibbing, Minnesota.

I think Minnesota's location—between the forest and the prairie, headwaters of rivers flowing in three directions, halfway between the North Pole and the equator, sitting in the geographical heart of the continent—gives the people of the state a unique balance and depth. I like to think these characteristics make Minnesota the spiritual as well as literal headwaters of North America. They also make it a great place to publish a national magazine, especially a general-interest digest. *Reader's Digest* started in Minnesota too, in 1921. There must be something in the water.

Bill Rothschild, my father-in-law, was a self-admitted East Coast, Ivy League snob. He was a Harvard overseer and led the university's capital campaign. When I told him we'd decided to stay in Minneapolis to publish the magazine, he said to me, with his vintage Long Island lockjaw, "I don't know how you can paaaw-sibly publish a naaa-tional magazine from anyplace but New Yawk."

Bill was visiting Minneapolis just after we'd launched the magazine, so I invited him to join the first session of the Alternative Press Reading & Dining Salon, a disparate group of media-savvy volunteers invited to discuss what they'd been reading, but more important, what they'd been "thinking and obsessing about lately."

After the two-and-a-half-hour session, which had been wide-ranging and fast-paced, Nina and I debriefed with Bill about the salon's cast of characters. They included Jerry Brown's renewable-energy adviser; an expert on systems theory and cybernetics; a former

Cargill grain trader turned advocate for sustainable agriculture; the author of a book on women's mystery cults in Crete; the Minnesota Democratic Party's candidate for the U.S. Senate; a Marxist middle school teacher; a librarian; a features writer for the *Minneapolis Tribune;* a stay-at-home mom; and several others.

Bill was most impressed with an articulate young man in a camel-colored cashmere sport coat. "Surely," he said, expecting the young man's pedigree to have some link to the Ivy League, "he's just got to be from Princeton."

"No, Bill," I said, "he's from Elmore, Minnesota, on the Iowa border. He's a hog farmer."

Then Nina added, "He listens to Brahms while he slops his hogs."

So . . . what is it about Minnesotans? Unlike New Yorkers, and Washingtonians and Los Angelenos and San Franciscans, Minnesotans know they're not living in the center of the universe. They're out there on the margins, on the edge of the great prairie, or deep in the North Woods. Like Nick Carraway in *The Great Gatsby,* their outsider status gives them a unique perspective, perhaps even a special insight. They become media-savvy sophisticates, keeping track of what's happening all over the world. They stay on top of what's going on in the arts, politics, fashion—just about any cultural realm you can think of—as well as or better than anyone else. Minnesotans are prairie polymaths. Cosmopolitans from the heartland.

This realization, that Minnesota was the best place to publish a national magazine, was liberating for me. I knew that if we were trying to publish in Boston or New York, I would impose standards of excellence and "slickness" on myself and the staff that we could never meet, let alone afford. And I knew that if we were publishing in California, I would be seduced by one idea after another and totally lose my objectivity. My Midwest inferiority complex evaporated overnight. I decided we couldn't do it anywhere but Minnesota. I asked Nina to give the state another three years. If she wanted to move after that, we would go wherever she liked. She agreed, and curiously, she immediately started meeting thoughtful, interesting women who cared nothing about yard sales, women who would become her lifelong friends.

19

OVER YONDER

The first *Utne Reader* office was a 1920s studio apartment complete with rusty toilet behind a cracked and broken bifold plastic door. Winds rattled the ill-fitting sashes of the double-hung windows. The ghosts of former tenants clanged on the radiator pipes. Our across-the-hall neighbor was one of the first franchisees of the new upstart Apple Computer. A Christian Science Reading Room occupied the storefront below Apple, and below us was the Linden Hills Natural Foods Co-op.

After publishing four monthly issues, we'd nearly run out of money. I realized that less than a third of the respondents to our free copy offer were actually paying for their subscription. We got dozens of letters from readers expressing their disappointment. One famous author wrote, "Don't give us abstracts, give us the thinking itself."

The message was clear—people liked the idea of an alternative *Reader's Digest,* but they weren't too wild about the snippets we were sending them.

We were faced with a choice: either close down the business or retool *Utne Reader* to make it a more fulsome fulfillment of the original premise. Like our readers, I wanted the thinking itself, not just a collection of short excerpts, so I decided to suspend publication and design a completely new magazine—one that I would like to read.

The new format was similar to that of *National Geographic.* The covers were full color, printed on heavy paper stock, and the inside was printed in black and white on newsprint. There were more than 120 pages of articles, columns, sidebars, and cartoons, some of them clustered around themes like green politics (nineteen pages) and sustainable shelter (twelve pages). It was a substantial read by any measure. We mailed the first issue of the redesigned magazine in the late summer of 1984 to everyone who'd responded to our initial mailing, whether they'd canceled their initial subscription or not. We glued a half-page note to the cover explaining to the readers that we didn't blame them if they didn't like the earlier newsletter format—we didn't like it either—and we asked them to take another look. "If you like what you see, please consider subscribing."

My brother Tom and his beloved kids, Emily and Christian, 1984

Just as our redesigned magazine was going to press, my brother Tom went to a spiritual festival attended by more than fifteen thousand people at Bhagwan Shree Rajneesh's ashram near Antelope, Oregon. The ashram was featured in the 2018 Netflix documentary *Wild Wild Country*.

At dinner in a huge dining hall called Zorba the Buddha, Tom grasped his throat and asked someone at the table to summon help as he dashed to the restroom. By the time the ashram's paramedics arrived, Tom was on the ground, unable to speak. They assumed he was choking and did a tracheotomy. By then it was too late. Tom had eaten a sauce that contained peanuts—his lifelong allergy and nemesis—and gone into acute anaphylactic shock. Had the medics given him a shot of adrenaline he probably would have survived.

I was on Cape Cod with Nina and our boys visiting Buff and his family when I got the news. My brother Bob flew immediately from his home in D.C. and gave the Rajneeshies permission to cremate Tom's remains. I flew to Minneapolis to collect Tom's wife, Robin, and their two young kids, Christian and Emily. We arrived at the crematorium just in time to witness Tom's body, covered with a mountain of flowers, wheeled into the flaming oven. Only by seeing his foot did I know that it was Tom on that slab. Fifty of Rajneesh's devotees, all of them dressed in orange or red, the Rajneesh colors, danced and chanted frenetically as the coffin was consumed by the fire.

Rajneesh's spokesperson told us that Tom had "achieved enlightenment by dying within twenty-four miles of the realized Master—Rajneesh." This sounded nonsensical to me. And she told us that Tom had decided, just a day before his death, and after years of ambivalence, to move to the ashram. Tom hadn't told Robin that, nor me. And I was disgusted by how shamelessly Rajneesh's lieutenants were exploiting Tom's death for their own purposes. When we arrived at the ashram, we were shown a video taken the previous day of the ceremony conducted to celebrate Tom's supposed enlightenment. Over ten thousand conference-goers participated, many of them touching, laying flowers on, and writhing around his open casket.

I was shocked and confused. My brother's life had been snatched away, and now, I felt, my grief was being stolen as well. I couldn't cry. I could only smolder with increasing anger at each new revelation. I asked to see the woman with whom Tom was dining when he ate the peanut sauce and was told she couldn't be found. When I persisted the next day, they told me they didn't know how to reach her—they only had her Rajneeshi name, and she had left the ashram that morning to return to Germany.

When Bob got back to Washington, he called me to say he'd been

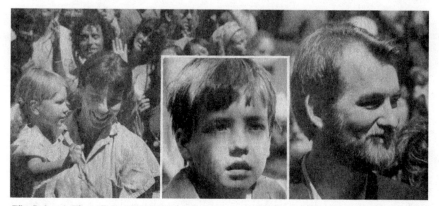

The Rajneesh Times (July 13, 1984) celebrated my brother's death as his "enlighten-ment." Said spokeswoman Ma Anand Sheela, "Anybody who belongs to Bhagwan (Rajneesh) and is totally devoted to him is inevitably going to be enlightened at the moment of death." Left to right during the funeral: Tom's daughter, Emily; his wife, Robin; son, Christian; and me.

thinking about the circumstances of Tom's death, and how badly the paramedics had handled the situation. He wanted to go to the Oregon attorney general's office and "get those bastards," he said. "We should sue them for wrongful death." In the middle of our conversation Bob suddenly shouted, "What the hell!?" It sounded to me like he was struggling with an intruder. After a minute Bob got back on the line and told me that a red bird had bashed itself into his window while we were talking. The bird, a cardinal, fell to the ground, then flew up and bashed itself into the window several more times. Bob was spooked. The red bird reminded him of the red colors worn by the followers of Rajneesh. Bob brought the conversation to an abrupt halt. "Maybe we better not mess around," he said. "Maybe Tom, or Rajneesh, is warning us to back off."

Robin, the kids, and I took turns holding the urn as we rode in the last vehicle of the funeral procession—thirty-four black limousines, one for each year of Tom's life, all owned by Rajneesh. I was a swirl of confused emotions. What was it about Rajneesh that appealed so strongly to Tom but left me so cold? Was I too uptight? Why couldn't I just cut loose and go for the ecstasy, like Tom?

As the funeral train snaked up the mountain behind the ranch, we passed Rajneesh's bandolier-wearing, AK-47-toting border guards along the way. The procession wound past an enormous natural stone arch and continued up to a plateau on which a line of towering juniper trees overlooked the ranch in the valley below. The ashram was built on the site of an old cattle ranch in the high chaparral of eastern Oregon. It looked like an Israeli kibbutz, with extensive irrigation feeding lush gardens of fruit trees, vegetables, and flowers. Out of respect for Tom, I wore a Rajneesh-colored pink shirt under my navy sport jacket for the burial service.

We were let out of the limo about a quarter of a mile from the grave site and walked a path flanked by thousands of devotees, two and three people deep on either side. The devotees, celebrating Tom's "liberation," chanted and leaped and pummeled us with rose petals. When we reached the grave, we found a twenty-piece band, with wild-looking musicians dressed in every conceivable color, including nonstandard blues, greens, and yellows, playing the ecstatic, chaotic meditation music.

There were three graves. On one side were the remains of the "Prince of Germany," a young man who had died at Rajneesh's ashram in Pune, India. Rajneesh's father was buried on the other. In the middle, a freshly dug hole awaited Tom's ashes.

I placed the urn in the grave, then stood back while prayers were said. I noticed that Tom's marker did not bear his family name, just his Rajneeshi name, Swami Dhyan Nirvesh. As the hole was filled, Robin danced in place, gently swinging Emily in her arms. In that moment I wondered, *What would Tom think of all this?* I had the surprising thought that he could not have chosen a better death, and that he was very pleased. But I felt devastated nonetheless.

The day after his burial, on the flight home, I opened the envelope containing the blueprints for the summer 1984 issue, the first in the redesigned magazine format. The printer had rushed them to me in Oregon. Tom had been involved in every decision having to do with the redesign. More than anyone, I placed stock in his editorial and artistic judgment. My first thought was "I can't wait for Tom to see these."

The dedication that introduced the issue read, "In loving memory of Thomas Carl Utne, aka Swami Dhyan Nirvesh." The words had been telephoned to our printer as the plates were being prepared for the presses. It was too late to do anything more than acknowledge that my brother had died.

It seemed as if *Utne Reader* was fated to happen, that it was an idea that fit the times, and whose time had come. When we sent readers the redesigned *Utne Reader*, in its new, 128-page magazine format, people actually paid for it, in droves. I think Tom would have been very proud.

During those first months of publication I saw Brenda often. She was my secret adviser. I usually found her working in her sunny second-floor studio, looking out over Lake Harriet, "like Captain Ahab, watching the whales spouting," she said. She wrote for local periodicals, lectured widely, and kept extensive diaries. She had causes to champion—women's rights, exercise and health, saving defenseless animals from vivisection and cruelty, stopping the proliferation of nuclear weapons, and ending war. And she stayed physically active. She swam several

The redesigned *Utne Reader*, summer 1984

times a week and often challenged me to a race across Lake Harriet. She had set three AAU swimming records in the over-eighty category, "because it took me longer to sink than the competition," she'd say.

Brenda maintained her house herself, changing her heavy storm windows atop a stepladder well into her eighties. At ninety, she fell from the ladder and broke her hip. She said the worst part of it was that she could no longer "dart from in between parked cars in the middle of city blocks and dodge oncoming traffic." But breaking her hip was really the beginning of the end.

In early March, I got word that Brenda wanted to see me. A young woman who was looking after her around the clock let me in. I found Brenda upstairs in bed, propped against the headboard, dressed in a loose flannel blouse and khaki pants, half under the covers.

"Eric," Brenda said, her voice weaker than I'd ever heard it, but still clear and direct.

"I'm glad you came, Eric," she said patting the bed. "Sit here, next to me."

"How are you?" she asked, with genuine interest. I don't recall what I said. I was trying to read how she was doing. She wanted to know about Nina and how things were going with the magazine. I gave her a short report. Then she surprised me.

"Jesus appeared to me last night," she said. This was not something I expected to hear from Brenda. She was a lifelong Unitarian who chided her fellow congregants for being afraid to say the "G-word" (*God*), and she loved Catholics for their "pomp and pageantry" and their love of Mary. But she didn't talk much about Jesus.

"It's amazing," she said, pointing to the foot of her bed. "He was right there."

"Did he say anything?" I asked.

"No," Brenda answered. "Or, yes and no."

She was clearly reliving the moment.

"I heard him in here," she said, pointing to her heart.

"I felt love coming from him, Eric. He was pure love."

She told me she felt reassured. Then she said, perhaps for the last time, "I can hardly wait to meet all those nice souls over yonder."

This time I believed her.

She seemed tired, so I decided to leave and let her rest.

"Goodbye, Brenda," I said, feeling a sudden wave of sadness.

George Herbert's words came to mind. Brenda had taught them to me. "Eternal restlessness will at last throw him to my Breast."

I squeezed her hand and kissed her on her forehead. "Time to rest, darling girl."

Brenda died the next day, on March 5, 1985. She is with me still.

"Listening creates us, makes us unfold and expand."
(Brenda Ueland, from her essay "Tell Me More")

20

MEETING THE SHADOW

One of the principal ways we monitored the zeitgeist and prospected for possible editorial ideas was with the Alternative Press Reading & Dining Salon. Robert Bly was a frequent participant. At one salon at my house, Robert showed up wearing a colorful Guatemalan vest that reminded me of Santa Fe goddess wear. His large presence and Minnesota farmer's twang filled my living room as he sounded off about one injustice after another and suggested articles from some of his

An early session of the Alternative Press Reading & Dining Salon

favorite journals, including the *Non-Violent Activist* and *Bulletin of Atomic Scientists*. This surprised me. I knew Robert was interested in politics, but for some reason I'd expected more psychological and spiritual references.

After the freewheeling editorial salon ended and everyone else had departed, Robert lingered, so I invited him to sit with me in the living room. I poured us each a shot of Norwegian aquavit, stirred the embers in our open-faced fireplace, threw another log on the fire, and settled in. I asked Robert what he'd been working on lately.

"Poems mostly, some translations, and a little book on the human shadow."

I knew a little bit about the shadow. Nina and I knew a Jungian analyst who talked about the shadow a great deal. I suspected mine was huge, fueled by my lifelong habit of denial.

"Men who have not faced their own shadow are a danger to themselves and to society," Robert said. "When a man falls in love with a radiant face across the room, it may mean that he has some soul work to do. His soul is the issue."

This got my attention. I'd fallen for many a pretty face across the room. Usually it ended there. Instead of pursuing the woman and trying to get her alone, Robert said, the man needs to go to a mountain cabin alone and listen to what his shadow has to tell him.

"That would save a lot of women a lot of trouble," he said, raising one eyebrow and giving me a sidelong glance.

"And a lot of men too," I added, thinking of my father, and grandfather, and brother Bob. Just about every other man, of course, except me (like I said . . . denial).

"I heard a famous Jungian say that the shadow is nothing more, and nothing less, than unexpressed creativity," I said.

"That's very true," Robert replied. "But you have to pass between Scylla and Charybdis and through a gauntlet of hungry ghosts to get to the creativity. You don't get there just by signing up for a weekend class in watercolor painting."

"Why is it so hard for me, and most of the men I know, to face our shadow?" I asked.

"Alice Miller writes about this in *The Drama of the Gifted Child*," Robert answered, sitting up, then settling more deeply into his chair. "She says, when you came into the world, you brought this amazing wild energy, well preserved from our mammalian inheritance, from a hundred fifty thousand years of tree life and five thousand years of tribal life, and you offered this gift to your parents. And your parents didn't want this incredible energy you brought in. They confused your exuberance for savagery. They wanted a nice tame boy. They wanted a nice obedient girl.

"You couldn't believe it," Robert went on. "That was your first rejection. You could feel it, and it was profound. It doesn't mean your parents were wicked. We do the same thing to our children."

This made sense to me. I remembered dancing like a whirling dervish in the kitchen for my mother and father as a five-year-old. My mother seemed delighted, but my father couldn't have been less interested. I got the feeling he wished I'd go away or simply disappear. I hoped I hadn't done the same to my boys.

"So to please your parents," Robert said, "you made up a false personality, and you survived. Don't blame yourself for that. You did the right thing. And the proof of it is that you're alive right now."

We both sipped our aquavit. I asked Robert why so many men seemed so confused today about what they were supposed to be. He said he thought the images we were given in high school didn't work, that the image of Eisenhower and his medals, or John Wayne and his horse, simply didn't work past the age of thirty-five.

"They don't work in your job," he said. "They don't work in your relationships, they don't work in marriage. They just don't work."

I thought of the models of masculinity I'd picked up in high school. Hugh Hefner surrounded by Playboy Bunnies in his Playboy mansion. James Bond outwitting villains and getting the beautiful women. Loving them and leaving them. The ideal man was cool, calm, detached, and in control.

"A lot of the men I know seem lost and confused," I said.

"Well, I think many men these days have a deep sense that they're inadequate," Robert continued. He said the typical man didn't have any close male friends and he didn't know why. He felt inadequate as a husband because his wife said he didn't talk about his feelings enough, but he didn't know what his feelings were.

"The typical relationship in the United States involves the woman trying to get the man to talk more, and the man fleeing," Robert said. "Are you with me? The man can't turn and face her because he doesn't know what he wants. And since the woman knows what she wants in a relationship, the man feels inadequate."

"Amen," I said. Robert was describing my relationship with Nina, and every other woman I'd ever known. I felt so inept at expressing my feelings, or knowing what I wanted, especially when I was in the grip of a strong emotion.

"I'm terrible at arguing," I said, feeling inadequate in that moment. "I just can't put my feelings into words. Instead, I get all tongue-tied and go mute."

Robert laughed and raised his glass, as if toasting me. "Exactly. You know, I say to women, 'Men are not hiding their feelings from you, it's just that when they look inside themselves, they don't see any-thing.' Believe me, I know what that's like. It's a feeling of numbness that comes early on in life, for a man."

We both fell silent for a minute. I felt the poignancy of a nation of frozen men, and for some reason chose that moment to stir the coals in the fireplace. I knew that feeling of numbness. I'd felt it many times in my life, perhaps most intensely when I felt ashamed. I told Robert about an incident that happened when I was twenty-one years old. I had fled the United States and gone to the northernmost town in Norway, where I stayed with my mother's uncle Bjarne. One night I had sneaked two girls into Bjarne's house. The next day, without letting on that he knew what I'd done, Bjarne told me to pack a toothbrush and come with him to shovel snow off the roof of his inland "hunting lodge."

"We traveled in silence for several hours," I told Robert. "First by ferry, then Bjarne's black Volvo station wagon. What was he thinking? I wondered. Why doesn't he speak? I hoped against hope that Bjarne didn't know about my escapade with the girls, or that he didn't care.

"We arrived at what turned out to be a very small cabin," I went on. "I climbed up on the roof and lingered there, shoveling and chopping while Bjarne prepared the usual dinner of cod with boiled potatoes and drawn butter. When Bjarne announced that dinner was ready, I reluctantly joined him in the cabin."

"I can see the whole thing," Robert said, encouraging me to continue.

"We ate in silence, our eyes never meeting," I continued.

"Yes," Robert interjected. "That's proper. The eyes are always lowered when shame is involved."

"My feeble compliments to the chef went unanswered," I said. "After our meal Bjarne sat on the floor directly in front of the blazing wood stove, leaned his back against the sofa, and drank most of a bottle of whiskey, straight from the bottle, in about ten minutes. He said nothing the entire time. I was relieved, thinking I'd dodged his rage. Just when I thought he'd fallen asleep, he opened his eyes, sat upright, looked into the fire, and spoke.

"'Eric, you have shamed me and my house,' Bjarne said in the most pained voice you can imagine. 'You have taken a girl into the room of my only son. You are no better than your father, your uncle, or your grandfather before you.' Then Bjarne leaned back and passed out."

"Gads!" Robert said. "Then what did you do?"

"I felt utterly exposed and ashamed. When I was sure Bjarne was asleep, I grabbed my toothbrush and slipped silently out of the cabin and began walking. I walked for hours through an endless forest of spruce trees that leaned helter-skelter under heavy snow, making them look like eerily shaped ghosts frozen in midmotion in the cold blue light of the full moon. I lashed myself with self-recrimination. 'How could I have been so ungrateful to Bjarne?' I thought. 'What a fool I am.' But I wondered, what did Bjarne mean that I was no better than my father, or Uncle Nels, or Sverre? What did he know about my own family that I did not?"

"Eric," Robert said. "This is a fantastic example of shaming. It's like a fairy tale. Your uncle's declaration was a kind of evil spell, an enchantment. You can overcome or reverse this enchantment. I can help you."

"You can?" I said, feeling sheepish, desperate, and hopeful all at once. "How?"

"First of all you have to forgive yourself. You probably internalized the shame you got from your parents and teachers long before Bjarne cursed you with his shame. That's what we all do to survive. What you did with those girls in Norway came from your false self. You don't need that false self now. But you have to go through the grief of abandoning it, or letting it die, or releasing it."

I heard Robert's words, but I didn't know if I could do what he was saying. When he said I could release my false self by "eating my shadow," he saw the puzzled look on my face.

"The shadow represents all that is instinctive in us," Robert said. "Whatever part of us our parents didn't like, whatever part of us that has a tail and lots of hair, we put in the shadow."

I wasn't sure I knew what Robert meant by the shadow. Was my habit of denial part of my shadow, I asked, or did it keep me out of touch with my shadow?

"You have to lift your eyes and focus them to see your shadow," he said. "For perhaps fifteen years I have been focusing my eyes as a sort of discipline, a spiritual practice," he said. "I focus on a pinecone, a bird's wing, a piece of amethyst.

"The idea is to make holes in your habits," Robert said. I still wasn't getting it. Robert suggested I do things to make my senses more acute, like keep a journal, play music, or create frightening papiermâché masks. Then he came up with a line I'll never forget.

"You could regard yourself as a genial criminal, or try being a witch at odd times of the day and develop a witch laugh and tell fairy stories," he said. "But you have to do it playfully."

I was ready. I could feel a weird cackle rise in me. If Nina weren't upstairs putting Sam to bed, I might have let it rip then and there.

"We could talk for a long time about all this," Robert said, as he rose from his chair. "But I have to go now." As I saw Robert to the door I thought, *I don't know what just happened, but I want more.*

———

In 1987 I was the father of three sons—Leif, Sam, and Oliver. My little family was beginning to look a lot like the one I grew up in—and I hoped that I was raising my sons differently from the way I was brought up. I hoped I wasn't infecting them with all the shame and other negative patterns I'd gotten from my parents, especially my father.

I was getting increasingly interested in "men's work." When I learned that Robert was giving a lecture I invited Leif, who was about fifteen at the time, to attend it with me. But it turned out to be more reunion than lecture. Held in the auditorium of a big suburban high school, the gathering was attended by men who had participated in one of the first of Robert's annual men's conferences at a summer camp. Leif and I were odd men out.

The men in the gym were boisterous and rowdy—lots of bumping and shouting and loud laughter. Robert calmed them down, then spoke about the need for men to get in touch with their feelings, especially their grief. He recited poems by Rilke, Machado, and Stafford, and some of his own.

At first I was skeptical of Robert the showman, which is who he became at the men's conference. He wore his white hair long and wild. His vest was an elaborate construction, making him look like a

Sam, Leif, and Oliver

cross between a Sami shaman and a Persian pasha. But when he recited Rumi, his hands tracing elegant mudras in the air, I was impressed. And his insights into mythology and grief, which he called "the male mode of feeling," struck me as truly original and pertinent to my life. I thought of Tom's death, my failed marriage to Peggy, and my estrangement from my father, not to mention the enormity of the harm humans were doing to the environment and to each other, and I realized I hadn't shed a tear over any of these. I carried an ocean of unexpressed grief. Could I dive into it without drowning?

This was still three years before the 1990 publication of his infamous bestseller *Iron John,* Robert's retelling of the Grimm brothers' fairy tale about the maturing of a boy into adulthood with the help of a wise mentor, Iron John, also known as the "Wild Man." When Robert asserted in the gym that day that boys need an elder's help to become decent, responsible, and mature men, I whispered, "Amen!"

Then Robert stirred up the group again, gathering everyone onstage for an insult contest, facing off, mano a mano, in verbal combat. The idea was to insult your opponent as eloquently as possible. The guy who could deliver the cleverest, most cutting, most withering blows with words, eliciting the loudest roar from listeners, would advance to the next round. It looked like good, clean Shakespearean fun, and very scary. "Thou art a reeky, ill-breeding maggot pie." "Oh, really. Your father is a frothy, flap-mouthed foot-licker." I wished I could do it, but I could not. Verbal combat was not my forte. It did not make me want to do men's work.

Why did I feel free and spontaneously expressive after doing Rajneesh's chaotic meditation but completely tongued-tied when faced with verbal combat? Was it the physical activity that got me out of my head, out of being self-conscious, that opened the floodgates and bridged the gap between feeling and verbal expression?

In 1989 I published an article about a men's workshop that had nothing to do with Robert, but it led to the very thing I feared during that conversation with him in front of my fireplace. The article made malicious fun of "men's work" in general, and the workshop's leader in particular. Though I was not yet involved in men's work, I was sympathetic to the movement's intent and reluctant to let our readers form an opinion about the entire men's movement based solely on a stylishly written hatchet job. So I asked Robert for permission to reprint a section of his "What Men Really Want" interview, the one that had been the lead article of the *Utne Reader* prototype, to complement and balance the nasty takedown. Robert obliged.

But the hatchet job wasn't the problem. It was a little sidebar in the same theme section by Robert's ex-wife, the writer Carol Bly. I failed to mention to Robert that Carol's piece would be on the same two-page spread as the excerpt from his interview. Carol called the men's movement "separatist, paranoiac, and regressive." When Robert saw the section, with his ex's criticisms running opposite his interview, he called me and exploded in my ear.

"Why the hell did you run that crap from Carol?" he wanted to know.

I was horrified. I had naïvely thought Robert would like the section. I thought he and Carol had divorced amicably, as Peggy and I had. After all, they'd appeared on a literary conference panel together just a month before. It never occurred to me that he'd be upset by Carol's critique, harsh though it was. But I was wrong, dead wrong.

Robert said he felt that I was trying to "exploit" his divorce by running it, and that the piece "belonged to the world of gossip." He called me a "yellow journalist" and told me he would have nothing to do with *Utne Reader* from that moment forward.

Overnight I'd lost a wise teacher and a budding friendship.

21

CULTURAL ACTIVISM

The first few years of publishing *Utne Reader* were rocky. *Reader's Digest, Time,* and *National Geographic* all threatened to sue us: *Reader's Digest* because we marketed ourselves as an "alternative *Reader's Digest*," *Time* because we used their "patented red border," and *National Geographic* because we used their "patented yellow border." We told all of them, "Yes, come on, please sue us." We wanted a David versus Goliath story to tell, but they all backed off.

A more perfect union: Jay Walljasper and Julie Ristau met and married at *Utne Reader.*

I didn't consider *Utne Reader* to be a political magazine—at least not in the sense that most people mean when they use the word. The mainstream media seem to define *politics* as "things having to do with Washington, D.C., or city hall." To them, politics means caucuses and sound bites and roll calls and referenda and lobbyists and shuttle diplomacy and redistricting and budget shortfalls. That was too many blue suits for me.

Utne Reader was more concerned with "the dailiness of life." In my editor's note in the summer 1984 issue, I wrote,

> We feel that politics is much more than choosing candidates at election time. It has to do with where we live and work, what we eat, where we go and how we get there, who we choose as intimates and friends, and what we hope for future generations. These are the issues of life. They transcend party politics.

This focus on the quotidian is what the Czech playwright and president Vaclav Havel called "the unknown life of society." Periodicals that address such personal concerns are labeled "lifestyle" magazines and are generally dismissed by the politicos as "nonpolitical," and therefore irrelevant.

Utne Reader was neither a political magazine nor a lifestyle magazine. It was a cultural magazine. Our beat wasn't high culture, or the New York arts scene, or the pop culture of *People* magazine. We were more interested in what we called "the emerging culture." When we covered political issues, we tried to give them a personal angle. When we covered lifestyle issues, we placed them in a larger political context. Havel called this approach "cultural activism," in which self-transformation underlies national transformation. "Even our own sexual liberation can profoundly threaten repressive regimes," he said. This did not sound like Ronald Reagan or *The New York Times* or most political journals. But the alternative press abounded with this more personal, more cultural approach to politics.

One of our signature editorial devices was what we called "theme sections." These were generally cover sections that included as many as a dozen articles and sidebars covering one topic from as many

points of view as possible, often extending to twenty or even thirty pages of the magazine. If the subject was political, we sought out and presented views from "left, right, and off-the-wall." We wanted source documents, in the words of the newsmakers themselves, not viewpoints mediated by pundits.

So, for example, if we were covering the immigration debate, we might run articles from the leftist *Mother Jones* and *The Nation*, as well

All the views fit to print.

Alice Kahn on the modern parent • Alice Walker on animal rights • Anne Finger on the sex lives of disabled people • Arthur C. Danto on art for activism • Barbara Ehrenrich on blue-collar feminism • Barbara Holland on living alone • Bill Moyers on our need for myth • Bob Black on abolishing work • Brenda Peterson on sacred sex • Brenda Ueland on the art of listening • Calvin Trillin on politically correct cuisine • Camille Paglia on date rape • Carl Jensen on news not fit to print • Carole Adams on the sexual politics of meat • Charlene Spretnak and Fritjof Capra on the Greens • Christina Kelly on our need for heroes • Christine Downing on menopause • Dana Ullman on wellness macho • David Maybury-Lewis on the importance of being tribal • Deborah Baldwin on push-button democracy • Deena Metzger on the holy prostitute • Don Hanlon Johnson on the loneliness of the male body • Dorothy Conniff on the problems with day care • Doug Henwood on business ethics • E. J. Dionne on why Americans hate politics • Ellen Herman on addiction to addiction • Frances Moore Lappé on the politics of eating • Gareth Branwyn on virtual community • Garrison Keillor on porch-sitting • Garry Wills on religion in American politics • Gary Snyder and Scott Russell Sanders on staying put • Gerri Hirshey on the tyranny of couples • Gloria Steinem on the new women's movement • Hazel Henderson on phony economics • Helen Cordes on Barbie's feminism • I.F. Stone on muckraking and the effects of pissing on a boulder • Ivan Illich on ritual's dark side • James Hillman on the anti politics of psychotherapy • Jim Hightower on grass roots prosperity • Joani Blank on outercourse • John Avedon on Tibet • John Callahan on welfare hell • Jonathan Rowe on Cuban baseball • Judith Guest on family systems • Julie Burchill on good reasons to despise the Greens • Jutta Mason on tea and community • Ken Kesey on the death of a son • Kirkpatrick Sale on the bioregional urbanite • Lars Eighner on dumpster diving • Laurens Van Der Post on the wilderness and why she carries a gun • Lou Reed on Vaclav Havel • Lynda Barry on jungle juice and getting loose • Lynnell Mickelsen on being a law-and-order liberal • Makau wa Mutua on Africa's democracy movements • Marcelle Clements on quitting smoking • Meredith Maran on living with fear • Miles Harvey on eco-warriors • Moira Farr on why twentysomethings hate baby boomers • Pat Paquin on the virtues of solitude • Patrick Breslin on

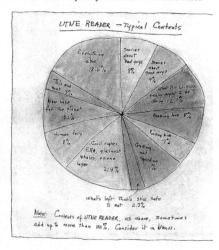

UTNE READER → Typical Contents

Everything else 18.6%
Stories about bad guys 8%
Stories about good guys 9%
What Bill Clinton really ought to do doing 12.1%
Making love 8%
Raising kids 7%
Getting and Spending 1%
Civil rights, ERA, glasnost, whales, ozone layer 21.4%
Human folly 8%
This and that 3%
New hope for the planet 13.1%

What's left that's still safe to eat 2.3%

Note: Contents of UTNE READER, as above, sometimes add up to more than 100%. Consider it a bonus.

legendary Irish storytellers • Paul Hawken on stopping junk mail • Quentin Crisp on the benefits of censorship • Ram Dass on how to help • Robert Bly on men's initiation rites • Robert Burrows on the risk of marriage • Robert Heilbroner on advertising • Robert McClory on the lure of gambling • Roberta Joseph on deciding against motherhood • Roger Swardson on careers in telemarketing • Russ Baker on controlling the CIA • Salim Mawakkil on the coming tribal wars • Sally Tisdale on women and pornography • Sandra Finzi on the inevitability of infidelity • Shelby Steele on white guilt • Starhawk on community rituals • Stephanie Ericsson on the agony of grief • Stephanie Mills on the art of salon-keeping • Stephen Levine on conscious dying • Steve Perry on rock writing • Studs Terkel on racial healing • Susan Faludi on the advantages of day care • Suzi Gablik on socially conscious art • Thich Nhat Hanh on Buddhism and social change • Tom Wolfe on the 21st century • Ursula K. LeGuin on reading aloud • Wallace Shawn on getting comfortable • Walter Truett Anderson on rethinking liberalism • Wendell Berry on why not to buy a computer • William Greider on how to save public schools • Winona LaDuke on the frontier mentality...

as from the center-right *New Republic* and the far-right *National Review*. But we'd also present arguments by the French conservative Jean-Marie Le Pen and the Louisiana right-wing populist David Duke, in their own words, so readers could see for themselves how compelling and seductive, or ridiculous and xenophobic, their positions were. This was like my mother keeping a copy of Adolf Hitler's *Mein Kampf* in the dining room bookcase "to hear the madness in the words of the monster himself."

We might also look for views from a resettled Somali living in Minneapolis or a deported California migrant farmworker or a traveling Buddhist pilgrim. The idea was to give our readers the whole picture and let them make up their own minds.

We got pushback from our colleagues and competitors alike on this approach, especially from the left. Progressive periodicals like *Mother Jones, The Nation, In These Times,* and others weren't accustomed to offering multiple perspectives. They tended to think that there was one right perspective, theirs, and everyone else's was wrong.

Our theme-section choices got me into trouble more than once. Some writers whose articles we ran in the theme sections on the AIDS epidemic, the environmental movement, prostitution, Alcoholics Anonymous, and liberalism hated having their articles juxtaposed with others that offered different perspectives. Still, we had an activist agenda, and we advocated for issues we cared about. That was the whole point.

For much of the late 1980s and the early 1990s, *Utne Reader* was the fastest growing general-interest magazine in America. In 1988 it had a paid circulation of 75,000. By 1990 it had grown to 175,000. And by 1992 the magazine sold 275,000 copies per issue, with an estimated 685,000 readers.

Utne Reader's offices were built around a central library. Over a thousand magazines were piled in wire baskets at one end of the room. Back issues of five hundred of the most frequently referred-to publications—at least a year's worth of each—were stored in plastic slipcases on the metal library shelves that lined the room.

The current issues of our favorites were displayed, face out, on easy-to-browse slanted shelves that circled the room, illuminated by overhead track lights: *Leading Edge, Mother Jones, Rain, Sojourners, New Age Journal, The Nation, Nuclear Times, The Progressive, CoEvolution Quarterly, Parabola, Nutrition Action, The Futurist, In These Times, Cultural Survival Quarterly, Laughing Man, The World Paper, Akwesasne Notes, Z, Big Mama Rag, The Guardian,* and many more.

Every two months, the editors and editorial interns, plus the staff librarian and the art director, would assemble around a long table in the middle of the library, the Big Rock Candy Mountain mother lode for magazine junkies, to pitch articles and hash out the contents of the coming issue. Mike and Tom, the ad guys, hovered in the threshold.

Each of the editors had spent a couple of weeks reading his or her favorite periodicals and leafing through the bins to find something, anything, that might be right for the next issue, or a future issue. Each

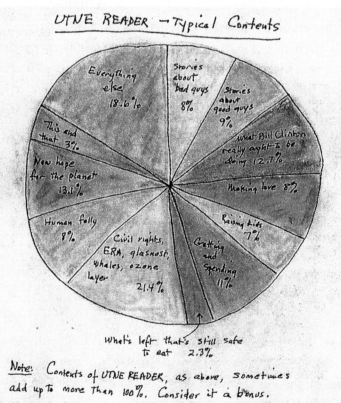

UTNE READER — Typical Contents

Everything else 18.6%

Stories about bad guys 8%

Stories about good guys 9%

This and that 3%

New hope for the planet 13.1%

What Bill Clinton really ought to be doing 12.7%

Making love 8%

Human folly 8%

Raising kids 7%

Civil rights, ERA, glasnost, whales, ozone layer 21.4%

Getting and Spending 11%

What's left that's still safe to eat 2.3%

Note: Contents of UTNE READER, as above, sometimes add up to more than 100%. Consider it a bonus.

editor then photocopied roughly twenty to thirty of their favorite articles, which they circulated to the other editors. By the time of the
meeting each of us had accumulated a foot-deep pile of photocopies,
which we piled on the table or stacked on the floor, and we pitched
our recommendations to each other over a two- or three-day mara-
thon. Here's what I recall from one pitch meeting, circa 1990:

"Whad'ya think of Babs Ehrenreich's piece on being an under-
cover waitress?" Helen Cordes began, looking up from her knitting.
Helen was always knitting.

"Fresh!" said Jay Walljasper, the magazine's executive editor. Jay
joined the magazine when it was just under a year old. He'd answered
our ad for a managing editor: "Applicant should have the background
and interests of a slightly skeptical, ex-radical, hippie, spiritual-type
magazine addict who's seen all the movements for personal growth
and social change and still has hope for the future."

Jay fit the bill perfectly. He had been a culture editor for the socialist newsweekly *In These Times* and associate travel editor with *Better
Homes and Gardens.* He was the one who worried over every line of
copy and wrote most of the magazine's headlines, subheads, photo
captions, and tables of contents. He assigned most of the "In Briefs"
and rewrote many of them, too. He edited the majority of the articles
and cover sections. I could tell that Jay hated that I got so much attention in the press when he was doing so much of the work behind the
scenes. I couldn't blame him.

"Have we got anything to go with it?" Jay added. "Maybe something from *Processed World*?" This was a San Francisco zine for dis-
gruntled office workers.

"Maybe we could find something in Gary Snyder's book *The Real
Work*," Helen said, "for a chop-wood, carry-water, Zen-type take on
service."

Helen had responded to the same ad as Jay, but when I first offered
her the job she decided to take a more secure position at *Mpls.St.Paul
Magazine.* She then came back a year later saying that she'd written
"too many articles about designer long johns."

"You know, it's possible to view so-called menial service work as

Going to the well: *Utne Reader* staff photo, circa 1990

a spiritual practice," said Jon Spayde, a freelance writer and copy editor. Jon was the office cutup, a literary Robin Williams, slipping from one to another of his dozen or so multiple personalities. In a perfect, high-pitched Japanese accent, he added, "Belly Zen, you know. Belly Zen."

"I've got a piece on Russian service workers," said Jay. "Apparently they don't believe in service. They're worse than the French. If you're in a Moscow restaurant and have the nerve to ask for your bill, they're likely to tell you to drop dead, or fuck off."

Then Tom McKusick piped in from the threshold, "Maybe Charles Bukowski could do something on service workers in Las Vegas. Or on life in diners after two A.M.?"

Tom was half of the magazine's two-person ad staff. The other half was Mike Tronnes. Mike made a place for himself by walking into the *Utne Reader* office and selling us on the idea that we needed a full-time ad director. A brilliant strategist and droll cynic, Mike seemed skeptical of Nina's and my new age interests and suspicious of our social milieu. His demeanor was sometimes churlish, and he seemed happy to play the role of the staff curmudgeon.

The *Utne Reader* ad guys: Tom McKusick and Mike Tronnes

Tom was Mike's much smoother, better-dressed, and more sociable compatriot. They'd met while working for the U.S. Postal Service. Together Mike and Tom were known as the "ad guys."

"I was thinkin' Lynda Barry or Roz Chast could do a bunch of cartoons to illustrate the section," added Helen, "and maybe the cover."

"Or Matt Groening," said Elizabeth Larsen, at twenty-six the youngest editor on the staff. "He could do something with Lisa from *The Simpsons* on the cover." As it happens, the character Lisa, Homer Simpson's brainy and principled daughter, later became an *Utne Reader* subscriber on the show.

"Have you got a cover line in mind?" I asked Helen. "Something provocative?"

"I was thinkin' somethin' like 'Fries with That? The Secret Lives of America's Service Workers.'"

"That's good," several people said at once.

"Let's see how the section comes together before we get hung up on any particular headline," I said. Truth be told, this was a delaying tactic on my part. I had another cover story in mind, but it was clear to me that now was not the time to bring it up. Besides, there were so many important issues we were tracking. The country was about to launch a war in Iraq. The ecological crisis was only getting worse. Corporations were shipping jobs overseas, busting unions, and automating factories. And working-class people, especially African Americans, Latinos, and the rural poor, were seeing their incomes fall and dreams evaporate. Not to mention the ongoing debates about abortion, pornography, gay rights, and animal rights, or the looming specter of nuclear winter and the emerging awareness of the AIDS epidemic.

Utne Reader staff salon, Loring Café, 1992

These phenomena and more were reported, discussed, and debated in the alternative press long before they surfaced in the daily newspapers or on the evening news. Racism, gun control, the downside of computer use, prison reform, terrorism, immigration, media monopoly, why Americans hate politics—it was all there on the pages of *Utne Reader*. It was almost inevitable that someone would start a magazine like *Utne Reader* to try to make sense of what was happening.

Then Mike grabbed the moment. "We got a query from AT&T's ad agency yesterday. They say they're thinking of running a two-page spread in every issue for a whole year."

The entire editorial staff's collective jaw dropped. We'd never had AT&T before. In fact, we'd had very few national advertisers, ever.

It was a challenge describing *Utne Reader* to prospective advertisers. Were we a "thought leader" magazine, like *Harper's* and *The Atlantic* and a host of partisan publications like *The Nation, The New Republic,* and *The National Review*? Or were we a "lifestyle" magazine, like *New Age Journal, Psychology Today, American Health,* and *Organic Gardening*?

We told advertisers we were both. We were a cultural magazine that viewed politics and lifestyle issues as essential and complementary interests within our larger purview. And we were "a lifestyle magazine for thinking people," we said. "A thought-leader magazine for people who act on their concerns."

"That comes to over $120,000 for the year," Mike added. "They want front-of-the-book placement."

"No way!" said Jay. "We're not letting those bastards anywhere near our magazine. They're one of the biggest, baddest corporations in America. Our readers wouldn't stand for it. We'd lose thousands of subscribers."

"It's not like they're selling liquor or tobacco," Tom said. "Where do you draw the line? We need an ad policy, and we need it yesterday."

"Why should we be all holier than thou?" asked Elizabeth. "Most of you guys drink and smoke, anyway. Why should the magazine be held to a higher standard than the readers hold for themselves?"

"Is it a product ad or an image ad?" asked Lynette Lamb, the managing editor. "We shouldn't take image ads. Only product."

"The readers want us to be pure. They want us to live the way they think they should," said Elizabeth. "Even if they don't." Then she added, with a pronounced, playful pout, "It's just not fair."

"Jah-vol!" Jon shouted. "Der readers are such nin-cum-poops!" He put on his best Herr Doktor Freud accent. "Dumkopfs!"

Amid a lot of grumbling, we agreed to meet again in a few days to hammer out an ad policy. Mike got back to the ad agency the next day saying we wanted to see the art before we'd accept the ads. And they got back to him the day after that saying, "We've decided that our campaign for AT&T is not a good fit with the *Utne Reader*. Thanks just the same." Rejected, again.

Our readers, not the advertisers, were the reason the magazine existed. The readers were right there in the name—Utne *Reader*. I began my editor's notes with "Dear Reader," just as Benjamin Franklin had in his *Poor Richard's Almanack*. Our readers cared about their magazine. Every issue we received scores and sometimes hundreds, and occasionally even thousands, of letters to the editor, addressed to U.N.C.L.E. (Utne Network for Communications, Letters, and Epistles). These readers expected to be listened to. And so they were.

Here's a sampling:

LEFT OUT

My problem with the *Utne Reader* is that the "alternative press" turns out to be, all too often, left-of-center. . . . I make no brief for the right. Most of those characters are beyond redemption. But . . . it simply is not possible that publications like *Inquiry* and *The American Spectator* have no contribution to make to the process of finding meaning and truth. . . . Don't forget that "progressive" has become a meaningless term co-opted by the left to signify "one of us" and has no genuine connection to anything real. Even if you can't shake off incipient leftism, I admire your attempt to launch your own project. Good luck.

Anonymous

Ed. Note: We subscribe to both of the above-mentioned periodicals, and scores more that one might place somewhere on the right side of the political spectrum. We have found articles in these periodicals worthy of excerpt or review in the past and will no doubt do so again. In our work we find that left/right dichotomies are rarely useful.

BEEN DOWN SO LONG IT LOOKS LIKE UP

I picked the *Utne Reader* out of my mailbox the other day and began reading while waiting for the "up" elevator. I got in but rode past my floor while reading. On my way "down" I missed my floor again, so I decided to sit and read in the lobby before making another attempt to get to my apartment. I find *Utne Reader* to be something like the vehicle Dr. Who uses in his travels—small on the outside, but big on the inside.

Charlie Beck, Mankato, MN

NAYS & PRAISE

Your latest issue came in the mail and I immediately TORE IT TO SHREDS!—Then I filed articles away in a dozen places—what a great magazine! You always have stuff I've never seen.

Lawrence R. Ephron, Berkeley, CA

UTNE READER ALL WET

To illustrate the regard in which I hold your magazine: after reading excerpts to a friend of mine I inadvertently left the issue outdoors on a rainy night. I subsequently ironed dry all 128 pages!

Frances Neill, Dobbs Ferry, NY

SAVING THE SEEDS

I thought you'd enjoy this example of modern-day networking:

A few days ago, on behalf of my Boston-based solar energy group, I called a research program out in Nebraska to ask them about a project of theirs which utilized do-it-yourself solar technologies for small farmers.

After chatting about solar a bit, my Nebraskan friend mentioned that his program had recently switched its emphasis from energy to water conservation. . . . Having just read an article in the *Utne Reader* ("Saving the Seeds," Feb./Mar. 1985), I hesitatingly asked him if he'd ever heard about the rediscovery of old seed strains that were more drought resistant than modern varieties (then started apologizing that I, a mere "city girl," could be so presumptuous as to bring it up). "Why no, I haven't heard about that," he said. He immediately asked with great interest, "What magazine did it appear in?" So I promptly sent him a copy of your article. Keep up the good work—you'd probably be amazed at how it gets passed around.

Barbara Brandt, Urban Solar Energy Association, Boston, MA

CANCEL MY SUBSCRIPTION

Last December I joined a tour of the Soviet Union, taking my latest copy of the *Utne Reader* along, and during the first week in Leningrad a charming physician from San Diego fell ill, and I passed the Reader along to him so that he'd have something to read. During the rest of the trip we often discussed what he'd read in your publication, and he decided to subscribe himself. In addition, he got my home address from the subscription label and contacted me when we returned. To make a long story only somewhat shorter, the relationship that began with the *Utne Reader* has flourished and on the 9th of June we were married in New Jersey, after which I joined him in San Diego, and will forevermore read his copy. Although it is my fervent hope that the Reader grow and flourish, I do think that one subscription is enough. You've not lost a subscriber, you've gained a family.

Peggy Hanisch, formerly of Long Branch, NJ

In the spring of 1986 the magazine went through an identity crisis. I announced to readers our intention to rename *Utne Reader* and solicited their suggestions, offering a lifetime subscription to the winner. Over a thousand readers responded, the clear majority recommending that we keep our original name. Ted Flicker of Los Angeles wrote, "Why would a bright gang like you guys want to change your name? . . . In the porridge-smooth world of journalism we need an occasional chewy lump. *Ut-nee*. What the hell is it? Just trying to pronounce it gets the mind working."

Marsha Gori of Lewisburg, Pennsylvania, wrote, "Knowing that Utne means *far out* in Norwegian is such a good conversation stopper. To be in possession of this translation is to dazzle friends, intimidate enemies, and unglaze the eyes of the disinterested." Janette Jamieson of Ventura, California, wrote, "'Ugh' is the most common sound in spoken English. . . . It is not a pretty sound. We produce it when hit in the stomach, or as we wake up, especially if we would rather keep on sleeping. So I say keep your crazy name."

The most compelling argument came from the vicar of St.

Andrew's Episcopal Church in Chicago: "Yes, it's time the magazine had a name which more clearly represents its purpose and content: Unadorned, uncanny, and underexposed UNDERCURRENTS, truthfully, trendily, and tidily told in THEMESONGS, nicely, narratively, and noisily NEWFANGLED, eagerly, engagingly examined in EXCURSUS. This is much too long, however, and can be abbreviated to *U.T.N.E. Reader.* Dropping the periods, for a better-looking cover, would give us *Utne Reader.* An admirable name, I think." For this, Reverend Grant Gallup was awarded a lifetime subscription.

22

THE NEIGHBORHOOD SALON ASSOCIATION

There I was on the biggest stage I could imagine—CBS's new late-night TV show *America Tonight*. I'd been invited to be a regular commentator on the show—I had three to four minutes to talk on camera about whatever I wanted. It was a journalist's dream gig, an opportunity to weigh in on the important issues of the day, advocate for my favorite causes, and help shape public opinion. Maybe I could even help change the world.

America Tonight was the network's answer to ABC's *Nightline*, which was killing CBS in the late-night ratings. The show was hosted by two of CBS's most beloved and heaviest-hitting personalities, Charles Kuralt and Lesley Stahl, and this was its first week. My producer was thirty-two-year-old Jonathan Klein, who would later become the president of CNN.

Klein had told me what to wear, how to sit, and where to look. My hair was combed, the makeup was on, and the mic was in position. "Lights . . . camera . . . *action*."

Just as the camera's red light blinked on, signaling that we were on air, the back of my throat clamped shut, hot and tight. My cheeks flushed, and my scalp and forehead burst into sweat—I looked like Richard Nixon in his infamous televised debate with John F. Kennedy.

I was on national television, in front of millions of people, and I froze up. Staring straight ahead, I could not utter even one word. It wasn't because I couldn't open my mouth. It was because I had just realized I had nothing to say.

That's how I remembered the interview. But it's not what really happened. It's what I *feared* would happen. Feared it so much that my recurring imaginings of a disastrous performance became etched in my memory. Etched so deeply, and replayed in my mind so often, that I thought they were real.

Almost thirty years later I contacted CBS to see if they had any records of that fateful taping. They told me they had three tapes, each about four minutes long. They all aired in the autumn of 1990. One was about junk mail, another about the alternative press in general, and the third about America's Third Great Awakening. According to Klein, "They all aired. They were all good. I was very happy with them."

It's funny, what we "remember," or think we remember. . . . In his memoir of the Vietnam War, *The Things They Carried*, Tim O'Brien wrote about memory, "All you can do is put things down as they come at you. . . . A thing may happen and be a total lie; another thing may not happen and be truer than the truth."

I finally watched the CBS tapes recently. The most embarrassing moment was in the segment on America's spiritual revival. I said that I considered myself a spiritual person but not a religious one. "I don't attend church but I do sing in a gospel choir, and my wife and kids and I go to Indian powwows." I was such a dilettante. I should have quoted Bill Moyers, who, just after airing his 1988 six-part series *The Power of Myth* with mythologist Joseph Campbell, to huge popular and critical acclaim, announced, "I've given up the beat of politics, I've given up the beat of international affairs, because 'America's spiritual quest' is the biggest story of the millennium."

I did not start *Utne Reader* because I was looking for a soapbox from which to broadcast my ideas. Almost everything I might want to say had been said better by other people anyway, so why not let them do the talking? Besides, nobody has sole proprietorship of the truth.

Sifting the good from the goofy

That was the magazine's fundamental editorial credo. No one point of view is the right point of view. The sum of all the points of view, added and considered together, comes closer to the truth. So who was I to bloviate on national TV about my particular take on the world?

My appearance on *America Tonight* marked a turning point. Things were starting to happen—invitations, interviews, and opportunities I would have never imagined, much less aspired to, to meet people and go places. I was not yet burned-out, but looking back, I can see that I was beginning to lose the run of myself.

That year I attended one of the first TED conferences on the convergence of technology, entertainment, and design. A previous TED conference six years earlier had been a financial dud, but this time things were different. Our host, the Missoni-clad architect and designer Richard Saul Wurman, told us he'd picked us—the five hundred "chosen ones"—from among the five thousand people who'd applied. "You're the ones I'd like to have at my dinner party," he said.

We'd each paid $695, which seemed to me an enormous amount of money, although in retrospect it was nothing compared to the price tag now. The conference would be three days of sitting in the auditorium listening to the likes of Apple's CEO, John Sculley, doing product demos, architect Frank Gehry complaining that his chair designs had become too successful, and keyboardist Herbie Hancock shooting the shit with record producer Quincy Jones. The World Wide Web did not exist yet. Apple Computer was struggling and about to lay off four hundred people in a personal computer market dominated by Microsoft and IBM. Google founders Sergey Brin and Larry Page were teenagers. Mark Zuckerberg was six years old.

We were not given name tags. Wurman wanted us to be open to the "serendipity of strangers." But I'd come all that way and paid all that money because there were a number of people at the conference I wanted to meet. So I went out and bought sticky-backed labels and a handful of Magic Markers and passed them around.

During the breaks, I started meeting people who introduced themselves as subscribers to the magazine. One of them told me, "What I like about the *Utne Reader* is that you introduce me to ideas and issues I didn't know I was interested in until you showed me that I was!"

By this point the magazine was six years old, and I was running into subscribers everywhere I went. They were invariably interesting. I began to toy with the idea of introducing the readers to each other, just as Bob Schwartz had done for the members of the Tarrytown Group. Who knew what good they could do together, I mused, or what mischief they might stir up?

The seed for this idea was planted back in 1977 when I interviewed Margaret Mead about tribalism and community for *New Age Journal*. Mead had said something during our interview that stayed with me:

"Ninety-nine percent of the time that humans have lived on this planet we've lived in tribes—groups of 12 to 36 people. The nuclear family only prevails during times of war, or in modern, western, urban society, which is the psychological equivalent of war, because it's the most mobile unit that can ensure the survival of the species. But for the full flowering of the human spirit," she said, "we need groups, tribes, community."

This idea struck me profoundly. I realized that most people in America had never experienced real community, and that most of us didn't even know what we were missing. It made me want to visit more indigenous communities and more places like Findhorn, which had been so important to me as I found my way from acupuncture to journalism.

As I met more and more of the magazine's readers, I began to wonder if they weren't some kind of tribe, or at least in need of one, and what might happen if they got to know each other. I resolved to help them meet, and to foment, as best I could, a nationwide community-building movement. So I began gathering articles for a theme section with the working title "Salons: How to Revive the Endangered Art of Conversation and Start a Revolution in Your Living Room."

At the next editorial meeting, we voted to run my pet "Salons" cover section in the March/April 1991 edition. In the issue, we introduced Margaret Mead's famous quote to the world: "Never doubt that a small group of thoughtful, committed citizens can change the world. Indeed, it's the only thing that ever has." And we ran an ad inviting our readers to send us their name, address, and daytime phone number if they wanted to meet other readers who lived in their zip code.

The magazine got a deluge of responses and we set up five hundred salons across North America. There were numerous salons in Manhattan, in the L.A. area, and in the Twin Cities. Within a year, nearly twenty thousand people had joined the Neighborhood Salon Association, meeting at least monthly in office conference rooms, church basements, coffee shops, and, mostly, in each other's living rooms.

One Utne salon member in Los Angeles took it upon himself to organize a meeting of representatives of each of the forty salons in the L.A. area. I had already planned to be in California on business at the time of the meeting, so I asked if I could sit in. We gathered in the

The issue that launched the salon movement

function room of his apartment building in Anaheim. When our host introduced me, I asked the assembled salonistas, "What are you doing in your salons?" One by one the salon reps stood up, introduced themselves, and spoke.

The first person was from the Culver City salon. She reported, "We get together every couple weeks in my living room to write to our local, state, and national politicians about issues that are important to us. We also write to the media."

The next person represented the Santa Monica "Table Tippers." "We were going to go camping together but it rained, so we had a pajama party."

Next to speak was an African American man from Long Beach. He said, "After the Rodney King beating by the police, and the resulting uprising and so-called 'riots,' we decided to start an 'enterprise incubator' in one of the burned-out storefronts in our neighborhood. The idea was to create a place where people could access technology to help them launch for-profit and not-for-profit initiatives in the neighborhood. We've already approached Apple and they've donated several computers for the project."

It went on like this around the room that night—inspiring ideas and galvanizing talk—as it did all across the North American continent. Hundreds of newspapers ran long features about the Utne salons in their cities.

When Jacqueline Kennedy Onassis read the salon issue of the magazine, she contacted me to discuss publishing a book on salons. We met in her office at Doubleday in Manhattan. I was more than a little daunted to be having an audience with the Queen of Camelot herself. Jackie, as she introduced herself, was dressed in a white turtleneck sweater under a tan wool jacket, with dark-brown slacks. She greeted me warmly from behind her desk, then came around to sit with me while we talked about the magazine, the role of salons in the French Revolution, and her favorite salon keepers from that era, specifically Madame de Staël and Madame Récamier. By the end of our conversation, it was clear that we wouldn't be working together. She wanted to publish a book heavy on the history of eighteenth- and nineteenth-century French salons, which I knew next to nothing about, whereas I wanted to ignite a cultural revolution, a community-building salon movement for the present day.

And a movement it was. Countless marriages, businesses, and nonprofit initiatives got their start in Utne salons. So did several schools and co-housing projects. The founders of the Blue Man Group met in an Utne salon in Manhattan. A number of large daily newspapers, including all seventy-seven newspapers in the Gannett chain, inspired by the Utne salons, started "discussion circles" for their readers.

I wasn't surprised. As Margaret Mead liked to point out, humans are social beings. We need to feel connected to one another. That's how our ancestors evolved. And there's nothing more social than a circle of people in conversation. But sometimes it feels like everything about our affluent and urbanized modern life in America conspires to *dis*connect us from each other, to make us feel isolated, alienated, and alone.

The nineteenth-century French sociologist Émile Durkheim, in his study of suicide, coined the term *anomie* to describe the characteristic tenor of modern urban life. It's the feeling of instability that arises when the social bonds between an individual and the community break down, when social standards and values are in flux, or when there is a general lack of purpose or ideals.

Perhaps this was what was going on in each of America's "Great Awakenings." Perhaps European Americans in the pre-Revolutionary colonies, and during the mid-nineteenth-century religious revival movement, were searching for true community. They were rejecting the rigid puritanical and Calvinistic values of the times and attempting to live more communally like their Native American neighbors. In fact, according to Sebastian Junger, in his book *Tribe: On Homecoming and Belonging,* thousands of white men and women joined Indian communities rather than staying in their own, whereas Indians almost never left their tribes to join white society. This emigration from the so-called "civilized" to the tribal left thinkers like Benjamin Franklin and Patrick Henry scratching their heads trying to explain such an apparent rejection of their society.

The Utne salons may have been, on one level, an antidote to the anomie, alienation, and loneliness that are endemic to postmodern, techno-industrial civilization. But because most of us didn't grow up in real communities, we don't know what real community looks like.

Most Americans these days live in networks, not communities. We tend to work, study, and socialize with people who are like ourselves. We rarely associate with people who are not similar to us in terms of education, income, age, race, physical characteristics, and worldview. We put our old people in nursing homes and our young ones in day-care centers. Lawbreakers are kept behind bars, and the physically disabled and the mentally ill are kept out of sight. We pay service personnel, often with tax dollars, to handle these "others" for us so we can get on with our careers and our personal growth.

The salons were my favorite part of publishing *Utne Reader,* but they didn't go over well with everyone. Shortly after the salon issue appeared, Erwin Knoll, editor of *The Progressive,* a national monthly based in Madison, said, "This is crap. With all the real pain in the world, to address such a trivial topic as conversation at a time like this, I find it faintly obscene."

But salons weren't about conversation, they were about *community.* Their popularity was symptomatic of a fundamental human need that only grows more urgent daily.

As soon as the salons were launched, we realized we were onto something big, though we weren't totally sure *what,* exactly. We hired a staff salon keeper and published a newsletter to try to capture some of the flavor of what was happening in the salons and to encourage members to go beyond talk, to engage in environmental or social justice work together. Many did. Some told us the salons were a kind of oasis in their otherwise overscheduled, hectic lives. To them, the salons were less about doing than "not doing," and more about creating a space where the participants could simply be together.

We also developed Café Utne, a lively and thoughtful online forum that may have been one of the first virtual communities. But the funny thing was, once we'd made the introductions and our readers had found one another, we were the odd one out—the matchmaker back in Minnesota. There was no reason for salon members to keep in touch with us. And we never figured out how to make the activity pay for itself. It was just a need that we saw and decided to fill. Many of the Utne salons and their offspring still meet to this day.

I loved introducing the readers to one another and hearing what they got up to together. The Utne salons anticipated Meetup groups and dating services, and the entire social media phenomenon. And yet, from today's vantage point, the need for human connection and real community only grows stronger.

23

THE MUD LAKE MEN

After my falling-out with Robert Bly I thought I'd never get involved in "men's work" again. Then, less than a year later, in late 1990, I hired Craig Neal, the former advertising director of *Organic Gardening* magazine, giving him my title as publisher. We moved him, his family, and 150,000 bees to Minnesota from Burlington, Vermont. The idea was that Craig would oversee the day-to-day business operations of the magazine, and help increase national ad sales, while I turned my attention to a number of new projects, like Utne Books, an Utne TV show on PBS, the online Café Utne, and several community-building initiatives.

Craig and I were the same age, and he was as drawn as I was to all things alternative, countercultural, and spiritual. In the sixties, Craig had also turned on, tuned in, and dropped out. You name the historic moment, and Craig, like Forrest Gump, had been there. He witnessed Martin Luther King, Jr., deliver his "I Have a Dream" speech on the steps of the Lincoln Memorial, worked in the food kitchen at Woodstock, got arrested for protesting the Vietnam War in Berkeley, and had a run-in with the law on a California Indian reservation. He helped start and lived on one of America's first hippie communes, in Vermont's Northeast Kingdom, where he shared meals and philosophical debates with a young Bernie Sanders. He was an early participant in Arica and in Da Free John's lectures, and did the EST training in New York City in 1978. He was my kind of guy.

When I learned that a new men's group was forming, I suggested to Craig that we join together. Our host and de facto leader was Will Winter, a holistic veterinarian and several-year veteran of Robert's mythopoetic men's work. We came to call ourselves the Mud Lake Men (other Bly-inspired men's groups in Minneapolis were called the Woolly Mammoths and the Cave Historians). We began with ten men, all middle-class, white, and middle-aged. We knew this was an awfully homogenous clique, but we couldn't find anyone else to join.

We met once every two weeks, on Wednesday night, in a space in Will's basement that we called "the kiva," from the Hopi word for an underground ceremonial chamber.

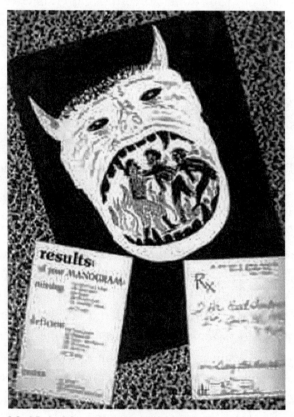

Mud Lake Men meeting notice, circa 1991

Each meeting began with nuts and chips eaten right from the bag while standing in the kitchen. Sometimes the teasing and joking turned homophobic. This sharing of feelings and being vulnerable with other men was new territory for all of us, and our insecurity manifested as sophomoric locker-room banter. Did *real* men really show their feelings to other men?

Then we descended into the kiva. Drumming, chanting, and poetry followed. We structured the meetings around themes: king, warrior, magician, and lover—the four male archetypes. We talked about relationships, parenting, mentors, rites of passage, and death, among other topics.

My favorite extracurricular activity with the Mud Lake Men was our occasional participation in the annual MayDay Parade. Organized by the Heart of the Beast Puppet Theater, the parade is a neo-pagan celebration of the return of the sun after Minnesota's long, cold, dreary winter. The parade begins at Little Earth, the largest urban Indian housing development in North America, and snakes its way through working class neighborhoods on Minneapolis's south side to Powderhorn Park, where a big pageant dramatizes the return of Father Sun and the renewal of Mother Earth with fifteen-foot-tall puppets and a cast of hundreds, while at least twenty-five thousand people chant and cheer from the park's broad hillside.

For one of the parades in the early 1990s the Mud Lake Men built a gigantic, papier-mâché effigy of Iron John, a massive, golem-like creature. We gave our Iron John bulging arms and legs, and an imposing torso, all on hinges so we could hoist him from his supine travel mode to stand and reach out to onlookers when we stopped in intersections.

I dressed as "Ironing John." My body was covered in cloth diapers held on with large safety pins. I wore an old-fashioned apron and a paisley bandanna tied atop my head. I carried a steam iron in one hand and a wooden-handled feather duster in the other, beating out the rhythm of our chant on the iron. When we raised Iron John to his full height in intersections, I'd prance up to onlookers like an errant clown and introduce myself. "Hi, I'm Ironing John. Is there anything

The Mud Lake Men with Iron John, MayDay Parade, 1991

I can do for you?" More than once I got back some variation of "You can drop dead."

Doing "men's work" changed my life. The part of me that sought recognition, acknowledgment, and affirmation from women found satisfaction instead through drumming, singing, and sharing poetry with men. My need to flirt evaporated almost overnight. The group introduced me to myth, ritual, and poetry. I developed some deep and lasting friendships. We were peers, members of the clan I'd been searching for. But to be a real community, we knew that we needed more diversity. For the full catastrophe, as Zorba called it, we needed women.

In 1992 I met Tashi Gyaltsen Gangzey, a young Tibetan who had recently emigrated from India as part of the Tibetan Resettlement Project, of which Nina and I were sponsors. At the time we met, Tashi was working at the Minneapolis Children's Hospital, in the hospital laundry, schlepping soiled linens. Tashi had trained for nine years as a painter of Tibetan thangkas (iconographic religious art) with one of Tibet's great masters in Dharamsala, the home of the Dalai Lama

and the center of the Tibetan diaspora. Tashi had a calm, gentle presence about him that the staff at the Children's Hospital recognized
when he first started working there. They soon asked him to be a
counselor, sitting with people who had been pronounced "terminal,"
or with people who had tried to take their own lives.

I asked Tashi what he did for these people. "Oh, I just talk about
how rare and precious a human life is." I asked him if he had a spiritual practice.

"Oh, I just think about death every day," he said.

Not long after we met, Tashi showed me some pen-and-ink line
drawings he had done to illustrate the story of the gingerbread man.
They were brilliant, combining the motifs of Tibetan religious art,
including stylized clouds, mountains, trees, and water, with the simplicity of the children's fable. I invited Tashi to work at *Utne Reader*, in
the art department, learning magazine layout and computer graphics.
I introduced him to an artists' agent, who helped him build a portfolio
and began circulating his work.

During this time, I developed an interest in Tibetan Buddhism,
especially tantra. I wanted to become an adept of Tibetan tantra. Tashi
and I soon began a business together. We would make high-quality rugs
in his aunt's factory in Kathmandu, Nepal, and sell the rugs via ads in
Utne Reader. We called our business "Tiger Rugs of Tibet."

The rugs were three by six feet, made of Himalayan wool, colored
only with nontoxic vegetable dyes, hand-knotted by Tibetans. No
child labor was involved. All the designs were based on ancient,
abstract Tibetan Buddhist tantric tiger patterns. They were meant to
be used as meditation rugs. Traditional practitioners performed tantric meditation rites on them.

Often referred to as sexual yoga, Tibetan tantra is based on the
principle that the separation of spirit and matter is an illusion. Practitioners of tantra use physical disciplines, such as breath control, visu-
alization, and certain sexual techniques, to transcend the illusion of
duality and achieve the ultimate state of bliss. This is not the frenzied
Dionysian ecstasy of Rajneesh's chaotic meditation, but rather the
perfect serenity of still, untroubled union with the divine.

I wanted to be Tiger Man—a Norwegian American Viking Tibetan rug dealer and tantra master. At the very least, I would have an excuse to travel to Nepal, and possibly Tibet. I read books on tiger rugs and Tibetan tantra by Tibetan scholars and tantric practitioners, including Namkhai Norbu, Keith Dowling, and Lama Surya Das.

Tashi and I ran a little ad on the pages of *Utne Reader* for several years and sold almost one hundred rugs. But eventually I realized that Tashi had no desire to be a rug dealer, or a commercial artist.

"What do you really want to do?" I asked Tashi.

"Oh, I don't know," he replied. He was clearly reluctant to tell me. But with more encouragement, and a little badgering, Tashi finally admitted, "I've always wanted to drive a city bus."

I never made it to Nepal, or Tibet, and I never became an authority on tantra. But Tashi got a job with the Minneapolis Transit Authority. He has been driving a city bus ever since.

Around this time Bob Schwartz invited me to speak at a course he was teaching on entrepreneurship at MIT's Sloan School of Management. I was billed as a "young entrepreneur who had an idiosyncratic dream and made it real," though by this time I was no longer young— I was in my mid-forties. The lecture hall was filled with nearly two hundred MBA candidates, a veritable United Nations of well-scrubbed, multiethnic young people in blue jeans and polo shirts. I told my story of starting *Utne Reader*. When I finished, Bob opened the session for questions from the students. A young woman leaped to her feet and shouted, "Me, me!" so I called on her.

"You're telling us to 'Follow your bliss!'" she started, spitting the phrase out with disdain. I hadn't used Joseph Campbell's famous admonition, but it had been in the air ever since Bill Moyers's popular interviews with Campbell a few years before. "You're a freak of the sixties!" the young woman continued. "If I start a business, whether I'm making widgets or making bombs, as long as I'm employing people I'm adding value to the economy, and that's good enough for me."

I was utterly speechless. I didn't know what to say. I couldn't believe someone so young could be so cynical. Then author Lynne Twist, a friend of Bob's who happened to be in Boston and came to hear my lecture, jumped up to speak. She came to the podium and said, "I've just returned from Oslo, Norway, where former prime minister Gro Harlem Brundtland held a conference about how to address the environmental crisis."

Lynne explained that Brundtland had called together a large group of former CEOs of Fortune 500 corporations, former heads of state, and Nobel Peace Prize laureates. An idea came out during the conference to create an "Earth Corps," a kind of Peace Corps for the whole earth. Volunteers from all over the world would work to reverse the environmental crisis. Young people from Africa would work in China, Chinese in France, and French in the United States. Everybody would go everywhere.

The lecture hall fell silent. Soon one hand shot up, then another and another. The first to speak said, "How can I join? The only reason I'm in school is because I don't know what I want to do with my life." Then the next, talking over the first. "The Earth Corps would be high adventure. It would make a real difference in the world." And then another. "And it would be our own thing, not something handed down to us by baby boomers. Sign me up!"

I never got to respond to the young woman who called me a freak of the sixties, but I was convinced that if I just had more time, and if we could talk one-on-one, I could show her so many examples of positive things happening in the world that she, or anyone with an open mind, could not possibly give up hope. Of course, all this was well before 9/11, before George W. Bush and the second Iraq War, before Facebook and smartphones, and the melting permafrost and President Donald Trump. Now I'm not so sure.

Sometime in 1992 frequent *Utne Reader* contributor Andrew Kimbrell, author of *The Masculine Mystique: The Politics of Masculinity*, told me he had attended a conference in California with Robert Bly. Robert had tossed off the idea that we're living in a "sibling society." Struck by the concept, I contacted Robert and proposed getting together for coffee. To my surprise he agreed to see me.

Robert and I hadn't talked in more than three years. This had been painful for me. While several of the guys in my men's group were regulars at Robert's annual Minnesota men's conference, I had stayed away so as not to upset him, and, truth be told, to avoid his legendary wrath. Several of the Mud Lake Men attended Sufi singing sessions in Robert's garage, sessions I would have loved to attend, and would have been welcome to join, but I'd chosen not to go.

Robert suggested we meet at Cafe Wyrd, a Minneapolis coffee-house. The place was dark and atmospheric, even in the late morning, and all of the tables were occupied, save for one right in the middle of the room, illuminated by a bright light directly above it. With a spot-light literally shining on us, Robert and I must have looked like two crows trying to make themselves inconspicuous in a flock of doves.

As soon as we'd gotten our coffee, I blurted something like "Robert, I hope you're not still mad at me for running that nasty little piece by Carol."

"I don't understand why you did it," Robert replied. "I thought you were a friend. Friends don't do things like that."

"I'm so sorry," I said. I should have left it there. But I thought I could explain. Maybe he'd understand my reasoning. I began talking about the "editorial mix," but Robert was having none of it. He cut me off. "Skip it. I'm over that. So . . . what was it you wanted to talk about?"

Relieved that Robert seemed to want to let bygones be bygones, I said, "Andy Kimbrell told me he heard you talk briefly about what you called 'the sibling society.' That's an intriguing phrase. I wondered if you'd tell me what you mean by 'sibling society'?"

"Sure," Robert said. "I use the phrase to suggest a culture funda-mentally without fathers, mothers, grandfathers, grandmothers, or ancestors. The thinking is horizontal. We have become a nation of squabbling siblings."

"You mean like Peter Pan in the song 'I Won't Grow Up.'"

"Exactly," Robert said. "We live in a culture in which we tolerate no one above us and have no concern for anyone below us. We live with, work with, and play with people just like us. We cast sidelong glances for direction, rather than looking up or down."

"But wasn't that the point of democracy? Or the counterculture?" I asked. "To challenge and break down traditional hierarchal forms, like the Catholic Church or monarchy, or even patriarchal thinking, either because they were unjust or because they had simply outlived their usefulness?"

"Well, it's true we've brought down hierarchy by questioning and challenging authority, but we have not replaced it with anything like true democracy. Instead, we have mass culture, consumer culture. We have no longing for the good, no deep understanding of evil. We shy away from great triumph and deep sorrow."

"Sounds pretty bleak," I said.

"Damn right it's bleak," Robert said. "What we are left with is spiritual flatness. The talk show replaces the family. Instead of art we have computers. In place of community we have the mall."

The conversation went on like this for two hours. At one point a woman with close-cropped hair and an army fatigue jacket came up to our table.

"Are you Robert Bly?" she said.

"So they tell me," Robert replied.

"I just want to thank you for your important work," she said. "My son is learning how to feel, thanks to you. Keep it up."

As she walked away, Robert leaned toward me and whispered, "I didn't expect that."

At one point I asked him what we can do about the sibling society.

"Forget about talk shows," he said. "Forget about crookedness, and rotten freshmen Republican congressmen, and retiring in Phoenix. Turn away from this completely and turn back and face the children and the ancestors."

As our time wound down, I was exhausted yet giddy, thrilled that we were talking again. And Robert's ideas about the sibling society seemed especially important to me. I asked him to write a cover story for *Utne Reader* about the sibling society. He said he'd think about it. A month later, he told me that he wasn't ready to publish anything on the subject. In fact, he worked almost full-time on it for the next three years. The book that resulted from this work would change my life.

24

UNDER THE VOLCANO

In 1993 I was invited to write a review of Tina Brown's *New Yorker* for the *Columbia Journalism Review.*

"Why me?" I asked editor Suzanne Braun Levine. After all, my beat was the counterculture and its alternative press, whereas *The New Yorker* was mainstream high culture, leaning increasingly toward pop culture.

"You're the perfect person to do it," Suzanne assured me.

"No," I pressed. "Why, *really*?"

"Because no one else will touch it."

I must confess I was not one of the faithful who read every issue of *The New Yorker*. Though I was a magazine junkie, *The New Yorker* had never been on my must-read list. The way I read it was to let the issues pile up (at my father's house) until someone told me there was something I just had to read—usually by Paul Brodeur, Bill McKibben, Pauline Kael, or John McPhee. I was content to wait for that happy confluence of truly stunning, important ideas and brilliant exposition, like Jonathan Schell's seminal *Fate of the Earth*, which ran in 1982 as a four-part series on the potential for nuclear war to destroy all humanity and possibly most life on earth. I'd pass on the five-part series on grain or the articles about "somebody's childhood in Pakistan," as Dorothy Parker once quipped about William Shawn's *New Yorker* of the sixties.

So while I was surprised to be asked to write the review, I jumped at the opportunity for an inside look at America's most exalted magazine. I was too curious, or perhaps too foolhardy, to decline. What was it about Tina Brown that commanded so little public criticism from the usually quick-to-shoot pundits of American journalism? Maybe I could learn something that would help in the running of *Utne Reader*.

After two visits to *The New Yorker*'s offices on West Forty-third Street, and a great deal of reading and phone work, I'd uncovered an organization rife with internal dissent. Scores of staff had been laid off or resigned. Many current and former employees contacted me, some anonymously. One gave me the staff directory, with a list of everyone's private phone numbers. A few spoke for attribution, but most spoke off the record.

The negative feedback I heard most often was that the magazine had been hijacked by Brown's need to create "buzz" and had thus become insistently, overwhelmingly topical. Even Brown's friends, like *Village Voice* editor Jonathan Larsen, said she had gone too far. "The magazine needed to become more topical," Larsen said, "but she's made it relentlessly so at the expense of the serendipitous, leisurely pace of her predecessors. You can find the topical anywhere, but not the timeless."

During a long and cordial interview, I asked Brown about the staff exodus. Among the many staff and regular contributors who'd quit in protest were staff writer Veronica Geng and Minnesota humorist and *A Prairie Home Companion* creator Garrison Keillor.

Brown claimed the transition was going smoothly. She said Keillor left because she hired someone who had written a column about him in *Vanity Fair* that Keillor found very, very offensive. "I wrote saying that I'm sorry you went before we had a chance to meet. And he wrote back that he hopes to publish something one day. I don't think there's any particular acrimony. He's a good writer."

When I later asked Keillor if Brown's account of his departure was accurate, he told me, "Tina Brown has a lot of nerve explaining why I left *The New Yorker* when she never bothered to ask me in the first place. I left because I love *The New Yorker* and because she is the wrong person to edit it. I didn't want to be on the premises to watch it suffer under her hand."

Keillor said the magazine he wanted to write for "is gone now, bought by a billionaire. . . . *The New Yorker* is a glorious and dear American institution, but Ms. Brown, like so many Brits, seems most fascinated by the passing carnival and celebrity show in America. Fiction, serious reporting, the personal essay, criticism, all that made *The New Yorker* great, do not engage her interest apparently. She has redesigned it into a magazine that looks and reads an awful lot like a hundred other magazines. The best writing to appear in Ms. Brown's *New Yorker*, in fact, was the section of tributes to William Shawn, which read like an obituary for *The New Yorker*."

Brown asked me what I thought about the old *New Yorker*. I said I admired it because it had the courage to disagree with the conventional wisdom even as it defined it. In its coverage of the United States' involvement in Nicaragua, Grenada, and the Persian Gulf, the magazine asked tough questions that few other mainstream publications dared to ask, just as it had earlier about McCarthyism, civil rights, and the Vietnam War. By allowing radical thinkers such as Michael Harrington, James Baldwin, and Barry Commoner to fling their incendiary ideas from its pages, *The New Yorker* of old consistently raised the level of the national conversation.

She also asked me what I thought she should do with her magazine. I told her I thought she could use more writing by women like Barbara Ehrenreich, Louise Erdrich, and Winona LaDuke. And I urged her to publish more from America's heretical visionaries and prophetic poets, like Robert Bly, Gary Snyder, and Stephen Mitchell. She thanked me, but took no notes.

My biggest takeaway from doing the article was the impression of sterility I felt in the *New Yorker* offices. Designed under the regime of Brown's predecessor, Robert Gottlieb, *The New Yorker*'s offices were not laid out to encourage intra-office schmoozing. The off-white linoleum floors and long hallways with endless closed doors were so stark that I expected a pair of the doors to burst open at any moment, orderlies rushing by with a patient on a gurney. The reception area was as barren as any other New York office reception area, except this one was devoid of reading material. There wasn't even a copy of *The New Yorker* in sight. The one space that invited conviviality was the open stairway between the sixteenth and seventeenth floors and the nearby library tables.

Still, it was a privilege to walk down those hallowed halls, to meet future *New Yorker* editor David Remnick and hang out with then executive editor Rick Hertzberg, and to see for myself how different those offices felt compared to the esprit de corps that I was trying to create at *Utne Reader*.

A few months after I wrote my review of Tina's *New Yorker*, *Utne Reader* turned ten years old, in February 1994. By any measure, the magazine was a wild success. It employed more than thirty people full-time. Each bimonthly issue generated press, sometimes a great deal of it. We were amplifying the voices of the alternative press, and connecting the readers with each other through the Neighborhood Salon Association. And we were growing. The magazine's paid circulation had grown to more than 305,000 (255,000 paid subscribers plus 50,000 newsstand sales), with an estimated 750,000 readers, and more than seven million dollars in annual revenues. To put those numbers in perspective, 300,000 was twice the circulation of *Harper's* and *Mother Jones* at the time, and three times that of *The Nation* and *The New Republic*.

But critics and staff alike were beginning to ask if *Utne Reader* had lost its magic. Some said it had become too predictable and not edgy enough. Others that it was not political enough. There were rumblings among the staff—talk of employee stock ownership, profit sharing, additional vacation time, and other benefits. I'd have been happy if we were simply breaking even, as long as we were publishing. My measure of success was simply that the magazine existed, that we were in print.

But I was feeling frustrated that my work life was so different from my private life. At home and with my friends, I felt I could let it all

One big dysfunctional family: *Utne Reader* staff photo, 1993

hang out. I could be playful and silly, indignant and outraged, earnest and sincere, befuddled and vulnerable. But at work I didn't feel able to show all of these sides. I tried to be collegial and to make editorial decisions by consensus, but some of the staff wanted me to be "the boss." Others wanted to turn the magazine into a democracy, or a collective. And some of the staff resented Nina's and my privileged status and more new agey interests.

I wanted the collegial feeling I'd experienced at *East West Journal* and *New Age Journal,* the intimacy and playfulness I felt at Findhorn, the camaraderie I felt among the Mud Lake Men. Was that too much to ask? Why couldn't we have a similar feeling in the *Utne Reader* offices? I wondered.

In my circles outside the magazine, we used the council process to build trust within the group. For some reason that now escapes me, I thought we could do the same at *Utne Reader.* Council could help us bridge the gulf between our personal lives and our work lives, I thought. This seemed like a good idea at the time. What was I thinking?

To celebrate the magazine's tenth anniversary, which came just at the time we were completing an expansion of the *Utne Reader* offices, I asked the entire staff to gather in our new library, a large rectangular room whose walls were covered in shelves filled with books and magazines. From the top of each wall, the ceiling sloped up in a high pyramid, at the top of which were steel girders that framed the building's eighty-year-old skylight. The slanting walls bore a gigantic, atmospheric mural, painted in crimsons and golds. We called the vaporous, Turneresque mural "Under the Volcano," and the room "the Crucible."

There we were, thirty of us, including our ad sales staff from the East and West coasts, gathered in a large circle, sitting on an ersatz Persian rug under the "volcano." This was the first time in our history that we'd gathered as one whole group.

I thanked the staff for their hard work, singling out several individuals for service beyond the call of duty. Then, feeling moved by the moment, and not a bit shy, I surprised myself and probably everyone in the room. I said that I believed we'd come to a crossroads, that even though it was my job to articulate the direction of the company, I didn't feel certain about which way to go. "We have no clear road maps to the future," I said. "We need a vision, and it can come to—and through—any one of us. We need to go forward with open minds, open eyes, and open hearts."

I hoped these words would inspire people's creativity and sense of community. Just as new ideas and insights regularly came from anyone in our editorial salons, so too could come a vision for the future of the magazine. But some people probably found my words deeply unsettling.

Then I lit a bundle of sage and walked around the circle smudging the space, and everyone in it, with smoke. I placed the sage in a large, candlelit crystal bowl in the center of the circle. The bowl had special meaning to me. It was made from the detritus of silicon chips used in the manufacture of computers, transformed through heat from industrial waste into a beautiful, resonant, translucent gong. It was our version of the Oscar statuette, inscribed and sent to the winners of the first Alternative Press Awards.

Then I sat back down and considered inviting everyone to join hands. This would be a first—we'd never actually held hands as a group. The *Utne Reader* staff was full of all kinds, some more touchy-feely than others. I'd never wanted to push anyone who wasn't so inclined into something so new agey as hand-holding. But what the hell, I thought. Schoolkids do it. Football teams do it. Why shouldn't we?

I silently took the hands of the people sitting on either side of me. To my amazement, within a few seconds everyone in the circle had done the same. I was both thrilled and relieved. I *can* have it all, I thought.

Just as I exclaimed, "We did it!" the crystal bowl burst into billowing smoke and flames. I leaped up and grabbed the bowl. Blowing on the flames only intensified the fire. The sage I'd dropped into the bowl had knocked the candle over, spreading wax across the bottom of the bowl and turning the sage into a hydra-headed wick. I rushed the bowl out of the library and, unable to douse the flames, dumped the burning wax into our new kitchen sink as the building's fire alarm went off. Everyone, including me, roared with laughter.

I reported this incident in my next editor's note and concluded the column by saying, "So be warned. As the *Utne Reader* staff joins together over the years to come, we're bound to generate some heat. May we also bring light."

GUIDING PRINCIPLES

So what have we learned in 10 years of publishing *Utne Reader*? Here are a few principles that we live by:

Start slow and taper off. What's the hurry?

If something's worth doing, it's worth doing poorly. The corollary to this is, learn how to say "good enough" (for now); you can always make it better next time.

If something's worth saying, it's worth repeating. Just because someone else published something first doesn't mean you shouldn't publish it too.

Edit for yourself, then give it to your readers. It's the difference between entertaining them and *delighting* them.

Read the alternative press. Because alternative press publications are *not* the journals of record. They're biased. They don't pretend to be objective. New ideas surface in the alternative press first, not in coverage by trend-watching journalists, but in musings and passionate polemics from the thinkers and visionaries themselves. The alternative press is where the emerging culture first reveals itself.

—ERIC UTNE
Utne Reader, March/April 1994

25

VISION QUEST

Late in the summer of 1995, I did a vision fast—four days with nothing but water in the high California desert above Death Valley. Doing the fast was Nina's idea. It was billed as a "wilderness family camp," organized and led by two old friends. Gigi was a free spirit who traveled the globe swimming with dolphins. Roger had interned at *New Age Journal* while he was a student at Harvard (mostly, his job as an intern had been to babysit Leif).

Squaw Peak, Inyo Mountains, north toward the White Mountains. Death Valley is to the east.

I was skeptical about vision fasts. I knew almost nothing about them and didn't feel I had a good reason or purpose to starve myself for four days. I certainly wasn't "crying for a vision," which was what Gigi and Roger told us was the state one should be in in order to get the most out of the ordeal. As far as I could tell, Nina wasn't crying for a vision either. Instead, we thought of the vision fast as something interesting to do on our family vacation. Nina and I had three children by now, all boys. Sam was thirteen years old, Oliver almost ten, and Eli four and a half. We brought all three and Jessica, their favorite babysitter. Leif couldn't join us because he was still in college, having dropped out for two years to work for Ralph Nader's PIRGs, then transferring to UMass Amherst, where he changed his major from music to poli-sci. As far as the younger boys were concerned, the choice had been between Disneyland and Death Valley, and their mother and I made the wrong choice.

The group included a dozen adults and their children. For the first four days we camped in the foothills of the Sierra Nevadas, on the edge of black and red lava fields. Gigi and Roger taught us wilderness survival skills—everything from how to light a fire without matches to how to treat sunstroke, heat exhaustion, and rattlesnake bites. And they led the adults in group conversations and one-on-one interviews to help us clarify our intentions. Why on earth did we want to spend four days alone, without food, in the high desert? they wanted to know. What exactly were we searching for?

I'd been a self-described "seeker" all my life, but what was I searching for *now*? As a child and teenager, I'd wanted to be a knight. Bravery, chivalry, valor, jousting, slaying dragons, saving damsels in distress— these were my Holy Grail, pursued mostly in my imagination.

When I was a teenager, Brenda encouraged my chivalrous ambitions. She admonished me to have what she called "that kingy feeling. . . . Everybody in the world should be great kings and queens," she told me. "Not meek but debonair, flexible, blithe, light-hearted, open, free. Suggestible, so that great ideas can enter you."

In my twenties, dreaming of transforming the techno-industrial system that I would later call "the Machine" and bringing on the love revolution, I'd made myself sick with drugs and worry about the Vietnam War. Michio Kushi's purpose for macrobiotics became my purpose in life—"to recover my lost memory and recall my largest possible dream." I wanted to be tuned in and obedient to natural law (but above and beyond man's law). I wanted to be knowledgeable about health and healing, and imbued with perfect intuition.

After my epiphany at Findhorn, when I was twenty-seven, I realized that seeing is a kind of conjuring, a creative act. Seeing the whole person, as I did when practicing acupuncture, or whatever I was doing instead of acupuncture, had a healing effect. I sought to heal society through journalism.

When I was in my thirties, my search took another direction. Bob Schwartz articulated it and embodied it. Bob was an entrepreneur, by his own definition "a person who has a vision and makes it real." He was an agent of change, a "poet and packager of the new social order." He foresaw what he called "the coming entrepreneurial revolution," and he saw me as a "visionary" magazine publisher and change agent. Rank puffery, but I'd eaten it up.

"See yourself as a warrior," Schwartz had said. "Understand the fear inherent in risk taking, accept it, and proceed *unafraid.*" This sounded like Brenda's exhortation, "Be great, be a king! Be a hero! We need you! The world needs you!"

When I met Nina, my search changed again. I wanted to do good *and* do well. I wanted my work to alleviate suffering and make a positive difference in the world, and I wanted to get rich doing it.

Utne Reader was my throne. The whole world was my domain. Editing and publishing the magazine gave me access. Anyone I wanted to meet seemed willing to see me. The magazine bridged disparate worlds: the New Left and the New Age, the mainstream and the alternative press, high culture, pop culture, and the emerging culture. My motto at the time was "When faced with a choice, always take both." Surely, that was a formula for trouble.

I saw my face in the media and my name in print. People even knew how to pronounce "Utne." The magazine was lauded in the press and nominated for the National Magazine Award for General

Excellence, twice. I was asked by journalists to comment on current events, sat on publishing and civic leadership boards and panels, and spoke at prestigious venues on all manner of topics. I was treated like a celebrity, albeit a minor one.

The climax of this phase before my vision fast, had been *Utne Reader*'s Visionfest, "an earth-shaking, tongue-wagging, soul-stirring, mind-bending, community-building celebration of ideas and vision," with presentations by twenty-five Utne Visionaries who could "change your life." The evening started at the Harvard Club and moved to New York City's legendary Town Hall. I was riding high on top of the world. I was also content. I had my health, a happy family, and a vital, supportive community. As far as I could tell, I wasn't searching for anything. Humpty-Dumpty must have had similar feelings.

During the preparation time for the vision fast, my purpose began to reveal itself. I realized I was just as estranged from wild nature as I had been when Peggy and Leif and I visited Dan Raincloud on the Red Lake Indian reservation in northern Minnesota, back when Leif was a baby. So one of my intentions was to learn to feel more at home in nature, and, perhaps, within myself.

Another intention was to deepen my connection with Nina and our boys as a family by doing something arduous and challenging together.

And finally, I wanted to contemplate what was next for me regarding the magazine. I hoped twelve days out of the office, including four days praying and fasting on the edge of Death Valley, would lead me to new insights and a renewed sense of direction for the company.

The children stayed at base camp with Gigi and Roger while the adults wandered a mile or two in various directions to do their four-day solo fasts. I spent my fasting days hiking the rugged Inyo Mountain terrain and seeking shade under piñon trees and giant cacti. I painted watercolor landscapes, read Chuang Tzu and the Bible, and wrote in my journal.

One morning, while hiking in the valley below my campsite, I came upon a tiny, slender, silvery-gray salamander. I would later learn it was the endangered Inyo Mountains salamander. I remembered the

Tracing of the outlines of the feather found on Day 5 (8/28) at Tinemaha Creek.

Today I told my story in council at Three Creeks to Gigi, Roger, and my fellow fasters Michael, Janet, Carol, Teresa, +Alan by

what I got mirrored back to me Roger + Gigi left me in tears -- I felt so seen and understood, so healed and loved. To see someone so deeply, so unconditionally, is truly an act of healing. I saw that in my faux acupuncture practice (I'd stopped using needles and would simply be with people -- and they'd heal themselves) when I was about 28-29. Seeing the true person the being they were born to be, is an act of healing and loving.

I told of hearing Gigi + Roger's call and answering it. I told of what I brought with me to the vision fast, what the ancient Bristlecones told me, what I prayed as I went out, the medicine I was given each day my death lodge with 200-250 people who I love, my purpose circle spent dancing all night, thinking of Brenda + Robert Bly and finally how Dan Rauncloud came to me.

Roger + Gigi saw me as a man who went out with an empty medicine bag and come back w/ an empty medicine bag, yet filled w/ the gift of healing + loving. They saw me as an

black-and-yellow-spotted salamanders that were stuck in the window well of my childhood home. Those creatures were out of place, exiled as they were by the fire-breathing earth graders that destroyed their swamp home. But these salamanders *were* at home. *I* was the exile, or intruder. I left them in peace and resolved to do what I could to protect their habitat.

On day three, I had a conversation with a desert jaybird, or rather a desert jaybird spoke to me. He landed a few feet from my head while I was half asleep under a juniper tree. As he pecked at a seed, he noticed me in the shadows of the tree. Then he turned sideways, fixing me with one eye, and I heard something. His speech wasn't audible in the jaybirds' usual shrill, piercing song; I heard him speak in my imagination. I don't remember what he said—I was gobsmacked, after all—but I felt acknowledged, creature to creature, and somehow welcomed. That was it—a five-second close encounter that would soon rock my world.

At night, I sat in my sleeping bag and watched the constellations come alive, identifying the few I knew—the Big Dipper, Orion, Leo the Lion—and tracking their mythic figures as they crept across the starry heavens. My ancestors must have navigated across the oceans by knowing these stars, I thought, and here I was, completely oblivious to their ways. I resolved then to learn the constellations and the night sky.

While Nina and I were out on our solos, the children whittled sticks, went on expeditions, and helped Gigi and Roger tend the basecamp fire. On the fourth day our boys decided to do their own vision fasts. Sam did a thirteen-hour solo—one hour for each year of his life. Oliver did a ten-hour fast, and Eli and Jessica went off with Roger's five-year-old daughter, Tara, to see if they could see bears. They didn't.

During my fast, I wrote a letter to my sons about my hopes for them. I told them that I didn't have much to give them other than what I already had: my genes, my patterns of avoidance and denial ("The sins of the fathers are visited on the sons for four generations"), a commitment to end these patterns in my lifetime, perhaps a keepsake or two, some memories, a few stories, and my love and blessings.

I wrote that I hoped each of them could do a vision fast someday, to contemplate his place in the world, to feel his connection with nature, to open himself to Spirit.

On the final night of my solo fast, I experienced the full moon as a living being, regent of growth, fertility, the tides, and dreams. I felt bathed in her luminescence, her glow a kind of blessing. Conscious of herself and me and the cosmos, she was infinitely patient, attendant to and totally in love with the Earth, just as the Earth was in love with her and the sun. I watched her approach, then slip below the western horizon, like a lidded eye slowly closing. I felt *seen* by her, and, as she bowed her head, a last flicker of connection, then she was gone. How

Bristlecone pines are the oldest trees on the planet.

could anyone believe that something or someone so present, so powerful, so generative, could be dead, a cold satellite, devoid of life? It's just not possible.

During the three days after the vision fasts, everyone, including the kids, gathered around the campfire several times a day to hear each other's stories. There were many adventures and insights to report. My sons listened in a way I hadn't seen before. They seemed more peaceful and present, and more interested than I had ever witnessed. Wanting to keep the magic going, I asked Gigi where she'd recommend we stay on our last night in Nevada before we flew home.

"Stay at Circus Circus Casino," she said. "It's like being inside a 3-D pinball machine."

I couldn't believe my ears. After what we'd just experienced, exposing our kids to a noisy, chaotic casino seemed like it would be a harsh shock to their systems.

"It's no use trying to preserve the magic spell that comes from being in the wild," Gigi explained. "Everyday reality will break the spell for sure. Circus Circus is just a fun way to do it."

One month after my vision fast, as I was standing on the sidewalk on Forty-eighth Street at Lexington Avenue in New York City, a gentle wind caressed my cheek, causing me to turn toward the breeze. As I did so, I noticed the full moon above the Chrysler Building. Immediately I was back on the mountain. Standing there in the heart of Manhattan, I realized that we are always in nature, wherever we are. What would it take to feel that connection every day, I wondered, in the city?

After the vision fast, I felt that I was on the threshold of a new chapter, one in which I would bring more of myself to my life, including the magazine. It was time to stop worrying about what other people thought of me. It was the same feeling I had had when I was at Findhorn: Damn what they think—I will be true to myself. I will let my light shine. Let it shine, let it shine.

Seeing the full moon above the Chrysler Building led to *Cosmo Doogood's Urban Almanac.*

In the next issue of *Utne Reader* I mentioned my vision fast in passing in the last paragraph of my editor's note. A cautionary voice told me to be more discreet, that this was not the place or time to mention having a conversation with a desert jaybird, but I couldn't see what harm it could cause. Besides, it seemed cowardly not to mention something that was so important to me. I chose not to listen to what my heart was telling me. I would come to regret doing so.

26

THE KING KILLER

The first sign of trouble had come five years earlier, in 1990, when an *Utne Reader* assistant editor told me that he'd gotten a call from a local alternative newsweekly reporter with a reputation for writing unflattering profiles of local personalities. The reporter had asked, "What's the dirt on Eric?"

Utne Reader had just gotten lots of positive press—in *Time* and *People* magazines and *The New York Times,* among other venues. Most of the stories focused on "the man behind the magazine," or "the Utne behind the name." I attempted to turn the attention from me to the rest of the staff. "It's a team effort," I protested. But with my name on the masthead, it was easier for writers to focus on me. Besides, truth be told, I liked hearing Bill Moyers call the magazine "an underground railway of ideas" and being called "a counterculture visionary" by *The New York Times.* The reporter told the staffer, "It's time to get the other side."

I asked the staffer what he said. "I told him I don't know any dirt about you. And that even if I did, I wouldn't tell him. I like my job."

I was both alarmed and relieved. I'd never been the object of an exposé, nor did I publish any—though we published a broad spectrum of opinion, we avoided character assassinations. In fact, the nastiest piece I'd ever published had been the one that made merciless fun of a men's workshop, in the same issue as Carol Bly's critical sidebar that led to the falling-out between Robert Bly and me.

But, to be honest, I did take guilty pleasure in reading gossipy "in-depth" profiles by writers like Dominick Dunne, Taki, Christopher Hitchens, and Leslie Bennetts in *Vanity Fair, The Village Voice,* and *New York* magazine. And I couldn't resist a bit of schadenfreude when watching Mike Wallace on *60 Minutes* induce some dissembling politician or corporate evildoer or flimflam artist to hoist himself by his own petard. I often wondered how accurate the stories were. Not very, I suspected.

And what of the unlucky schmuck whose life was splayed out for all to see—how did Wallace's victims feel being so publicly dissected? For me, it was the stuff of nightmares.

As usual, I comforted myself with denial: It could never happen to me.

Roughly once a year from 1990 to 1995 the reporter called the *Utne Reader* office asking to interview me. I always declined his requests. Why should I talk with someone so clearly out to get me? Then one day he called my assistant to "check a few facts." I assumed what he was working on would end up being a five-inch story in his paper's media column. It was the cover story.

The headline read, "The Trouble with Utne." An odd (I thought) caricature of me filled the tabloid's cover. The subhead read: "Eric Utne has become a self-appointed guru to the questing hip-oisie. But critics say the *Utne Reader*'s founder is a hypocritical flake, a new-age Teflon editor who co-opts critics and *converses with rocks,* but declines to speak with reporters in his home town. Has the *global village idiot* gone off the deep end?"

Inside, the article led with the following: "Critics say success and privilege have put *Utne Reader* founder Eric Utne at odds with his politically correct mission. Former magazine staffers portray an office rife with dysfunction. Onetime *Utne* fans mourn its current direction. Local reporters complain that Utne won't talk to them."

Suddenly, I was off my high horse. I felt blindsided and wounded by the article, though I should have seen it coming. Being called a

Twin Cities Reader

NOVEMBER 8–14 1995

Show

THE TROUBLE WITH UTNE

Eric Utne has become a self-appointed guru to the questing hip-oisie. But critics say the *Utne Reader*'s founder is a hypocritical flake, a new-age Teflon editor who co-opts critics and **converses with rocks**, but declines to speak with reporters in his home town. Has the **global village idiot** gone off the deep end?

BY JON TEVLIN PAGE 10

"hypocritical flake who *converses with rocks*" hurt. He'd taken my remark about my vision fast totally out of context, just to make me look bad. The article was a bitter brew of leering innuendo and unattributed aspersions but thankfully little substance.

Nina responded with this letter:

> *I won't get into the particulars of the article except to offer that anyone who knows Eric could testify to the fact that though he is completely impossible, he has a few redeeming qualities. . . . In case you run this letter, here's a public thank-you to all those who don't believe everything they read. I extend my condolences on your severe case of cynicism. In all sincerity, I wish you a speedy recovery of hope and good will.*
>
> *Nina Rothschild Utne, Minneapolis*

Still, there was some truth in the piece. The office *was* rife with dysfunction. There was an undercurrent of deep cynicism among certain staffers, a contingent whose jokes were nihilistic and mean, often at the expense of others in the office. Worse, I was complicit in creating the cynical atmosphere—I laughed at the cynics' cruel jokes, often in spite of myself. It wasn't safe for anyone to stick his or her neck out, to reveal an enthusiasm, without risking ridicule.

But the criticism that I was a hypocrite seemed to me groundless and unfair. I never presented myself as a guru or expert on anything. I had a lot of confidence, but it wasn't in myself, it was in the ideas we were promoting in the magazine: holistic journalism, cultural activism, participatory democracy, slowing down, reducing the scale of our institutions, building community one conversation at a time. *Utne Reader* aspired to a journalism of healing, offering a range of perspectives from a variety of sources about political, social, and cultural issues. It was produced by a committed staff who were sometimes a contentious lot. We strived to live up to our mission—at times we succeeded, at times we failed. But I believed that what we were doing was worthwhile.

When I dug up more of the reporter's writing, I decided that he was a talented stylist who had inadvertently done me a great service. I'd been editing and publishing *Utne Reader* for twelve years. I had gotten full of myself, impressed with the magazine's success. I needed to have some air let out of my sails, to be brought down to earth. Still, I hated the reporter for doing it.

Besides my personal travails, the economics of magazine publishing had grown increasingly difficult. The costs of printing and postage kept going up, and readers had become less responsive to our subscription appeals. This wasn't unique to *Utne Reader,* or even to magazines. People concerned about the environment were rejecting junk mail en masse. Greenpeace, which relied heavily on direct mail at the time, saw its membership shrink from 1.2 million members to fewer than 200,000 in a few short years. Many magazines and nonprofits whose members were environmentalists were forced to shrink operations or to shutter their doors.

In addition, Café Utne, our attempt to publish a digital version of the magazine and serve an active community of online readers, proved to be too far ahead of its time. The magazine lost half a million dollars on the effort in less than a year.

Perhaps most significantly, Nina and I were having our own troubles. I decided it was time for me to leave the magazine and focus on my family. I hired Hugh Delehanty from *Sports Illustrated* to be the editor. Hugh was co-author, with fabled Zen basketball coach Phil Jackson, of the book *Sacred Hoops*. And I hired John Sheehy, who was the founding general manager of Time Inc.'s *Health* magazine, to be the publisher.

In my penultimate issue as editor in chief, I told the readers in my editor's note that I was taking a one-year sabbatical starting in April 1996. "After twelve years, I'm ready for what I'm calling my 'walkabout.' I don't know what I'll be doing yet, so it feels a bit like stepping into the void. I know I'll take some real one-on-one time with my wife, Nina, and with each of my children. And I'll travel some with Nina and some on my own. But beyond that I'm leaving things wide open for now. I may file the occasional report in these pages, and I may not."

In the next issue, my final one as editor, I ran an excerpt from Robert Bly's new book, *The Sibling Society*, for the cover story, with the headline "Are You Grown Up Yet? (Do You Know Anyone Who Is?)" I included an interview that I did with Robert for the section and ran a photo of the two of us on the balcony of his Greenwich Village apartment, commiserating together about old times. In my editor's note I explained that it was only fitting for the cover story in my last issue to be written by Robert, for his work had been the lead story of the prototype issue and a leitmotif weaving in and out of the magazine for much of its twelve years.

Publishing the excerpt from *The Sibling Society* was my final editorial act before setting off on my sabbatical. I felt great satisfaction knowing the cover section represented a healing of the rift between

Robert Bly and I reminisce in his New York City apartment.

Robert and me, a reconciliation that I'd worked hard to achieve. I wanted to give Robert's book, which I considered his magnum opus, a proper launch. Perhaps we would help it become a bestseller, and perhaps we'd help our readers, and the culture, to "grow up."

In the very next issue, the first under Hugh's editorship, and just three months after the *Twin Cities Reader* profile of me, Hugh published a letter from a reader accusing Robert of sexual misconduct, of having sex with his daughter's friends.

I was unaware of the letter. I was in a remote corner of New Mexico, starting my sabbatical with a ten-day silent meditation retreat. I had neither seen nor heard about the letter, and Hugh ran it without my knowledge or consent. When I arrived home, Nina was waiting for me at the front door. The look on her face told me something was terribly wrong. As I set down my suitcase, she handed me the issue. It had been shipped to subscribers while I was at my meditation retreat.

"Here," she said, as I hugged five-year-old Eli, who'd thrown himself into my arms as soon as I walked in. "Take a look at the first letter in U.N.C.L.E. [Utne Network for Communications, Letters, and Epistles—the magazine's letters section]."

I sat down in the living room with Eli on my lap and took a deep breath. The lead letter carried the headline "Grow Up Bob."

"You cannot claim elder status while you're seducing your daughter's friends," the letter read. "You cannot mentor young men if you are their rival for sexual partners."

I was dumbfounded. Could it be true? Had Robert succumbed to the predatory behavior of so many gurus and spiritual teachers? How did Hugh know? Nina couldn't answer my questions. She had only just been alerted to the letter by my assistant, Jeanne Hoene, when she'd dropped off the copy about an hour before I got home.

I called Hugh immediately but didn't get an answer. Then I started down the staff phone list. I just had to know what was going on. After calling three editors who didn't pick up, I decided to wait until morning to contact Hugh.

I didn't sleep that night. All I could think about was Robert. Had he seen the letter yet? If so, what was he going through? He had been a mentor to me. He showed me that it was possible, even necessary, to be both political and spiritual at the same time. He made me proud to be Norwegian. He introduced me to men's work. And he opened the door to feelings I had never allowed myself to have before. And now something I'd created had slandered his good name.

When I finally reached Hugh by phone in the morning, he said it never occurred to him to fact-check the letter. "I had no reason to doubt that the letter was true." He seemed dismissive of my concerns, as if I was making a big deal out of a non-issue.

As soon as I got to the office, Jeanne told me she'd gotten a call from Robert's lawyer. When Bly saw the issue he "went ballistic," the lawyer had told her. He said the letter was "rank character assassination, a low-level lynching." The lawyer said Robert was going to sue the magazine and me for libel, slander, and defamation of character. "He told me you might as well hand the magazine over to Robert right now," Jeanne said, looking as if she was about to cry.

Feeling shaky, I went to the U.N.C.L.E. editor's desk, found the actual letter, took it into my office, and read it several times, still in shock and disbelief about its contents and what Hugh had done with it. Had anyone bothered to check out the letter writer's allegations? Had anyone tried to reach me? Then I tracked down her home phone number through directory assistance and called her to find out what she was talking about. To my surprise, she picked up the phone. I asked her if she had proof for her allegations.

"Allegations!?" she replied. "I wasn't talking about Robert Bly specifically," she said. "Bly is just a symbol of older men who pursue younger women. It was nothing personal," she said. "Bly's famous for leading the men's movement, and men do things like this. That's why I chose him." She added, "I didn't mean any harm."

The accusation was groundless. But Robert was so well-known, and so identified with the men's movement, that he'd become its symbol and lightning rod. The letter had been published, and the damage had been done. How could this happen? And to a man whom I respected and admired—even loved? Once again, my magazine had betrayed and dishonored him.

I, of course, was to blame. I was the majority owner of the magazine. It had my name on it. And I had hired Hugh, so I was responsible. How I wished I could rip my name from the cover. How I wished I could fathom the letter writer's bizarre and dangerous logic—since a few men do it, she figured, then all men must do it too, especially a leader of the men's movement, whom I knew to be a happily married man.

Betrayed and humiliated, I marched into Hugh's office as soon as he arrived. I was outraged. "How could you publish something so accusatory without making sure it was true? Were you trying to damage Robert? Were you trying to undermine me? Were you trying to destroy the magazine?"

Hugh just shrugged. "I blew it," he said. "Let me see if I can fix things."

"You've done enough damage already," I snapped. "I'll take it from here."

I contacted Robert's lawyer, told him about my conversation with the letter writer, and promised that we'd run apologies from the magazine and the letter writer in a prominent place in the next issue.

Highlighted in a box and headlined "Retraction and Apology to Robert Bly," the text ran on page 5. It said, in part,

> *We wish to apologize to Mr. Bly, and to the readers of* Utne Reader, *for running this scurrilous and groundless accusation, and for our inadvertent complicity in the media's ongoing campaign of male-bashing in general and Bly-bashing in particular.*

The letter's author wrote,

> *To Mr. Robert Bly, his wife, daughters, and other concerned family members, please accept my abject apologies for a misguided and overwrought letter. . . . I totally misrepresented you in a thoughtless manner. . . . I included you in a group to which you do not belong. I wanted to take issue with what you were saying, not with you personally, and I botched it miserably.*

When we published the retraction, Robert graciously withdrew his threatened suit. It all happened through his lawyer, who told me Robert was too angry to speak with me.

I was then faced with a decision: dismiss Hugh and retake the reins of the magazine, or go through with my sabbatical. After the nasty profile in the *Twin Cities Reader,* and now accusations from friends and strangers that I was a "king killer" for slandering Robert, I felt punch-drunk. I was an empty shell, completely useless to the magazine.

Besides, during my meditation retreat I realized that I'd made a mess of my life. I'd broken Brenda's two commandments—no lying and no cruelty. I'd done both. Repeatedly. I'd gotten full of myself. I'd started thinking that I was special, that the rules didn't apply to me. That I could be rich and famous and not let it go to my head. That I could be the boss and still be part of the team, the owner and a mensch at the same time. That I could make a difference in the world and get rich doing it. That I could succeed and people would somehow be grateful to me.

I wished I could just disappear. Fade away. Start over somewhere else.

I took a walk around Lake Harriet, contemplating my decision. I wished I could talk with Brenda. I remembered her telling me a line from Blake when I was twenty years old, "Sooner strangle an infant in its cradle than nurse unacted desires."

I wish I'd never heard that line. I'd left a trail of carnage in my wake by acting on my desires—two failed marriages, four sons confused about their father, lots of people hurt and angry with me.

I heard myself say aloud, "What the hell did that line even mean?"

And then I heard Brenda's voice, as clear as if she were standing right next to me, whispering in my ear, "We've all got regrets, Eric. Sometimes we have to do the wrong thing to find what's the right thing."

Then, a heartbeat later, she added, "It's what we do with our misdeeds that's important. You can turn them into gold."

I decided then that I couldn't go back to the magazine. I needed to change my life. I chose the sabbatical.

IV

COMING HOME

27

STAY-AT-HOME DAD

During my "sabbatical" Nina and I switched roles—she took the reins of the magazine, guiding it through particularly difficult terrain, while I became a house-husband and stay-at-home dad. I did most of the shopping and cooking, packed school lunches, scheduled playdates, and drove the boys to their lessons. I planned birthday parties and coached their sports teams in the neighborhood park leagues. It was a relief to forget about printing costs and libel suits and employee benefit packages. I attended the occasional business meeting for the magazine, when they happened in our kitchen, but mostly I'd exiled myself from the business.

One Sunday morning, I attended the mostly black True Apostolic Assembly Church in my mostly white Minneapolis neighborhood. The church had received numerous citations for violating anti-noise laws after neighbors complained about the volume of the music coming from the 230-member congregation. Some neighbors said they didn't like the high-decibel singing and preaching, others the drums and amplified electric guitar—especially during evening rehearsals in the summer, when the church windows were left wide open. Reverend Robert Wesley Hill, pastor of the church, was jailed overnight for ignoring the citations. On release, he admitted the church's services were loud. "The spirit of God raises up a spiritual and emotional level. . . . It's just like when people get excited about a football game or a basketball game. We are vocal and we do make a joyful noise."

The moment I entered the church I was greeted by a woman about my age who offered a welcoming handshake, introducing herself as "Sister Alice." She ushered me to a pew, then sat beside me and asked me about my interest in the church. I told her I was a neighbor and just wanted to hear the music. Sister Alice sat with me for the next hour and a half. Reverend Hill's sermon was punctuated by boisterous cheers and "Amens" from the congregation and the choir. A Bible-slapping, pulpit-pounding, charismatic preacher, Reverend Hill radiated filled-with-the-Holy-Spirit rapture. His volume, pitch, and cadence rose and fell and rose again to a full crescendo, whereupon he swooned and pitched backward in a kind of mosh-pit dive, only to be caught midflight in the arms of three young women from the choir, who stood on the chancel behind him.

At one point, the congregation was invited to "testify." I felt everyone's eyes turn to me, then move on to a young black man standing across the aisle. Reverend Hill asked if anyone wanted to be baptized. Within minutes, the curtain behind and above the choir was drawn back, revealing a large aquarium. The young man was now dressed in an orange flight suit and accompanied by an older man whom I took to be a deacon of the church. As the choir and congregation sang, and Reverend Hill recited scripture, the man received a full-immersion baptism. Soon thereafter the service came to an end. As we filed out of the church, Reverend Hill and the choir formed a receiving line, greeting each departing parishioner with "God bless you, brother" and "Christ be with you, sister." I was greeted by the only other white person I'd seen in the church, a woman about my age who was a member of the choir. She stepped toward me, shook my hand, and asked my name. When I told her she said, "Utne, as in *Utne Reader*?"

"You read the magazine?" I asked.

"Why yes, I do," she replied. "Or rather I did. I used to subscribe."

"When did we lose you?" I asked.

"Oh, about three years ago," she said.

"And when did you join the church?"

"About three years ago" came the reply.

And then it struck me—maybe I needed to let go of my old life too, my *Utne Reader* life. Not necessarily to join the True Apostolic Assembly Church, but maybe I needed to get out of the world of ideas and into the realms of soul and spirit, out of my head and into my heart.

One of the benefits of this new stay-at-home-dad routine was having more time with my boys. Leif was away in college, so I only saw him intermittently. But Sam, Oliver, and Eli, when they weren't in school, were my nearly full-time companions.

We lived in a big old high-ceilinged house on a curving street about a block from one of Minneapolis's many lakes. Shortly before Eli was born, we'd remodeled the house, removing a wall between the kitchen and dining room, creating a large space where everything in our lives seemed to happen. The room was divided down the middle by a long butcher-block peninsula with a cooktop stove in the middle of it. I called the room the Circus.

I remember one evening scene that was typical: I was chopping veggies for dinner—root vegetable soup, roast chicken, and pressure-cooked brown rice. Nina was at work. Oliver (eleven) and Eli (six) were shooting a grapefruit-sized basketball at the mini–basketball hoop mounted on the wall at one end of the room. Felix, the rescue dog who looked like an Irish border collie in a golden retriever's body, and Luna, the fleet-of-foot ball of feline tortoiseshell fur, were curled together on the built-in sofa, each with one eye peeled for errant balls. Oliver had made ten shots in a row. Eli patiently awaited his turn to shoot. He wouldn't dream of asking for the ball while Oliver was in the zone and just might be setting a new world record for consecutive swishes.

Just as Oliver was about to take another shot, Sam (fifteen) entered the room, directly beneath the basketball hoop. He was wearing a black top hat, black tuxedo with tails, and white gloves. The room fell silent. The only sound was the occasional jiggle of steam from the release valve on the pressure cooker.

"Ladies and gentlemen . . . ," I announced in my best P. T. Barnum ringmaster voice, going with what appeared to be happening. "Put your hands together and give a warm welcome for the most incredible magician in this corner of the galaxy, the one and only Sammy Mambo."

Without speaking, Sam let the applause subside, then placed a small folding table with a pitcher of milk and a folded newspaper in front of him and proceeded to perform two tricks that we'd never seen before. One involved pouring the milk into a rolled-up newspaper and making the milk disappear, and in the other he materialized a white dove (two of which lived in a cage in the corner next to the stereo and kept producing eggs and occasional hatchlings). Sam concluded the second trick by tossing the dove into the air, and poof, it vanished as a white silk scarf floated gently to the floor. Magic!

Nina and I were not always in sync with each other in our parenting styles. She was more likely to bark out orders and raise a ruckus if she walked into a scene that she thought needed attention, like the boys watching TV while the kitchen counter and sink and table sat cluttered with dirty dishes, or a messy room that needed cleaning, a lawn that needed mowing, leaves that needed raking, or a sidewalk that needed shoveling. I was more likely to start the cleanup myself, and then (hopefully) get the boys to join me.

But our finest hours together were the births of our three boys, all of them with the help of midwives. Nina trusted me completely during her labors. All the hurt and pain and nonsense of our day-to-day melodramas disappeared in those moments of real-life drama.

One particularly excruciating instance of real-life drama occurred on a family vacation in Hawaii when fourteen-month-old Oliver pulled a pot of hot steeping tea off a table and scalded his entire torso. Sequestered in an isolation ward in a Maui hospital, we had to decide whether to allow the hospital to give him a HyperTET shot, which

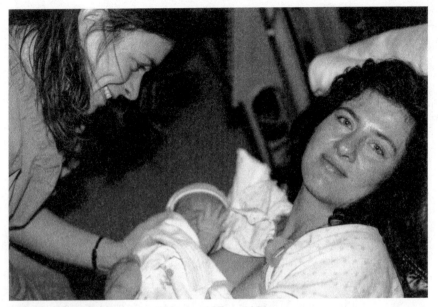

Midwife Maggie Pastarr with Oliver and Nina, 1985

was a blood product and could contain the AIDS virus. This was early 1987. HIV/AIDS had only recently entered the public consciousness, or at least ours. There was the very real possibility that the blood was tainted. After much discussion and soul-searching, Nina and I decided to go ahead with the shot. Fortunately, the donated blood turned out not to be infected.

Perhaps the worst part of the ordeal for me was watching Oliver get his bandages changed every four hours. He howled in pain and confusion as the nurses tried to gently lift the clinging cloth from his raw wounds. His look said, "Why are you hurting me?" I couldn't stand it. Against the advice of the doctors and nurses, and Nina's concerns, I insisted on helping the nurses change Oliver's bandages. The hospital staff didn't want Oliver to associate such extreme pain with me, his father, but I didn't want Oliver to feel abandoned. Oliver squeezed my thumbs as I looked into his eyes and tried to be a comforting presence, just as I had done during the births of Leif and Sam. And it worked—he found his strength to get through the pain.

The cause of Eli's trauma was more mysterious. He was three years old. We had been visiting friends in Florida. By the eve of our last day there, Eli developed a painful rash in his armpits, then his groin. We rushed him to the local emergency room the next morning. Their diagnosis: Eli was having an allergic reaction to the PABA-based sunblock we'd used. They gave him a steroid shot and painkillers and urged us to seek further help in Minneapolis.

By the time we got home, Eli was exceedingly uncomfortable, the rash had begun to spread over his entire torso, and he was running a fever. A friend and neighbor who was an urgent-care doctor came over to have a look. He said that Eli would probably be OK at home as long as we bathed him frequently, coated his sores with antiseptic to prevent infection, and made sure he got plenty of fluids and calories. But by the next day Eli was getting worse. His skin was literally shedding—peeling off his neck, shoulders, armpits, and groin. The rash was moving like a burning tide out to his legs and arms. And he was in agonizing pain. We were giving him morphine for the pain but that made him too drowsy to take in liquids. Nina arranged for him to be admitted directly to the burn unit rather than going to the ER but we had to go while the doctor was there. I resisted going, I was afraid of losing control of his care, but at the last possible minute, I capitulated. We rushed him to the burn unit of the local county hospital, where the nurses admitted him immediately.

Eli's chest was raw and blistered. His torso looked like Oliver's had, but Eli's burn was coming from the inside. The doctors chose to give him liquids and let the fever run its course, just as our neighbor had advised. His primary care nurse, who was pregnant, signed on for duty the next day, even though it was her day off, so she could look after Eli. She cleaned his skin and changed his bandages while I tried to comfort him. After another trying day, Eli still wasn't eating, and it was difficult to get him to take any liquids. From the looks on the nurses' faces, though they wouldn't say so, I could tell they were afraid we might lose him. I refused to believe it.

That night Eli shed the outer layers of his skin like a snake. The last bits came from his fingers and toes, peeling off like translucent latex gloves and socks. Oliver and Sam came to the hospital to visit Eli the next morning. When Oliver offered his sick brother a piece of bread, Eli devoured it ravenously. We all burst into astonished laughter, then tears of amazement and relief. It was only then that we knew Eli would be all right.

The doctors theorized that Eli had contracted a staphylococcus infection, the same kind that killed *Sesame Street* creator Jim Henson. The infection led to a kind of toxic shock that could have been fatal. Nina was a lioness throughout both boys' ordeals. There was no way she was going to let either one slip away without doing everything humanly possible to save them. In the end, we thanked God, and the boys' very vigilant guardian angels, for protecting them.

By the time Sam and Oliver were teenagers and Eli was eight, the constant debriefing about all that was happening at the magazine was wearing thin. It was hard to have my advice solicited, then ignored. Though I'd exiled myself from the magazine I'd founded and built, and I missed all the excitement, the creative challenges, and the occasional accolades, the truth is I was enjoying parenting my sons more than anything I had ever done.

Family portrait, with Felix (*left*) and Ozzie (*front and center*)

28

THE EYES OF THE HEART

Sometime in late 1998 or early 1999 the administrator at my kids' Waldorf school asked me if Nina and I would like to host a visitor who was coming to town to give a lecture.

"Sure," I said, "who is it?"

It turned out to be Joseph Chilton Pearce, who wrote the cover story of the first issue of *New Age Journal,* published some twenty-five years before, in 1974. I hadn't seen or heard from or about Pearce since, but soon he was sitting at my dinner table. When I told him about my interest in all things heart related, Pearce told me about the HeartMath Institute and urged me to go. After a brief investigation, I did.

The HeartMath Institute, Pearce explained, was a group of ex-hippies who had developed a few simple, heart-focused techniques that helped practitioners shift the locus of their attention from the head to the heart. They'd found that these techniques helped people boost their immune system and lower their level of cortisol, the stress hormone associated with the fight-or-flight response. HeartMath published its findings in the *American Journal of Cardiology* and taught its techniques to police, firefighters, all four branches of the military, teachers, nurses, and competitive athletes, among many others, to help them make better decisions in stressful situations. They also taught their techniques to schoolchildren to reduce their stress and anxiety levels while taking tests.

I went to HeartMath several times, first on my own, then with Nina, and then I organized a gathering there for a dozen friends from around the country. I went again for three weeks on my own to get to know the community and see if they were living what they were teaching (they were). HeartMath's retreat center was the site of a former Boy Scout camp, under the redwoods not far from Santa Cruz. I came to practice their Freeze Frame and Heart Lock-In techniques every day.

A few months later, I attended a lecture by Dennis Klocek about the "evolution of consciousness" at City of Lakes Waldorf School, the school Nina co-founded and our kids attended. Dennis was teaching "Goethean Studies" at Rudolf Steiner College in Sacramento at the time. In his lecture, he said that the majority of humanity has evolved from a kind of dreamy, intuitive, tribal connection to nature, spirit, and each other to what we have now in the West, which he characterized as scientific, materialistic, individualistic, and rationalistic.

Klocek said the tribal sense of community based on blood kinship that had prevailed for millennia is being replaced by individuation, the process so celebrated by Freud and Jung. Klocek asserted that individuation represents a step beyond tribalism because it allows each individual to develop his or her unique gifts and capacities. But, he said, individuation comes with a sense of isolation, atomization, alienation, and loneliness.

Then he said, "Here's the good news. Individuation is not the end point of evolution."

Humanity's task now, Klocek said, is to go beyond individualism to what he called "brotherhood"—for individuals to develop communities "based not on physical proximity or blood relations, but on spiritual kinship."

Yes, I thought, this is what I'm looking for—a community of people who *choose* to be together. This is what Margaret Mead was talking about when she told me that humans are tribal beings. This is what I saw at Findhorn. This is what most of our ancestors had, and certainly what most indigenous people had, before the industrial revolution and the global market economy gripped the planet and tore communities apart. This is what Brenda was talking about when she told me that we were "closer than kin." This was the "spiritual kinship" that Klocek meant by "brotherhood."

As Klocek described the future, he said we would need to learn to "see with the eyes of the heart." The phrase leaped out at me, probably because it had something to do with the heart, and since my sabbatical, especially since visiting the HeartMath Institute, I'd become interested in anything and everything having to do with the heart.

I raised my hand mid-lecture and asked Klocek if he would accept a question. He said, "Sure," so I asked him what it means to "see with the eyes of the heart." His response: "People who see with the eyes of the heart see the consequences of their actions before they take them." I found myself blurting out, "I could use some of that."

Soon thereafter, I unearthed a book I'd purchased and attempted to read nearly twenty-five years before, when Leif was just three years old and entering a Waldorf preschool. I'd decided to find out about the ideas of Rudolf Steiner, the founder of Waldorf schools. I'd been told that *Knowledge of Higher Worlds and Its Attainment* (now called *How to Know Higher Worlds*) was Steiner's most accessible book, but I'd found it impenetrable.

This time, twenty-five years later, when I read my same mildewed copy, the words leaped off the page and spoke right to my soul. I devoured every sentence. Something felt different this time around.

I was especially interested in Steiner's notion of "heart thinking," his idea that thought not balanced with warmth of heart risks turning cold and abstract, whereas feelings not guided by the rational mind risk turning into out-of-control emotions and passions.

Around this time, I attended a graduation party for the daughter of one of Nina's fellow founding mothers of City of Lakes. Two teachers from the school cornered me at the party. One of them said, "Eric, next year's seventh-grade teacher just told the school he's leaving, and we were talking about who could replace him when you walked in. We think you should teach!"

"No way!" I brushed them off with a laugh. But the seed was planted, and over the next few days the thought of teaching at my kids' school took root. I couldn't shake it. Could I really teach a class of seventh graders? Isn't middle school the hardest age? Was I really done with publishing? Could I get ready in *less than three months?*

In the days that followed, I remembered that I had teachers on both sides of my family—my father's two sisters were both teachers, and his father (my grandfather) was a superintendent of schools in northwestern Minnesota. And I learned that my mother's grandfather was a schoolteacher in the Far North of Norway. Teaching was in my blood. When I was honest with myself, I realized that something in me had leaped up in response to their challenge, declaring, "Yes! I want to teach! I should teach! If it's right, I will teach!"

A few days later, I contacted the school's administrator and asked if the position had been filled yet. It hadn't. A few days after that I was interviewed by the school's teacher search committee. I told them that I wanted to be of service, and if the committee determined that I was the right person for the class, I would be delighted to teach. Then I suggested something that a few years before would have been too hokey to even imagine—I proposed that we all meditate on the question together.

We sat in a circle, lit a candle, and closed our eyes in silence. I asked my heart whether it was right for the students, and me, and the "greater good," that I be the class's teacher. Then I simply listened. Perhaps I, or someone in the group, would get some sort of sign, I hoped. Within a few minutes, I noticed a kind of golden inner glow, tinged with viridian green, centered around my heart. It seemed to shout a resounding "Yeah!" When we opened our eyes, we all agreed that it "felt right" for me to be the coming fall's seventh-grade class teacher.

Teaching was very hard work. I was scrambling to prepare for class every waking minute, often until two o'clock in the morning, then I was up again at seven. If I was an hour ahead of the students, I felt lucky. Fortunately, I had attended three week-long seventh- and eighth-grade Waldorf teacher-training intensives, one in New York and the

My first blackboard drawing, after Michelangelo

other in California. And I had several mentors among my colleagues and my children's past teachers who generously shared with me their lesson plans and advice.

About two months into that first year of teaching, I gave my students an in-class writing assignment. One of the students, Elliot, just laid his head on his desk. I went over to him and asked, "What's the matter, Elliot?"

"I can't think of anything," he moaned. Elliot was the only child of two computer programmers who'd divorced and remarried. Elliot looked like he spent a lot of time in front of a computer screen. Each summer his parents sent him to computer programming camp. He had a collection of twenty-five gaming platforms, which was all he ever wanted to talk about.

Later that day, I took the class to Fair Oaks Park, a rolling, tree-covered park across the street from the Minneapolis Institute of Art that serves as the school's auxiliary playground. As we strolled the two blocks, I found myself walking next to Elliot.

"Elliot, I have an idea," I said, as an intuition came to me in that moment. "Let's do an experiment. For the next month or so, until winter holiday break, how about you don't look at any TV, computers, or game platforms on school nights? You can do whatever you want the other nights, but nothing on school nights. What do you say?"

Elliot said, "I'll think about it."

The next day all four of Elliot's parents came to my classroom for a previously scheduled parent-teacher meeting. I asked them why they enrolled Elliot in a school known to be averse to electronic media and technology. "To create balance with the rest of his life," one of his dads replied. When I told them about Elliot's and my conversation, and my suggestion that Elliot avoid screens on school nights, his birth mother asked nervously, "What did Elliot say?"

"He said he'd think about it."

"Well," she said, "I'll support that."

Within a week Elliot's imagination came alive. He was designing his own board games and participating in class like never before. But as soon as Christmas came our experiment ended. Elliot was inundated with electronic gifts and screen games. We had to start over.

One of the reasons I wanted to teach in my kids' school was to learn more about Rudolf Steiner's ideas. Besides founding Waldorf education, Steiner invented biodynamic agriculture, anthroposophical medicine, and the "threefold social order." Biodynamic agriculture works with the rhythms of nature, sees the farm as a living being, and has higher, stricter standards of purity than the USDA's lax standards for organic produce. Europe's best wines are all certified biodynamic by Demeter International. Anthroposophical medicine is the original holistic medicine, combining homeopathic remedies and other integrative practices with conventional allopathic techniques. In the 1920s a rising Adolf Hitler considered Steiner's ideas antithetical to his own and tried to suppress Waldorf schools and other Steiner initiatives. Among Steiner's more intriguing concepts to me was the idea of Ahriman, the regent of "cold evil." Steiner said Ahriman's influence could be seen in the mechanization of our economic, governmental, and cultural lives and in the "denial of spirit" by conventional science. Steiner's Ahriman was the very Machine that Thoreau, D. H.

Another blackboard drawing after Michelangelo

Lawrence, and so many others had warned about and that I'd tried to destroy in the swamp as a twelve-year-old.

To my great disappointment, there was very little talk among my fellow teachers about Steiner's ideas. Mostly, we teachers didn't have time for edifying readings or philosophical discussions with our colleagues. We were simply too busy to do anything more than prepare the next day's lesson plan.

Later that year, when things were going especially badly with one of my students, Nina chanced upon a verse by Steiner from the bottom of one of her piles. It was called "Faithfulness." It came at a particularly low point in our marriage. For the next year and a half, we recited it out loud to each other every night, as if we were saying a prayer. It was the last thing we did before we fell asleep. The text goes like this:

> Create for yourself a new, indomitable perception of faithfulness. What is usually called faithfulness passes so quickly. Let this be your faithfulness: you will experience moments, fleeting moments, with the other person. The human being will appear

to you then as if filled, irradiated, with the archetype of his or her spirit. And then there may be, indeed will be, other moments, long periods of time when human beings are darkened. At such times, you will learn to say to yourself, "The spirit makes me strong. I remember the archetype. I saw it once. No illusion, no deception shall rob me of it." Always struggle for the image that you saw. This struggle is faithfulness. Striving thus for faithfulness you shall be close to one another as if endowed with the protective powers of angels.

The "Faithfulness" verse helped me navigate the trickier shoals of both my marriage and my teaching. It reminded me to see a more complete, healthy, and whole human being when I looked at my wife or my students. When Nina and I fought, I began to see her not as a menacing harridan ready to rip out my throat, but as the Divine Feminine, who in that particular moment had chosen to manifest as Kali, a wrathful, vengeful aspect of the deity (who wanted to rip out my throat). I realized I would never change her. Instead, I learned to say (to myself), "Bring it on," not defiantly, but with genuine sincerity, even gratitude. "Bring it on."

In Waldorf schools the teacher moves with the class, ideally from first grade all the way through to eighth grade, which means that the teacher learns the curriculum *with* the class. Steiner's curriculum has an age-appropriate theme for each grade. The first-grade curriculum is rich in fairy tales, folk tales, and nature stories. The fifth grade concentrates on Greek, Indian, Persian, and Egyptian history and myths. The theme for the eighth grade is revolution—the American and French ones, and the American Civil War. I had no idea what kind of revolution I was in for.

29

TEACHING REVOLUTION

On the first day of school a boy in my eighth-grade class spat in a girl's face. The next day, a girl who had been in the class since kindergarten told me she was leaving the school because the other girls were being so mean to her. The class was in chaos. The revolution had clearly begun.

During the summer I had attended another teacher-training intensive and had been forewarned, and I thought thoroughly prepared to deal with the tumultuous changes my thirteen- and fourteen-year-old students would be experiencing. Kids go through tumultuous changes. Their hormones would be pumping. Their limbs would seem to grow inches overnight. Cliques would form and disband and reform by the hour as they learned how to bond, or to wound, with words.

I had been contemplating these upheavals during the summer and was considering introducing a form of group conversation called "council" to manage and, with any luck, shift the social dynamic. I had learned to use council with the Mud Lake Men, and I was convinced it could help my students "listen from the heart and speak from the heart." Rudolf Steiner taught a similar form of active listening that he called "Goethean conversation," in which each person tries to enter into the feelings and thoughts of the other, to develop true empathy and compassion.

I decided the time to introduce the council process had come. That night I searched through my house looking for objects with which to make a centerpiece for our conversation circle. I found a candle, a cloth, a stone, a shell, a feather, and a pinecone.

On the way to school the next day, there wasn't much traffic. It was a warm early-autumn morning. I switched on Minnesota Public Radio. "It's going to be unseasonably hot today," the host said, "with a high of eighty-three degrees Fahrenheit." Then a National Public Radio announcer interrupted. "We have breaking news here. It's 8:52. We understand a plane crashed into the World Trade Center a few minutes ago. We don't know any more than that. We don't know if it was a commercial aircraft . . ."

Before I reached school, the second tower had been hit. There was talk among the teachers of terrorism. By the time my students arrived, half of them had heard that one of the towers was down, but that's all we knew. I felt a familiar sense of vertigo as we were swept up in the swirling confusion of distant unfolding events. Instead of turning to the media, and watching or listening helplessly, my intuition told me that in this moment the class should stay together and turn to each other.

"Today is a day you will never forget," I told the students as soon as we'd gathered, thinking of the day John F. Kennedy was assassinated. "Today may be a turning point in history. You will remember what you were doing today for the rest of your life."

Then I led them from our basement classroom to a small space in our old building's fourth-floor attic, where a ring of chairs that I had set up for council awaited them. We sat with the lights turned off, the candle burning in the center. While the chaos and confusion escalated around the world, we sat in a circle of silence. Inwardly, I thanked the students' guardian angels for providing this way to comfort the children at this time.

"Today we will talk about how we want to treat each other, and how we want to be treated," I began. We all knew something momentous was happening in New York. And we all knew that we were far enough away from those events that we were safe. It would take months and years to realize how much our sense of safety and security was shattered on that day, wherever we were.

After laying out the ground rules for council and pausing for another minute of silence, I passed the talking stick to Sarah. Everyone, it seemed, had put the events in New York out of mind. The trouble in our classroom was pressing enough.

"I wish people weren't so mean," she started out. "Sometimes it seems like people just don't think you have any feelings." She let her words hang in the air, then handed the stick to Lily, sitting to her left.

Lily held the stick for a minute, seeming like she was about to speak several times, then she decided otherwise and handed the stick to her left. "Pass," she said.

As the talking stick moved around the circle, first Martin, then Bruno, then Philip did likewise. "Pass." "Pass." "Pass."

Then the talking stick came to Rachel, the girl who'd told me she was leaving the school. "I used to love it here," she whispered, her chin quivering. "But now I can't stand coming to school," she said, tears forming in her eyes. "I've never felt so all alone. Everyone's so mean."

All the girls began crying. Sniffling and nose blowing went right around the circle. There was not a dry eye among the boys either. As the talking stick moved around the circle a second and then a third time, everybody spoke.

"I'm sorry, Bridget," said Philip, the class's most mercurial and, for me, most challenging boy. "About the spitting, I mean."

Bridget looked at Philip across the circle and gave him a half smile, then lowered her eyes. Other apologies, echoes of Rachel's pain, more tears, statements of regret and resolutions to do better followed one after the other. Long silences that might have been uncomfortable seemed fine, even savored. Waves of sadness, regret, and relief followed one after the other as we floated together in a salty sea. The students listened to one another. They felt each other's pain. Life in our classroom, and the country, would never be the same.

Much to my regret and I'm sure to that of others in the class, Rachel did leave the school. But there was no more spitting and each week for the rest of the year we met in a circle for ninety minutes.

At the end of eighth grade, I took the class to Death Valley for our class trip. The kids had raised their own airfare and travel costs by selling cheese pizza, carrots, and apples to the rest of the school every Wednesday for the entire year.

Parents were not allowed to come on the trip, though I did discreetly invite one of the fathers, who I knew to be an experienced camper, to join us. We had two skilled wilderness guides—a married couple, with their toddler—who were experienced in leading rites of passage. They taught us outdoor survival skills and led our rituals.

Aristotle, who was an initiate of the Greek mysteries, maintained that it was "not necessary for the initiate to learn anything, but to receive impressions and to be put in a certain frame of mind by becoming a 'worthy' candidate." I hoped our nine months of studying initiation rites and five days of learning survival skills had made my students "worthy candidates."

On the fifth night, we had our last supper before the kids went out the next morning on their solos. Each of them would be alone. They would have nothing to eat or drink but water for twenty-four hours.

I hoped these twenty-four hours would be the centerpiece of the students' passage from childhood to adolescence. We'd studied rites of passage in other cultures throughout the year. Each student had picked a culture—Egyptian, Jewish, sub-Saharan African, Greek, Viking, Native American—and reported on their initiation ceremonies and rites of passage for twelve-to-fourteen-year-olds. Our last supper and the twenty-four-hour solo fast would be the culmination of nine months of preparation.

This is what I longed for when I was a thirteen-year-old. That was when my parents divorced, and I became "the man of the house." Without realizing what I was missing, I craved adult interest and guidance. But just when I needed to be close to adults and be shown my role in my community, my parents were separating, and my world seemed to be splitting apart.

After our last supper, we formed a circle for council, each student declaring whether or not they were going out and why. No one was obliged to do the solo. Elliot had announced at the beginning of the year that he wasn't doing any rite of passage.

"Ninety-nine percent of Americans have never been initiated," he had said, parroting a statistic I had mentioned in class. "So why should I?"

Just before we left on our trip, Elliot decided to come. "But," he said, "I won't be doing the solo."

When the talking stick came to Elliot, he took it and just sat quietly. Elliot had a gift for the dramatic. As he sat there, a scorpion crawled through the circle. Everyone was so well prepared in survival first aid that no one even flinched. We just watched in silence.

When the scorpion left the circle, Elliot spoke. "I'm going out." Long pause. "Because I don't want to."

Elliot had found his courage, and his will. "Yes!" I said under my breath.

The next morning everyone went out, spreading across nearly a mile of remote backcountry. Each child carried a drop cloth, a sleeping bag, and a gallon of water. Some had notebooks and colored pencils. That was it. Everyone was out of sight and hopefully out of earshot of everyone else. Back in Minneapolis, their parents held a twenty-four-hour vigil, praying that their children would survive their time in the wilderness with Mr. Utne. Shortly after dawn the next morning, the students found their way back to base camp, one by one. They were welcomed back into the threshold circle by our guides, who bathed them in sage smoke and blessed them with a prayer. All of them had survived, thank God, and they were all uncharacteristically quiet.

After a hearty breakfast, we spent the day hearing each student's story. I looked closely at each one as they spoke, wondering if they'd changed in any way. I couldn't tell if they'd learned anything, but it was clear they'd all become "worthy candidates." They seemed confident, more themselves somehow, certainly capable of assuming the roles and tasks of the next stage of life.

We drove across Death Valley the next morning and spent the day taking in the neon sights and overamped sounds of Las Vegas, a city that truly never sleeps. We walked the crowded streets, floated in the canal at the Venetian, visited the Calder exhibit at the Bellagio, and rode the rides at Circus Circus. By the time we got back to Minneapolis, the class had become family. Many of the students have stayed in touch with each other, and with me, to this day.

In Waldorf schools, the teacher is neither a repository of facts nor a special-interest authority, teaching today what he or she taught last year, or last period. Instead, the teacher strives to learn *with* the class. The *striving to learn* that the teacher models for the students is what's so important.

After graduation I knew I wouldn't be coming back to teach next year's first grade. The Waldorf curriculum is very different from those of conventional public and private schools in the early grades, especially in its unique, unhurried approach to reading. I thought I would need at least a year or two of training to teach the early grades' curriculum. Besides, those adorable and adoring first graders, who learn by imitating their beloved teacher, were for some reason much more intimidating to me than squirrelly, unruly seventh and eighth graders.

Teaching was the hardest work I'd ever done, and the most rewarding. My students taught me far more than I taught them. My class allowed something in me that had been stuck since I was thirteen to get unstuck. They helped me thaw parts of myself that had been frozen since I was their age. My tears came back.

And I learned about being a mentor. In his book *The Snowy Tower,* English storyteller Martin Shaw writes: "How many men and women in later life find the mentor within themselves? . . . There is an owl in an old woman just ready to come out and hoot. . . . If no youth gather at the mentor's door to ask 'please, tell me a story,' then some vital seed remains unhatched in the elder, something remains un-blessed in them and they go back to the remote and the football game. Everybody loses."

Did I learn from my teaching to see with the eyes of the heart, to see the consequences of my actions before I took them? A little, I think. I know I learned to sense what the students were feeling and to feel their struggles as if they were my own—like when I suggested to Elliot that he take a "screen fast" on school nights, and when I introduced the council process on 9/11, and when I decided to create a rite of passage for the class in Death Valley. In each of these situations, I

"Teaching isn't about filling buckets; it's about lighting fires."

trusted my intuition, which I now know is what it means to see with the eyes of the heart.

I also learned, yet again, just how powerful the council process can be. There's nothing like deep, attentive listening to one another to bring a group together. It's the very basis of community.

And I learned that I didn't need to fix my students' problems. In fact, I discovered I *couldn't* fix their problems, and that it wouldn't serve them even if I could. They had to work through their own life lessons. But I could let them know that I was there for them, and that I saw them, and that I would listen.

At my going-away party, my colleagues presented me with a yearbook that included inscriptions like these: "It's been a joy to have your spirit lifting our school (and choir)." "You have been a healing balm during a time we so desperately needed your vision and joy." "You are a crazy driver, a born leader, and a very kind soul." And "You had a clear vision and went for it, and that was the key that allowed the gift to enter each one's life, including my own. . . . We all want to see what you'll do next."

I brought the yearbook home and showed it to Nina. "Look, I *can* work with other people," I said. "They actually *like* working with me." Then I added, "I just need to *not* be the boss."

30

PARZIVAL

In the fall of 2002, shortly after my two-year teaching stint was completed, I attended my first Minnesota Men's Retreat. I'd always wanted to come to these five-day feasts of myth, ritual, and camaraderie, filled as they were with friends from the Mud Lake Men and other men's groups. But I'd kept a respectful distance because I didn't want to upset Robert. We'd had two fallings-out. I didn't want to risk a third.

"I'll say that line again." Robert Bly gives a reading.

But this time I couldn't resist. The theme for the retreat was the legend of Parzival, with Robert presiding. And Martín Prechtel, an Austrian spiritual teacher who had trained for many years in the mysteries of Guatemalan shamanism, was to tell the entire Parzival myth over the conference's five days. It would be a deep dive into the story of the quest for the Holy Grail.

I knew something of the legend from my work as a Waldorf teacher and from my readings of Rudolf Steiner, who called Wolfram von Eschenbach's version of the twelfth-century tale "the first modern myth." I'd participated in a study group that read and acted out each of the book's sixteen chapters over a several-month stretch. I loved the story. In some ways, Parzival's story seemed like *my* story.

Parzival is a popular romance from the Middle Ages about a callow lad who feels called to become a knight and embarks on a quest to find the Holy Grail. His path takes many twists and turns in which he gets himself and the people he meets into a lot of trouble. On his journey from "dullness to doubt to blessedness" he tends to get distracted by his attraction to beautiful, alluring women and attacked by belligerent, competitive men. During long periods, he even forgets that he's on a quest. Eventually, through a series of encounters with people who either love him or want to destroy him, Parzival accomplishes his quest, frees the people, and fulfills his destiny.

I saw myself in Parzival's story. From my first encounter with Prince Valiant in the Sunday comics, I'd been a knight on a quest, a seeker, and occasionally a finder as well. During my adventures and misadventures seeking romance, then healing, then fame and fortune, and later seeking enlightenment and redemption, I stumbled upon *my* Holy Grail. But like Parzival, I wasn't ready to claim it. There it was, right under my nose, but I didn't have the eyes to see it, let alone the wisdom to possess it.

The conference was everything I'd hoped it would be. Robert was cordial, and for this I felt relieved, if not fully forgiven for what he had suffered at the hands of *Utne Reader*. Mostly I gave him a wide berth. I was astounded by Martín's thorough scholarship, his capacious memory, and his flamboyant showmanship. He tossed his wavy shoulder-length, straw-colored hair from side to side as he conjured his characters like a medieval troubadour. He gave them flesh with fabulous flourishes on his flamenco guitar. With his melodious voice, he was a minnesinger from the Black Forest. He used unexpected, unfamiliar words and gave new meaning to familiar ones. In short, he was spellbinding.

Martín began his telling of the legend as the book does, before Parzival was born. It took a couple days for Martín to get to two of Parzival's most important encounters—the first with Cundrie, the hag, and the second with Trevrizent, the hermit.

At a critical moment in the story, when Parzival was enjoying undeserved public acclaim, Cundrie burst in on King Arthur and his knights of the Round Table to speak the hard truth.

Cundrie, the "loathly messenger of the Grail," was so ugly that she had the snout of a pig and wore her long eyebrows in braids. Without any props or makeup, Martín transformed himself into Cundrie before our eyes. Cundrie chastised Parzival:

> You think me an unnatural monster, yet I am more natural and pleasing than you. You who were in the presence of the ailing fisherman [the Fisher King] and failed to ask him the compassionate question that could heal him and thus free him from his sighs! He showed you his burden of grief and still your heart remained closed. You should have taken pity on his distress. May your mouth become empty, I mean of the tongue within it, as your heart is empty of real feeling! A curse on the beauty of your face. . . . Did a word escape those glorious lips of yours? Nothing. . . . You were probably too busy gazing into a mirror to notice.

Cundrie certainly knew how to burst Parzival's bubble. My Cundrie moment was the take-down cover story in the *Twin Cities Reader*. My motives, my character, even my inner life was attacked and ridiculed. Like Parzival, I was pulled off my high horse.

And my public comeuppance was doubly painful because it was

followed soon after by the slanderous letter that was so hurtful to Robert, and our subsequent falling out.

Then Martín shape-shifted into Trevrizent, a very different kind of mentor than Cundrie. Trevrizent was an old hermit who had been a knight, seen the world, experienced its pleasures and disappointments, and knew "how to read the stars." Trevrizent was worldly-wise yet had chosen a life of simplicity and contemplation.

Like Cundrie, he served as mentor to Parzival at a key juncture in the young man's life. But Trevrizent's truth telling was kinder than Cundrie's tough love. He gently guided the youth to speak his own truth, and to accept responsibility for his misdeeds and the pain he had caused others, and then to forgive himself. As Brenda had done countless times for me, Trevrizent gave Parzival the rare and precious gift of deep listening.

Again, Martín was totally convincing. By feeling his grief, Parzival found his heart, which enabled him to feel empathy for others' pain. This was the key that eventually led Parzival to ask the question "Uncle, what ails thee?" This simple, compassionate question healed the Fisher King and allowed Parzival to complete his quest and claim the Holy Grail.

Each mentor, said Martín, provided Parzival the kind of mentorship that was needed at the time. Cundrie's public scolding of Parzival deflated his self-importance just at the moment when he was feeling most full of himself. She awakened Parzival to his mission, from which he'd gotten distracted, and sent him back on his quest.

Robert had done the same for me when we had our fallings-out, exploding with anger and accusing me of trying to bring him down. Those accusations hit home. I was forced to confront my motives and I began to imagine how my actions affected others before I acted.

Trevrizent, on the other hand, provided encouragement and a receptive ear just when Parzival was at his lowest point, filled as he was with self-loathing and existential despair. Trevrizent listened as Parzival unburdened himself of his own story and confessed his sins. Only then could Trevrizent teach Parzival about the mysteries of the stars and the history of Parzival's own family. This was the kind of listening that Brenda had given me so often. Only *after* Parzival felt deeply seen and heard could he hear the wisdom that Trevrizent had to offer.

Martín's virtuoso performance brought Parzival and his two mentors to life. I realized that the magazine had lost its magic because *I* had lost my magic. My marriage was running off the rails because I had avoided dealing with certain patterns and issues between Nina and me that needed my attention.

At the retreat's concluding banquet, Robert came up to me at the dessert table. No one else was within earshot.

He asked me, "Why did you do it? Why did you trade your integrity for journalism?"

I was dumbfounded. I didn't know what Robert was talking about. Was he still mad at me because I had run the piece by his ex-wife, Carol, criticizing the men's movement? That was in 1989. This was 2002.

As I groped for words to answer Robert's question, I couldn't help but notice the phrase of a song wafting up from the basement where a group of men had gathered to sing. The refrain ran, "The distance between us is holy ground."

"Why did I publish Carol's piece?" I replied. "I did it because it made for a better read."

That sounded harsh, I realized. But it had been a strictly editorial decision, if such a thing is possible. I included Carol's piece because it made for a more interesting and nuanced section about the men's movement, a subject that had become controversial by the time we published it. I felt the needs of the magazine trumped Robert's and my personal friendship.

As soon as the words were out of my mouth, I wished I could reel them back in. I realized how harsh they sounded. How unfeeling.

I could tell my answer wasn't having the effect I'd hoped for. Robert was getting more angry.

And then I had a Parzival moment. I saw beyond Robert's anger to the pain behind it, the pain my actions had caused him. By not telling him I was going to put his ex-wife's scathing critique of the men's movement alongside his interview, which would have been the honorable thing to do, I'd deprived him of his freedom, and put a knife in his back.

Robert just looked at me, his eyes scanning my face like searchlights, as if he was trying to find something. I imagined him asking, "Is anyone in there?"

"I did it because I wasn't thinking," I said. "I lacked empathy."

Then I added, "I never asked, 'What ails thee?' I'm sorry I didn't."

Then Robert turned without further comment and went back to the festivities.

After the conference, I wrote the following poem and sent it to Robert.

BETRAYAL

How can I sing in his presence
When the very sight of me
Causes my elder brother,
Whom I have betrayed,
So much pain?

How can I comfort this woman
Mother of my children,
When every tender word,
Every gentle touch
Causes her heart to break
And the wailing to return?

The one who could betray
So unthinkingly, so unfeelingly,
Thrived on numbness, frozen memories,
Unfelt anger, hidden grief.
Now, his own singing, tenderness, and tears
Melt the betrayer back to life.

How can I sing in the presence
Of the ones I have hurt?
How can I not?

Over the next few months I kept running into Robert—around a neighbor's kitchen table after a poetry reading, at a book signing, in the aisle at the grocery store, at his eightieth birthday celebration, or on a walk around Lake of the Isles—and every time our paths crossed he acted as if he was genuinely glad to see me. He wanted to know what I was doing and how life was going. He even came to my sixtieth birthday party and participated in a ritual in which he and the other elders present reached out and pulled those of us turning sixty that year across an imaginary line into elderhood.

Robert and Ruth Bly at my sixtieth birthday party

In other words, Robert couldn't have been more magnanimous. The tolerance and forgiveness he gave me were unexpected and undeserved. He went out of his way to ask me, with real interest and concern, "What ails thee?" and "How can I help?"

As I think about it now, those questions were completely in character, for Robert was a true knight. His generosity was outsized. King-sized.

Robert's fellow poet and across-the-street neighbor Jim Lenfestey sums up my feelings about Robert better than I can. Jim's poem "Old Poet at a Coffee Shop" includes these lines:

The age of poets is over with this man. . . .
There will be no more tall as he,
Able to see so far.

31

A LOTTA JUBILADA

Nina and I divorced in 2008. It took us a while to get there, beyond the acrimony, and we needed help from friends who knew and loved both of us and our sons. Our sons were the key. When our mutual friend Richard Perl offered to serve as our mediator, we both jumped at the opportunity. Richard is a businessman and lawyer, not a divorce specialist, but he'd been a family friend for over twenty-five years, and was "Uncle Richard" to our boys,

Richard's strategy was to keep reminding Nina and me that he loved both of us, and our sons. I began keeping a photo of Sam, Oliver, and Eli in several places around the house and in my wallet so I'd be reminded of them throughout the day. Keeping them in mind enabled me to make concessions to Nina that I wouldn't have considered otherwise. I suspect the same is true for Nina. I know it's a cliché, but it's true—we did it for the children.

Around the time my marriage was unraveling, I turned frequently to my sister, Mary, for counsel and support. Mary was the wisest and most generous person I knew. And the most fun. When we were young, I was Mary's confidant, confessor, and protector. She called me Rickey Roo. She cut me enormous slack and made me feel as if I could do no wrong (dangerous!). Nina and our boys could always tell when I was talking with Mary by my conspiratorial tone of voice and hysterical laughter.

Our parents were alcoholics and Mary experienced severe physical and psychological childhood abuse. Seeking understanding and escape, she became a book reader and a rebel. When she was just sixteen she and a friend met Frank Zappa at a Mothers of Invention concert. Enthralled, Zappa soon thereafter recorded "The Nancy & Mary Music." Mary skipped her senior year in high school, passing up full scholarships from several Ivy League colleges to attend the University of Wisconsin, where she had to pay full tuition, which drove our parents crazy. She got her PhD in social psychology, creating for her thesis "an equity theory of intimate relationships."

In 1979, Mary got a job with the Police Foundation in Newark, New Jersey, and I helped her find an apartment in my building on the Upper West Side of Manhattan. Mary and I cooked for each other, watched our favorite TV shows, and attended gallery openings and book launches together. We took long walks, and hung out together just like we did growing up. When she took a new job and moved back to Chicago just before Christmas, she was alone for the holidays for the first time in her life. She wrote to me:

> *I didn't call you guys at [*brother*] Bob's because I was feeling so lonesome for you all. . . . I knew that when I heard your voice Eric—you who always encourage my sentimentality—well, I'd turn to mush and cry and cry. . . . Boy do I miss you all-of-a-sudden! Ache-ies! Last year was great, Eric. Thank you so much. Mush! Mush! (Self-consciously gushy here . . . how to end?) I love you!—Mare*

During the 1980s and '90s Mary underwent psychoanalysis with unrelenting determination, seeing her therapist four days a week for most of seventeen years. She directed her extraordinary compassion and insight to helping society's least fortunate, including the urban poor and the homeless, and especially children. In 1999 Mary became the executive director of the Collaborative for Academic, Social, and Emotional Learning (CASEL), an organization whose formation was inspired by Daniel Goleman's 1995 bestseller *Emotional Intelligence.* With CASEL colleague Roger Weissberg and others, Mary proved that emotional skills like self-awareness and empathy are critically important to student success, raising academic test scores while reducing violence, bullying, and drug use.

While directing CASEL, Mary wrote an article called "Reimagining Education" that I find particularly touching. In it she envisioned a world where ". . . children feel safe, the environment is supportive, and parents are fully engaged." That's *not* the world Mary (and I) grew up in.

Mary didn't consider herself an artist, yet she was a wonderful singer and pianist, with long, graceful, piano player's fingers. She filled her home and clothed herself in soft pinks and baby blues. She picked an Irish restaurateur named Bob O'Brien as her mate. Turned out that he was not only the "real mensch" family man she had in mind, he was also brilliant—her perfect match. They were utterly devoted to each other. Her proudest accomplishments were her two beautiful children, Ingrid and Conor.

Mary was diagnosed with breast cancer in the mid-2000s. After her initial diagnosis I thought she would travel or do some of those other things people never seem to get around to. But she wanted to work—advancing social and emotional learning was her life mission—and to simply hang out with her husband, kids, and friends. Drinking pinot grigio on her front porch with her book group, or watching *American Idol* in bed with her husband and grown kids, was Mary's idea of bliss.

Mary fought her breast cancer like a tiger. She tried everything—chemo and radiation and an anti-cancer diet that looked very much like macrobiotics. She learned to meditate and tried guided imagery and took lots of herbs and supplements. She sought counsel from a psychic. She slowed down and savored life more.

We thought she had beaten the cancer, and that she'd have many more years to live. But when new malignant cells appeared in her brain in early 2010, Mary's health declined rapidly. I spent a lot of time at her side for three months, and then she was gone.

The wound is the gift: Mary Utne O'Brien and her husband, Bob O'Brien.

After Mary died, on April 28, 2010, I ran around the country giving speeches about God knows what—Waldorf education, community building, social entrepreneurship—I don't remember. Each speech ended up being about Mary. She was all I could think about. Then I got pneumonia for most of July—fevers of 104.5°F for five days, two rounds of antibiotics over twenty days. My doctor told me I would have died without the antibiotics. Part of me wanted to die—living without Mary seemed somehow disloyal to her, and pointless.

Mary taught me the truth of the medieval alchemical maxim that "the wound is the gift" through the way she lived her life. That the handicaps and hardships life deals us have the potential to be transmuted into something precious, like lead into gold. Bucky Fuller transformed his blurred, presbyopic eyesight into a vision for the geodesic dome. Viktor Frankl transformed his internment in Nazi

concentration camps into existential therapy. Nelson Mandela transformed twenty-seven years in prison into the Truth and Reconciliation Commission.

Mary transformed her difficult childhood into a compassionate
protectiveness for children and spent her lifetime equipping them with
the sorts of survival and coping skills that she had to learn on her own.

In her last days, barely able to speak, Mary told me, "I haven't
completed my assignment." I think she did. She transformed her
childhood wounds into a gift for all children, becoming in the process
a Queen of Hearts. Mission accomplished—the rest of us can take it
from here.

When I said goodbye to her for the last time, Mary pulled herself
out of a near coma to give me a big kiss. It was a kind of blessing, letting me know it was all right for me to go. That's when my floodgates
opened. Mary died the next day, as the full moon rose above Lake
Michigan, surrounded by Ingrid, Conor, and husband, Bob, who
reported that Mary crossed over with a smile on her face. She was
fifty-seven.

During the mid- to late 2000s I started several initiatives bringing
young people and elders together to listen to each other and do something for the greater good. None of the initiatives took off, so after
Mary's death I turned my attention to writing a book about growing
older and becoming an elder. It was not going well. Most of my baby
boomer friends couldn't bear to think about getting older, let alone
identify themselves by any of the most common age-related terms,
like *elder, senior citizen, retiree,* or *older person.*

Then, in 2011, I took a six-month break from the eldering book to
publish Fridtjof Nansen's love letters to Brenda. Many Norwegians
consider Nansen the greatest Norwegian who ever lived. Athlete, Arctic explorer, artist, scientist, statesman, humanitarian, winner of the
1922 Nobel Peace Prize, Nansen is Norway's greatest hero and favorite son. He and Brenda met in New York City in 1929, when he was
sixty-seven and she was thirty-seven. They had a two-day love affair,

and then a yearlong, transatlantic correspondence until his sudden death from a heart attack.

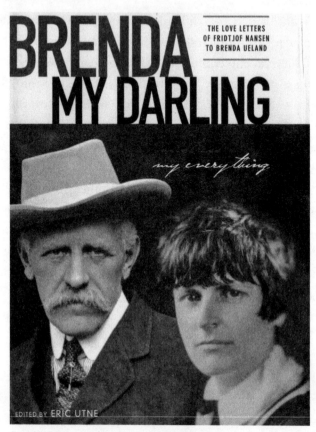

Fridtjof Nansen's love letters to Brenda Ueland

I don't remember when I first learned of Nansen's letters to Brenda. It may have been in late 2006, around the time that I joined the board of the Nobel Peace Prize Forum, a consortium of five midwestern colleges with Norwegian roots that hosts an annual peace conference featuring the previous year's Nobel Peace Prize winner.

Brenda saved Nansen's letters for many years, then gave them to the Minnesota Historical Society. After I read Nansen's letters to Brenda (hers to him were probably destroyed by his family after his death), I considered publishing them. They are some of the most eloquent love letters I've ever seen, filled with passion, candor, and longing.

Why did I want to publish the letters? I wanted to introduce Nansen to Americans, and Brenda to the Norwegians. I grew up knowing nothing about Nansen, but as I read about him, I realized he was a real hero. According to Brenda, he was held in such high regard by Norwegians that after Norway won its independence from Sweden in 1905, they asked Nansen to be their king. He declined but said, "I'll find one," and he did. He got Denmark's Prince Carl to agree to become King Haakon VII of Norway, on the condition that the people would have to elect him and there would be no other aristocracy, just the immediate royal family.

So I wanted the world to know about the Norwegian who had been offered a kingdom and declined. And I wanted the world to know that this man had been my step-grandmother's lover. I also wanted the world to know that she had inspired him to write some amazing, romantic letters. (Hers to him must have been incendiary.) And, truth be told, I wanted the reflected glory, both as publisher of Nansen's love letters and as step-grandson to his muse.

Perhaps I also saw in this project an opportunity to heal my own ambivalence about being Norwegian. I wanted to claim my Norwegianness and wear it proudly. Say it out loud and proud, *"Jeg ar Norske!"* "I am Norwegian!"

After launching the Norwegian edition in Oslo in late October, I was contacted via email by my first U.S. customer, Jeri Maeve Reilly, on November 11, 2011 (11/11/11). She wanted to know how she could get a copy of the English-language version, which wasn't out yet. How did she know the book even existed? I looked her up online and saw that she was a writer and editor. The photo on her website revealed that she was beautiful. I wrote her back and invited her to coffee.

A longtime fan of Brenda's writing, Jeri worked for the Minnesota Historical Society, where Brenda's papers are kept, and had learned from a colleague that the Norwegian edition of my book had just been launched. Our first date was an afternoon walk in mid-December.

When we returned to Jeri's apartment, she offered me a cup of tea. I happened to be on my way to a holiday office party and had a bottle of wine in my bag. "How about that?" I asked. Jeri looked at the clock and replied, "I can drink wine at three-thirty in the afternoon, I'm a *jubilada*." I got the bottle from my bag.

Simply irresistible: Jeri Maeve Reilly's picture on her website

"What's a *jubilada*?" I asked.

Jeri explained that she'd recently resigned from her longtime job as the historical society's speechwriter and board liaison. Since then she'd been asked by several people if she had *retired*. Her answer to them had been something like "Please, don't use the word *retired* with me. I don't know what word you should use, but it's not *retired*."

We were standing in the kitchen with the still-unopened bottle of wine between us. Jeri then told me how her sister had returned from Europe bearing a new word. "The Spanish," she said, "call their retired persons *los jubilados*—the jubilant ones."

"That's it!" I practically shouted. "That's the magic word I've been looking for."

I'd been struggling to find the right term, and this woman, whom

I'd met through our mutual love for Brenda, was offering it to me. In that moment, Jeri became Calliope herself, the muse of epic poetry.

Well, that lovely bottle of Stag's Leap got opened, one date led to another, and we began writing the *Jubilados' Manifesto*. Jeri found the following line by Irish poet Dave Lordan. I think it defines perfectly the *jubilado* approach to life: "a giddy relinquishing of certainty and control and a launching into the numinous unknown."

But then we got stuck. I assumed I'd hold the copyright but Jeri insisted it be shared, since we were co-authors. I was worried about repeating the mistakes I'd made working with and owning publishing ventures with Peggy and Nina. What if we split up? I worried. What would happen to the book? Who would own it?

I was leaving town soon to visit my son Leif and his family in Guatemala. As the date approached with no progress in our copyright negotiations, I began to get anxious. I started having pains in my chest and erratic heartbeats. They were so bad that I called my doctor and went to see him the day before my scheduled departure. He gave me a stress test and pronounced me fit to travel.

Still, when I arrived in Guatemala I was a basket case. I couldn't do any of the activities Leif had arranged, including hiking to the top of a nearby volcano, leaping from a cliff into Lake Atitlán, and hang gliding. All I wanted to do was vegetate. Leif's wife suggested I have a session with the Chocolate Shaman.

"Who's the Chocolate Shaman?" I asked.

"He's an American guy named Keith who does healing rituals with Mayan chocolate," she told me. "But I've never gone to him."

I had no interest in seeing some guy who was ripping off Mayan traditions for his own profit. But the next evening, Leif and I ran into Keith as he was striding up the street. He didn't seem as reprehensible as I'd feared. I decided to attend a session.

When I arrived at Keith's modest home, or shack, really, the ritual was about to begin. There were about a dozen people, mostly tattooed and pierced twentysomethings who looked like they'd been living out of their backpacks for years. Last month they had been in Bali, or

Goa, or Sayulita, and next month they'd be in Berlin. There were a couple of wealthy-looking Mexicans, a middle-aged woman from Spain, and an American woman about my age.

The ceremony was simple. Keith prepared a vat of hot chocolate, then served each of us, one by one, talking all the while. He called the chocolate "love grade," and he invited us to season it with milk, honey, and cinnamon. Then he launched into a wide-ranging soliloquy about the history, biochemistry, and health benefits of chocolate. And he riffed about spiritual relationships.

"Right now you are in a spiritual relationship with lovers, business partners, friends, family, even teachers . . . also truly with your health, wealth, and creative expression," he said. "*Spiritual relationship* is a catchy phrase for life. But if I called it life, you wouldn't be here."

Over the next six hours Keith lectured, turning from time to time to one or another of the participants and asking if they were open to doing a one-on-one. If they were, Keith asked a few questions, then offered some advice. About halfway through the session he turned to me.

"Would you like to talk?" he asked.

"Sure," I said.

"You're having an issue with a woman," he said. "Right?"

"Yes," I answered, wondering how he knew.

"I just want you to know that it's perfect just the way it is. The issue that you're struggling with is exactly the issue you came here to deal with in this life, and your relationship with this woman is your opportunity to face that issue and learn from it."

Then he added, "I can't see how it's going to work out, but this is an opportunity for you. Are you willing to go for it?"

"Yes, I am," I said, wanting more than anything to believe that he was right.

As soon as I got back to Minnesota, Jeri and I did a chocolate ceremony—that is, we drank hot chocolate together. As the love-grade chocolate warmed our bodies and cleared our thoughts, we talked about the *Jubilados' Manifesto* and the terms of our collaboration. We both realized that the project was not a business to either of us. It was a mission. This felt like a major breakthrough to me. I wished I'd done the same with the ownership of *Utne Reader*. The magazine was a mission, not a business, and it should have been a nonprofit.

Free of our more prosaic concerns, Jeri and I proceeded to fall in love. Within a few months, we were living together.

The book, as of this writing, is still gestating. It is our progeny: a manifesto for life in the sixties, seventies, and beyond. We believe that it's meant to be, and that we are meant to write it together. It is our labor of love.

32

BECOMING AN ELDER

September 2012. I was in a group of seventy people gathered at Three Creeks Ranch in Big Pine, California, not far from where I did my vision fast in the Inyo Mountains, and where I'd brought my students for their rite of passage. The home of Gigi Coyle and her husband, Win Phelps, Three Creeks is a rare oasis in that dry place.

We had traveled to Three Creeks from across the country and around the world, all of us involved in teaching or supporting the council process and wilderness rites of passage. Gigi and Win had invited us there to consider the questions: "What's going on in your life right now?" and, most especially, "What's calling you?"

I'd known Gigi for nearly thirty years. Picture a flaxen-haired Annie Oakley, riding on the back of a wild dolphin. Gigi is a co-author of *The Way of Council,* a past president of the Ojai Foundation, and a leading expert on intentional community and intergenerational collaboration.

Our group of seventy people was standing in two concentric circles inside the Heron Council Hut, a nautilus-shaped meditation chamber made of earth-filled bags piled on top of each other, its walls sealed with a smooth adobe finish, its roof shingled with recycled license plates. The hut served as chapel and sanctuary, a lovingly polished gem in the California desert.

Marlowe Hotchkiss atop the Heron Council Hut, Three Creeks Ranch

We'd been working with the four directions during our retreat. The previous day, when we were in the west, the direction of darkness, dreams, and decay, we heard four impeccably researched and movingly delivered presentations on the state of our world. Afterward I felt devastated. When each person had a chance to speak, I heard myself say, "I feel hopeless."

Later that afternoon, having worked with the north's qualities of wisdom, responsibility, and will in the morning, we turned our attention to the east, the direction of vision, spirit, and renewal. Those in the inner circle were standing on the pounded earth floor, and those of us in the outer circle were standing atop the built-in adobe bench that rings the interior space. In a few words, each of us offered a prayer or declared his or her intentions for the future.

The last person to speak was Tara, daughter of Roger, one of our hosts. Roger is an old friend who was my guide, with Gigi, for both of my vision fasts. He worked as an intern at *New Age Journal* in the mid-seventies, when he was a red-haired, ponytailed philosophy student at Harvard. On this day, Roger was a shaven-headed businessman, a longtime practitioner of Buddhist meditation, and a leader in the sustainable forestry and environmental movements.

Tara was twenty-one, and I'd seen her only a few times since she was a five-year-old and her father led me on my first vision fast. During the four days that I was in the wilderness, Tara and my son Eli had hung out together.

The youngest in the group by ten years, Tara appeared reluctant to step into the circle. When she did, she moved quietly to the center, sat down facing the open fire, and played with it, burning twigs and dry grass in the flames, then flicking drops of water from a nearby bowl onto the coals, creating the occasional hiss and pop. This is the sound of salamanders, I thought, the fire spirits.

Tara seemed in no hurry. After about ten minutes, without saying a word, she got up and began circling the fire, surrounded by the tired but transfixed assemblage. A few in the group were in their eighties, and they'd been standing for over an hour.

Finally Tara spoke. "I need your help," she began. "I don't know what to do with the chaos coming toward us." She was referring to the presentations from the previous day that had focused on the state of our world—our beleaguered water, the proliferation of waste, the continuing oppression of women and the persistence of war.

"I need you who are older to be *elders*," she said. "I need your wisdom and guidance. Please help me."

My thoughts went to the chaos erupting at the time in Gaza. American troops and civilians were still being killed in Afghanistan. The excitement over the Arab Spring and Occupy Wall Street movements was long past. The European debt crisis continued unabated, with Spain and Italy joining Greece on the precipice of collapse. The richest 1 percent of Americans were getting richer while 47 million Americans relied on food stamps. Congress was in gridlock, unable to accomplish anything. Global climate collapse was accelerating at an alarming rate.

On top of all this, the world's population had exceeded the earth's capacity to support it. I had just read a UN Population Fund report saying that we had reached and surpassed 7 billion people on October 31, 2011. Some estimates predicted more than 12.5 billion by 2050.

Our gathering at Three Creeks came to an end shortly after Tara spoke. On the plane home, Tara's words came back to me. "I need you who are older to be *elders*. I need your wisdom and guidance. Please help me."

I still felt hopeless. It's too late to save the planet, I thought, from the "Great Disruption." Author Paul Gilding coined the term. In his book by the same name he predicted that Tara's generation will experience global climate collapse, major species extinction, massive migrations of human beings, escalating armed conflict, and great loss of human life, possibly of billions of people.

But Tara's words ignited more than hopelessness in me. She kindled a spark. I felt called by her to become an elder. But what does it mean, I wondered, to be an elder in twenty-first-century America?

Elders were the community organizers of tribal society. They were the storytellers, the masters of ceremonies, the peacemakers, and the mentors of their communities. Author Marlowe Hotchkiss writes, "Elders had the critical job of safeguarding the [group's] collective memory." The elders presided over home births, the initiation and apprenticeship of the young, the group's shared spiritual and ceremonial practices, rites of passage, weddings and funerals, and the collective legacy of the tribe's songs and stories.

Hotchkiss writes, "The proverbial village that it takes to raise a child is the same village it takes to grow an elder. These are circular, reciprocal roles. One could equally say, it takes a child, or an elder, to raise a village."

One of the most essential roles of the elder is to see and listen to the young. Done with attention and care, this kind of mentorship can be a blessing, both for the mentee and the mentor. But baby boomers and members of the Greatest Generation have abdicated their role as elders, and all of us, young and old, are suffering from this lack.

In Greek mythology, Odysseus put his old friend Mentor in charge of his son, Telemachus, when he went off to fight the Trojan War. As Telemachus's tutor, Mentor became a second father to the boy. A mentor is an experienced and trusted adviser. To mentor is to advise—the origin of *advise* is the Old French *aviser,* based on the Latin *ad* ("to") plus *visere* ("to see"). The mentor is a faithful and wise counselor who provides encouragement and practical advice, helping mentees see themselves and the world anew.

I thought of the mentors in my life—Brenda, Michio, and Bob Schwartz—and the gifts they bestowed on me. Brenda gave me her unflagging courage, her belief in the creative power of listening, and her conviction that "death's a joke. I can hardly wait to join all those nice souls over yonder." Michio gave me his eclectic sensibility, his skepticism of conventional wisdom, and his unquenchable curiosity. He taught me to trust my own intuition, and my appetite. Like Brenda, he saw potential in me that was far beyond my ability to imagine. Bob Schwartz gave me his grandiosity, his need to see the big picture, and his flair for showmanship. He helped me believe in myself.

And Robert Bly—who I'm reluctant to claim as a mentor but who taught me so much—gave me my grief, my tears, and his forgiveness. He and Brenda helped me find my pride in my Norwegian heritage, and what it means to have "that kingy feeling."

Many of us think that mentoring is all about telling compelling stories that convey the hard-won lessons we've learned in life. But mentoring starts with *listening*. It's not until a young man or a young woman feels truly seen and heard that they too begin to truly listen. And that kind of listening is seeing with the eyes of the heart.

Perhaps most meaningful to me, each of the mentors in my life knew how to bless.

I remembered the blessing Brenda inscribed for me when she gave me a copy of her autobiography, *Me:* "To my incomparably handsome grandson, so strangely full of lightheartedness and grandeur at the same time. . . . There is a star on his forehead and his existence cheers up the world. I love him day and night and in the middle of the night."

I could dismiss Brenda's inscription as insincere flattery, the kind of puffery Bob Schwartz used to such good effect when introducing people. But I think it's more than that. Who would not flourish when fed such rich, warm broth, so generously ladled? Perhaps Brenda was seeing my archetype: the person I was born to be. Perhaps she was seeing me with the eyes of the heart.

There's something in all of us that wants to believe about ourselves what Brenda told me she saw in me, and to make it real. I've longed to be seen like this all my life. This is what elders can do for youngers, especially in these "hopeless" times—see their archetype, their essence, their courageous, noble, swashbuckling self. Give strength to their sword arm. Help them to see that they have a star on their forehead, and that their existence cheers up the world.

33

THE UTNE MEN'S SAGA

What's it like to be a young man in the time of the #MeToo movement, a time of reckoning when models of masculinity and male-
dominated society that are at least five thousand years old are being
swept aside and young men in their twenties and early thirties are
being called a "lost generation"?

Utne men: Leif, Sam, Mateo (Leif's son), me, Oliver, and Eli

Many young men today are feeling hopeless. They're confused about what it means to be a man, estranged from politics and public life by the polarized, belligerent behavior they see coming from Washington and the media, unsure how to behave in the presence of women, depressed and overwhelmed by accelerating climate disruption and looming global climate collapse, burdened by debt and discouraged by an unfair, volatile, and rigged techno-industrial system, and distracted and in some cases spellbound by the siren call of their handheld smartphones and sixty-inch flat-screen TVs.

In November 2015, well before the #MeToo movement began, the author Charles Eisenstein circulated a description for a webinar he was organizing called "Masculinity: A New Story." He invited men and women to join him in a series of live calls and online discussions. Here's the passage from Charles's invitation that intrigued me:

> As I inquire more deeply about masculinity—what it has been, what it could be—I realize more and more acutely how damaged it is in our society. . . . For many men, including myself, childhood and particularly adolescence was an intensive training in emotional shutdown. Unfortunately, that which is suppressed tends to come out in another form: explosive rage, aggression, violence, ambition, or, turned inward, depression, heart attacks, addiction. . . . I think I speak for many men when I say, we want to feel again. We want to be fully alive again. We want to heal from the damage of patriarchy, and we want to express our masculinity in ways that serve life, not destroy it.

I shared this statement with all four of my sons and suggested we participate in the webinar together—one session per week for six weeks, each session lasting nearly three hours, followed by our own Utne men's Skype call. To my delight, they were all up for it.

The webinar was very rich. How many fathers get to talk with their sons about love, intimacy, and family? About partnership, fatherhood, and work-life balance? About the shadow aspects of masculinity? About male privilege, insecurity, and emotional shut-down? About how to heal the damage that has been done to women and the earth by toxic, violent masculinity? I never talked about any of these things with my father.

The follow-up Skype calls with my sons took the form of council and began mostly as check-in sessions in which we brought each other up to date about what was going on in our lives—our relation-ships, work, health, and so forth. As each of us spoke, the others would listen in silence. Issues we were struggling with would bubble up. After two hours or so, all of us would invariably feel thoroughly seen and heard.

After Skyping regularly with my sons for about a year, I began to appreciate how well each of them seems to be handling being a man these days. All of them are socially skilled in ways I am not. They all seem committed to radical honesty and transparency, almost as if to say, "Look Dad, it's possible to be honest and open and have what you want." I have much to learn from them.

On November 22, 2016, I received an email message:

On Utne family history:

Hello, I am a Norwegian farmer, and I recently found a letter from my great grandmother's sister. It was written from Minnesota on the 4th of July, 1888. Thorine had just given birth to her son Theodore (1888-1943). Her husband was Oliver Martin Utne (1848-1930). Are they your ancestors? I have some unidentified pictures I am trying to find out more about, attached.

Regards, Jostein Matre

I replied that day, sending photos of my great-grandfather Oliver, my grandfather Theodore, and others. I asked, "Where is your farm? Do you know the Utne farm near Sarpsborg? Do you know any Utnes?"

Jostein responded, still on November 22:

Hello, Thorine, who wrote the letter on the 4th of July 1888, was the wife of Oliver Utne, so we are related. In a few hours I will bury my father, but I will come back with more information.

Regards, Jostein Matre, Sarpsborg

Thus began a correspondence with a relative whom I'd never met and didn't know existed. Coincidentally, my thirty-five-year-old next-door neighbor in St. Paul, Minnesota, just happened to be from Sarpsborg, where my father's family and Jostein are from. When I told him about Jostein's email, he told me he was going home to Norway for Christmas and offered to bring whatever I might want to send to Jostein. I packed up six back issues of *Utne Reader* and, on an intuition, a copy of a piece I'd co-authored about Waldorf education.

Two weeks later, Ole returned from his trip with a large glass jar filled with amber honey made by the bees on Jostein's farm, which turns out to be next to the Utne farm from which my great-grandfather and Jostein's great-grandmother's sister emigrated back in 1886. Golden honey, a gift from the Norske ancestors, ambrosia from the gods.

Jostein wrote early in the new year to thank me for the magazines, and then he said, "We have been parents in the local Waldorf school since 2002, still are." My long-lost Norwegian cousins Waldorfians? Of course!

On May 17, 2017, I wrote to Jostein and told him I'd been thinking about how much fun it would be to meet him and his family, and to see the ancestral family farm. I asked if he'd be there at that time the next year. Jostein wrote back the same day:

My plan is to be here, and we have room for all of you. I am looking forward to show you the area, and spend some evenings around the fire in our garden. . . . I suggest that you stay here for a week. . . . You can also take part in the work on the farm. The lambs are born in April, and May is the time to bring them out to the pasture for the first time. They are joyful little creatures, curiously exploring the world for the first time.

Imagine how thrilled I was. I immediately contacted Leif, Sam, Oliver, and Eli, forwarding Jostein's invitation. If they could find the time, I told them, I would find the money for all of us to go. To my surprise, they were all down with it. Each of them would carve two weeks out of the busiest years of their lives to go to Norway with their old man.

Over the following months Jostein and I corresponded about our children and our ancestors, among other things. Inspired by Jostein's genealogical research, I attended meetings of the Norwegian American Genealogical Society in Minnesota and received a great deal of help from members tracking my mother's family in the Far North. But it was Jostein who discovered that the farm where my mother was born has a burial ground on it dating from A.D. 340. The graveyard, found during road construction in the 1980s, had been used for more than a thousand years, then forgotten. Archeologists excavated, documented, and then reinterred the remains of up to thirteen hundred people, some of them possibly my pre-Viking ancestors from as many as ninety generations ago. Who were they, I wondered, and what were their lives like? So we decided to add my mother's homeplace in the Far North to our itinerary.

After a good deal of correspondence with Jostein, we had our plan. My sons and I would rendezvous in Iceland on May 11, 2018, and proceed to Norway together. Our fourteen-day itinerary would begin in Sarpsborg, where we'd stay for a week with Jostein and Gerd, visiting Oslo each day to see the sights and rendezvous with old friends I'd met while serving on the board of the Nobel Peace Prize Forum, and meeting new ones, like a young couple who wanted to make a feature film about the love affair between Brenda and Fridtjof Nansen. For our second week we'd fly to Tromsø in the Far North, then drive through Sami country and the coastal mountains to Melbu, my mother's birthplace in the Vesteralen Islands.

My goal was to make a pilgrimage to the ancestral farms of my father and my mother, to connect with long-lost cousins in the South and the North, to get a sense of the zeitgeist in Norway through conversation, to experience the midnight sun, and for my sons to meet a number of their contemporaries with whom they might develop ongoing friendships. I also wanted them to experience the seventeenth of May celebration in Oslo, and to be proud of their Norske heritage.

Then, a few days before our departure, I got this email from Jostein:

> *Hello, Eric. Earlier this month I found out I have cancer, and I will start radiotherapy on the 7th of May. We still want you to stay in our house, but I will not have as much time with you as I had hoped. You have to explore more of the area on your own. The therapy will make me sick, but since you come in the beginning of the treatment, my doctor has said it probably will be no problem. Looking forward to meet you.*

> *Regards, Jostein Matre*

Cancer! Oh my god! Should I cancel our trip? I did not want to impose on Jostein and Gerd, so I found a place to rent near their farm through Airbnb and booked it for the week we'd planned to be with Jostein. But Jostein, and then Gerd, insisted we stay with them. I kept the booking just in case. The place was called Utne Camping, and, as it turns out, it was built on the old Utne farm. Still, my hope and intention was that we would stay with the Matres, and that the Utne men would be a healing presence for Jostein.

34

IT'S THE DREAM

If Jostein was feeling weak from the radiotherapy, he hid it well. He and Gerd made us feel completely at home. They gave us a tour of Østfold county's rolling hills, broad river valleys, and powerful water-falls. Jostein introduced us to the farmer on the old Utne farm, walked the ancestral lands with us, and presented us to his cows and sheep. We shared many meals together, and we even stayed up late in the garden talking around the fire.

The boys and I commuted to Oslo each day. The thousand-year-old city sits at the north end of the Oslofjord, wrapped around the Brygge Harbor and surrounded by extensive forests and parkland. Nineteenth- and twentieth-century governmental buildings, the uni-versity, and countless museums and churches are interspersed with gleaming corporate headquarters, the new Oslo Opera House, and the towering Holmenkollen ski jump. We had lunch with the director of the Nobel Peace Prize Institute and sang in the Emanuel Vigeland Mausoleum. We explored Brygge Harbor, toured the Storting (parlia-ment), and dined in the famous Theatercaféen, and in Middle East-ern restaurants in Grønland. We discussed the #MeToo movement, immigration, the effects of Norway's sovereign wealth fund, also known as the Oil Fund, and Norway's role in geopolitics with every-one we met.

The saga begins at the old Utne farmstead in Sarpsborg, Norway.

When my sons weren't launching Frisbees off the top of the opera house or the ski jump or the Vigeland Monolith in Frogner Park, they were biking around Oslo (with me trailing behind), or leaping into the harbor at Sørenga Sjøbad (with me snapping photos).

We saw Nansen's ship the *Fram* and Munch's painting *The Scream*. We connected with my cousins from my mother's side, met a leader of

Taking a leap of faith: E, S, L, and O in Oslo harbor

"men's work" in Norway, and traveled to Lillehammer to see my friends at the Nansen Academy.

We timed our visit so we could be there during Norway's Constitution Day, Syttende Mai, the seventeenth of May. The day was sunny and warm. Norwegian flags were flying everywhere and the lilacs were in full bloom. The traditional children's parade brought an estimated half million people to the city center, we were told, many of them gathered in front of the royal palace to watch the king and queen review the parade from the royal balcony. The king tipped his top hat as the children pranced by with their teachers and schoolmates, tooting their trumpets, beating their drums, and shouting, "Hip, hip!"—with the crowd shouting back, "Hoorah!" The city was overrun with blond-haired women and girls who looked just like my sister, Mary, and my nieces Ingrid and Emily, every second or third one wearing a colorful *bunad*, the traditional peasant costume, each one with embroidery, fabric, and jewelry specific to a particular region, town, or fjord.

I was also struck, and heartened, by how many children and adults of different ethnicities—African, Latino, Middle Eastern, Chinese, South Asian—were joyously flaunting their *bunad*s, or wearing their

Utnes in their skivvies

own national costumes, while waving the Norwegian national flag. I was reminded of the Twin Cities' Tibetan community and the Tibetan women in their traditional *pangden* aprons. These children did not fit the Scandinavian towhead stereotype—perhaps they were from immigrant families or were adopted from abroad—but they were proud to be Norwegian, and all of them were *my* people.

Every other woman wore a *bunad*.

On day eight, we left Jostein and Gerd and headed north. We flew to Tromsø, stayed overnight with a friend, then drove the next day through Sami country to my mother's birthplace. Melbu is a tiny town on tiny Hadseløya Island, surrounded by bear-trap jaws of jagged mountains to the south, east, and north, and the Atlantic Ocean to the west. Connected by modern bridges and a ferry to the mainland, Melbu couldn't be more picturesque with its neat, white farmhouses, red dairy barns, and round-the-clock, early-summer sunlight. We stayed in the home of Per Helge Kristoffersen, an Airbnb owner who moved with his wife, Solveig, to their cabin in the mountains to let us stay in their house, which was less than a mile from the farm where my mother was born. Word soon got out that we were on the island,

and my third cousin, Björn Myhre, stopped us on the road and invited us to his house for coffee and cake. We stayed in Melbu three days, eating seagull eggs, exploring the island, and meeting the local farmers who seemed interested to meet us, the descendants of long-gone-away neighbors.

On our last day in Melbu, Sam led us on a hike up a hill that rose steeply above and behind the ancestral farm to a waterfall that seemed to burst directly out of the side of the mountain. When we'd all reached the waterfall, that is, when I caught up to my sons, Sam handed each of us a postcard-sized piece of heavy card stock and a Sharpie, and he asked us to write a message to his unborn son, who was due at the end of August. Sam and Molly wouldn't tell us the name they'd chosen for their baby, but Molly called him Pizza. Why Pizza? "Who doesn't like Pizza?" was Molly's reply. Sam suggested we address our messages to "ZZ."

Each of us wandered off to find a boulder on which to sit and write. In my note, I included two of my favorite poems, *It's the Dream,*

Messages to Sam's unborn son, whom we now know as "Fizzy"

by Olav H. Hauge, translated by Robin Fulton, and a fragment of *A Cradle Song,* by William Butler Yeats.

After thirty minutes or so, Sam gathered the cards and placed them into a small treasure box, and sealed it in a ziplock plastic bag. We circled up in a five-man embrace, and each of us said a blessing. Then Sam began digging in a rocky place somewhere near the waterfall.

As he moved stones and scraped the earth, his brothers joined him. I turned and looked out across the sea to the mountains of the Lofoten Islands. Below me, a little to my right, was the farmhouse where my mother was born. Across the field the hidden, early medieval graveyard. The stream next to me tumbled down the hill and meandered to the sea. Out across the Hadselfjord loomed Strøna, the pyramid-shaped mountain that rises nearly three thousand feet out of the sea, all of it awash in the amber glow of the midnight sun.

I felt the stillness, the immensity, and the remoteness of that place, and something opened in me. Something I'd been holding for as long as I could remember released and settled. I breathed deeply, and felt a sense of familiarity, as if I'd been here before, or known this place for a thousand years. A circle had closed. In that moment, I felt at home.

Later that day, as I savored our adventure, I felt a sense of accomplishment. I'd gotten my sons to a place of their origins. My work was done, in a way, my life complete. Someday in the distant future, ZZ—whom we now know as "Fizzy," short for Julius Felix Skaar Utne—will follow his father's map, with or without Sam, to find the hidden treasure and thereby connect with his uncles, his grandfather, and his ancestors from above the Arctic Circle.

On our last night in Norway, we were sitting outside a courtyard pub in Oslo when a very dark-skinned man with graying dreadlocks tucked loosely under a tam-o'-shanter ambled regally up the plaza toward us. We all fell silent. He was sporting a T-shirt emblazoned with the image of Afro-beat legend Fela Kuti, the Nigerian bandleader and human rights activist.

"Ahhh," said the stranger when he reached our table, quickly taking the measure of our little group, "a father and his sons searching for their roots in Norway." His deep baritone sounded to me like Oxbridge English.

"How are you this blessed evening?" he asked.

We invited the man to join us, which he did, sitting directly across from me. He told us his name is Abuwa Edema.

"In Nigeria, where I grew up, we didn't have written laws. We learned them orally, by heart. My great-grandfather, Numa Edema, issued the proclamation that abolished the slave trade in Nigeria, and in doing so angered many elite Nigerian families.

"My great-grandfather was a brave man," he continued. "I think of him often. It's good to remember the ancestors.

"I'm writing a book about my life," he said, which startled me because I'd been writing this book about *my* life for the last five or six years and felt no closer to being finished with it than when I started.

"I'm writing it as fiction so I can tell the truth," he said.

Hmmm . . . maybe I should try that, I thought.

Abuwa has lived in Norway with his Norwegian wife for thirty-five years. His son, Numa, is a popular recording artist who performed at the 2016 Nobel Peace Prize ceremony. "I almost lived in the United States," he told us. "I could have several PhDs by now if I had accepted the scholarships I was offered. But I preferred to live in Norway."

Abuwa told us his dream is to cook for anyone who comes to his home. "You don't have to be rich to do that, and everyone's welcome. I am a black man and you are white, but we are the same. We are human beings."

Every once in a while he'd pause, reach across the table, and flick me on the forearm, saying, "Know what I mean?" Then he'd give a sigh, tilt his head, and continue with his stories. He listened as well as he talked. The conversation went on for more than an hour, maybe two. We talked about politics, food, writing, race, and the ancestors,

Fast friends in the Oslo night: Abuwa Edema and me

among other topics. I could tell from my sons' occasional comments, and the looks on their faces, that they were enjoying Abuwa's riffs as much as I was.

Shortly before leaving, he said he wanted to talk about what it means to be a man these days.

"When I was young, I had big muscles," he said. "I thought I needed to be strong to be a man." He flexed his biceps as if he were lifting weights. "But Jesus was meek and mild, like a lamb. So was the Buddha. I finally realized the important thing is to have dignity and self-respect."

At this, Abuwa stood up, gave each of us a big hug, posed for a picture, and sauntered off into the night, leaving five grateful Utne men behind. His parting words: "Because I know who I am, I am free."

I remembered Brenda telling me the same thing. She was talking about the inscription above the entrance to the Oracle of Delphi. "Know Thyself." Amen!

And I remembered asking my Tibetan friend Tashi if he had a

spiritual practice. "Oh," he said, wagging his head from side to side the way Tibetans do, "I just think about death every day." This was at least twenty-five years ago, and his reply struck me as somewhat morbid at the time. Not so anymore. Now I live with the thought of death almost daily.

I'm not sanguine about the prospects for the future of life on earth. I think we may even be on a path toward near-term human extinction. But if you think about death every day, and live as if you could die at any moment, which is of course the truth of the matter and has always been, life gets more precious. You savor the moments you have and treat others, and yourself, with more loving kindness.

Jostein made it through his cancer treatments. In June he told me:

I am now having lazy days resting at home after the intense radiotherapy. I am at my weakest now, expecting to be a little better next week. . . . [If] you are coming back [I] hope you will stay with us.

And on January 1, 2019, he wrote:

Looking back on 2018, I had a good year blessed with a lot of support from family, friends, colleagues and our great health care system. . . . I am in good health, and getting stronger every month. . . .

Bless Jostein's soul. He knows how to live with the presence of death every day. Inspired by his example, and Abuwa's, I'm now more alert for ways to love my loved ones, and everyone else, as best I can. In the face of my imminent demise, instead of being a "feverish, selfish little clod of ailments and grievances complaining that the world will not devote itself to making me happy" (as George Bernard Shaw put it), I want to go out the old Viking way, wielding a splendid torch and singing my death song.

"Bring it on," I'll shout. "Bring it on. Today is a very good day to die."

35

FALSE PROPHETS

On October 13, 2018, the day of the Full Hunter's Moon, my youngest son, Eli, and I attended the fiftieth-anniversary celebration of the *Whole Earth Catalog*. I got us invited to the private all-day program and festivities at Fort Baker in San Francisco by telling the organizers that I was Stewart's "softer, less scientific, more new agey protégé" and that "I would not be the techno-skeptical, neo-Luddite publisher/editor that I am today were it not for Stewart Brand."

In truth, I was there under false pretenses. I was on a reconnaissance mission. I wanted to see the leading thinkers and advocates of the techno-industrial state up close, from the inside. And I wanted Eli to get an inside view with me. I felt like Frodo Baggins with his young accomplice Samwise, deep inside the Black Gate of Mordor. Thanks to the One Ring, we were invisible.

Stewart's motto for the *Whole Earth Catalog*, "We are as gods and might as well get good at it," rings differently to me now than it did when I first encountered it. With his many books and Long Now Foundation, Brand has become the techno-industrial system's highest-leaping cheerleader and one of the Machine's principal spokespeople. He gives talks all over the world arguing the case *for* nuclear power, geoengineering, and GMO crops. Underlying Brand's worldview is a fundamentalist's faith in technological progress. Now he says things like "Once a new technology rolls over you, if you're not part of the steamroller, you're part of the road."

During the afternoon workshops, I watched a presentation about Brand's latest project, called Revive & Restore, which aims to "de-extinct" the woolly mammoth, the passenger pigeon, and other bygone species by gleaning their DNA from fossils and museum specimens, reassembling them, transferring them into their closest living relatives, and then releasing the resulting offspring into the wild. What Brand and his colleagues are doing to protect the habitats of currently endangered species, such as the African lion, the Siberian tiger, and the Arctic polar bear, I do not know.

Another of Brand's enthusiasms, the 10,000 Year Clock, is under construction now on the Texas-Mexico border inside a mountain owned by Amazon founder Jeff Bezos, who has invested $42 million in the project. Bezos calls the clock "a symbol for long-term thinking."

Brand was once my exemplar. When I made the pilgrimage to Gate Five in Sausalito for my audience with Stewart, shortly after

Stewart Brand, me, and Eli, at the *Whole Earth* fiftieth

co-founding *New Age Journal* in 1974, I considered him a wizard, as brilliant as Gandalf himself. Mostly I wanted his blessing for my new venture, which he generously gave. In the years that followed, I found many of the contributors to *New Age Journal* and *Utne Reader* on the pages of his catalogs and journals, including Bucky Fuller, E. F. Schumacher, Michael Phillips, Stephanie Mills, Ivan Illich, and many others. For this I thanked him at the party.

Eli and I spent much of the day with two old friends of mine whom I hadn't seen in years, and who hadn't met each other until I introduced them that day. We'll call them Samwise and Strider. Strider is a Northern California writer whose work has appeared in the *Whole Earth Review* and a variety of environmental and politically progressive magazines. He and Eli had met years before at a Bioneers conference and stayed in touch. Samwise is a professional party organizer and techno-skeptic who felt compelled to infiltrate the party for the same reasons I did—he wanted to see his former heroes, up close and personal.

Brand spent much of the day surrounded by a posse of his technophilic compatriots—Howard Rheingold, Art Kleiner, Peter Schwartz, and a clutch of West Coast entrepreneurs, authors, and business consultants, most of whom advocate for technological "solutions" to environmental problems. Some, such as Google engineer Ray Kurzweil, author of *The Age of Spiritual Machines,* envision a near future in which human beings merge with their "precious" machines so that illness, old age, and death become things of the past. I don't think Kurzweil was at the party but he would have fit right in. He even boasts that he intends to live for seven hundred years and resurrect his dead father. "I think people are fooling themselves when they say they have accepted death," Kurzweil says. "There will be no distinction, post-Singularity, between human and machine."

At the center of Brand's crew stood Gollum, aka Kevin Kelly, a former editor of the *Whole Earth Review,* co-founder of *Wired* magazine, and author of the book *What Technology Wants.* In J.R.R. Tolkien's *Lord of the Rings,* Gollum was a hobbit who had been corrupted by the One Ring, which he referred to as "my precious." The Ring extended Gollum's life far beyond hobbits' natural limits and twisted his body and mind, so that he "loved and hated the Ring, just as he loved and hated himself."

I'm probably being unfair to Kelly. He's probably a perfectly nice person. But when he writes about "the technium," a global, massively interconnected system of technology, "which is now on the verge of taking on its own life and its own mind," Kelly sounds very Gollum-like to me. Surely the technium is the latest incarnation of Ahriman, the regent of cold, mechanical evil that Steiner foresaw. The technium is a good thing, Kelly believes, because it is "as great a force in our world as nature." Trying to resist the march of the technium is futile, Kelly argues, because "technology has its own imperative." Instead, we should "listen to what it wants" and "surrender to its advances." This will "unleash human potential" and lead to "deep progress" as we merge with machines and become greater than we could possibly imagine. Kelly concludes, "We can see more of God in a cellphone than in a tree frog."

I'm sorry, but I don't think so. The technium, and the singularity, are just the ultimate delusions of a civilization built on the belief that humans are meant to dominate nature, and the fanatical faith in the technology that is driving us toward extinction.

At one point in the afternoon, Samwise approached Eli and me excitedly and said, "You've got to meet Anna Wiener. She covers technology for *The New Yorker*, and she's here writing a piece. She's young, but she's one of us."

I thought I understood what Samwise meant by that, but I wasn't sure how he knew she was "one of us." I asked him to introduce us, but alas, we couldn't find her. A week later her piece came out. She wrote:

> As I sat on the couch in my apartment, overheating in the late-afternoon sun, I felt a growing unease that this [Stewart Brand's] vision for the future, however soothing, was largely fantasy. For weeks, all I had been able to feel for the future was grief. I pictured woolly mammoths roaming the charred landscape of

Northern California and future archeologists discovering the remains of the ten-thousand-year clock in a swamp of nuclear waste. While antagonism between millennials and boomers is a Freudian trope, Brand's generation will leave behind a frightening, if unintentional, inheritance. My generation, and those after us, are staring down a ravaged environment, eviscerated institutions, and the increasing erosion of democracy. . . .

Brand, Kelly, and company are not asking whether the techno-industrial machine is worth fixing, or what the alternatives might be. Not one of them is pointing out that climate chaos, species extinction, mass migration, and global conflict are inevitable consequences of the techno-industrial system itself. Instead, they are working to jury-rig the system with heroic life-support interventions meant to prolong a deadly and dying way of life.

As *Whole Earth*'s fiftieth-anniversary festivities were reaching a crescendo, Kelly, Brand, and a dozen other old-timers stood pressed together at the center of the heaving crowd. Eli and I decided it was time to go. As I squeezed past Kelly, he recognized me.

"Eric Utne!" he said, grinning incredulously. "What are *you* doing here?"

"Just passin' through . . . ," I said, tossing off a wave like R. Crumb's Mr. Natural.

On the way home, our Lyft driver, a twenty-five-year-old named Miguel from Sacramento, asked, "What was the event?"

"The fiftieth-anniversary party of the *Whole Earth Catalog*," Eli said.

"What's the *Whole Earth Catalog*?" Miguel wanted to know.

"You've never heard of it?" I asked.

"No. Should I? What is it?" Miguel asked, a little defensively.

"It started out as the bible of the love revolution, the counterculture, and the hippie back-to-the-land movement," I said. "That was fifty years ago. It turned into a promotional rag for personal computing.

Now it's Apple and Google and Facebook and the rest of Silicon Valley."

Eli asked Miguel if he did anything besides drive for Lyft.

"I'm a baker in San Francisco," he said. "I like working with bread because food brings people together. It's all about community for me."

"I'm with you, Miguel," said Eli.

"Me too!" I added. It's not about the Machine. It's about community.

A couple of years ago I attended a program at the Walker Art Center in Minneapolis that was very different from that Fort Baker event. It was part of an exhibition called *Hippie Modernism: The Struggle for Utopia.* The event was a celebration and reunion for some local countercultural antiwar activists from the late sixties and seventies. Unlike the *Whole Earth* party, which was almost entirely old white men congratulating themselves and each other for transforming the counterculture into the cyberculture, the gathering in Minneapolis emphasized political organizing and included a diversity of speakers. One young Native American man caught my attention when he said, "You baby boomers have forgotten who you are. It's time to step back up and finish what you started."

Right on, man! I thought when the young man spoke. *Far out!*

His words, his challenge, stayed with me for days afterward and they linger still. "Finish what you started." What happened to our ideals and values? When did we buy into the system that we knew was wrong? Now, when some young people say, "OK, Boomer," I can't blame them. We old ones know better, or at least we should. We need to get back on the barricades. We need to do whatever we can to support the young people who are so courageously taking on the techno-industrial machine that is destroying everything that is precious and good and life sustaining.

The hippie back-to-the-land movement of the sixties and seventies, combined with grassroots political organizing, really was the way to go. We need to regroup. We need a hyperlocal Green New Deal. We need to come together in diverse, intimate, place-based communities. We need to segue now from the techno-industrial market economy to its sequel—much smaller-scale, less energy-intensive, more localized communities that prize food growing, knowledge sharing, mythmaking, musical celebrations, and convivial neighborliness. This is the only kind of a society that might survive the rocky climacteric that already is upon us.

Do I have hope now? If hope means the expectation that someone (a new president), or something (geo-engineering or some other techno-fix), is going to save us—then no, I'm hopeless, or rather "hope-free." I like Vaclav Havel's take on hope:

> Hope is not a prognostication—it's an orientation of the spirit. . . .
> It's not the conviction that something will turn out well, but the
> certainty that something makes sense, regardless of how it turns
> out.

Lately, I've been surprised to occasionally find myself having feelings that seem very much like hope. Hope when I meet young activists organizing to stop the Line 3 oil pipeline that Enbridge wants to build across northern Minnesota, and hope when I meet a young woman studying acupuncture and Chinese medicine in Bloomington, Minnesota. Hope when I meet young people and old people learning together how to live the zero-waste lifestyle, and learning to use their hands to plant rooftop gardens in Berkeley. Hope at the birth of my grandchildren, and the children of strangers and friends. New life and young life and hope itself give me hope.

But perhaps these feelings aren't hope. Perhaps they're something else entirely. New life elicits in me a fierce protectiveness, an instinct to nurture and to defend. Innocent life calls forth in me a combination of courage and curiosity that I didn't know I had, and very probably didn't have before it was summoned.

Perhaps these feelings are love. Love is active, something you make, moment by moment and day by day. Love for each other, and love for the earth. These days—to think on what we love and what is being lost—love more often feels like grief. I guess I'm with Derrick Jensen—when hope ends, action begins.

This is my prayer: May our actions come out of hopelessness. May our actions be expressions of love.

FAR OUT MAN

Going to Norway with my sons helped me to know myself, helped me realize I'd been looking for my place, my family, my community, all my life. I'd been searching for people with whom I could feel, as Brenda put it, "closer than kin."

And yet, thanks to our Utne men's saga, I feel closer to *my* kin. I feel I know each of my sons better now than I ever have. They're all unique and marvelous combinations of the masculine and the feminine, they all know how to feel, and I'd say they all express their masculinity, their femininity, and their humanity "in ways that serve life, not destroy it," as Charles Eisenstein put it. And I like hanging out with them more than with anyone else. Our Utne men's Skype calls continue monthly to this day.

And even if feeling "closer than kin" is reserved for a special few, I'd like to feel "as close as kin" with everyone.

First my father and then Robert Bly told me *Utne* is old Norse for "far out." *Lexico,* the Oxford online dictionary, defines "far out" as "unconventional or avant-garde, as in 'far-out politics': marked by a considerable departure from the conventional or traditional."

I can own that. But then the *Merriam-Webster* dictionary gives these synonyms: *bizarre, cranky, crazy, curious, eccentric, erratic, funky, funny, kinky, kooky* (also *kookie*), *odd, off-kilter, off-the-wall, offbeat, out-of-the-way, outlandish, outré, peculiar, quaint, queer, queerish, quirky, remarkable, rum* [chiefly British], *screwy, spaced-out, strange, wacky* (also *whacky*), *way-out, weird, weirdo, wild.*

Hmmm. . . . If that's what *Utne* means, I don't want to be Utne anymore. I don't want to be "far out" anymore. I want to claim my place in the family of things. I want to have a family feeling with everyone and every living thing, with "all my relations," as the Lakota put it.

But I like the part about "far out" meaning "avant-garde." The definition of *avant-garde* reads: "an intelligentsia that develops new or experimental concepts especially in the arts: advanced, cutting-edge, progressive, state-of-the-art." Now, *that's* far out! By that definition, I've been far out ever since I can remember. Far out when I was trying to save the swamp from the Machine. Far out when I was taking and distributing magic mushrooms. Far out when Toad told me that I could be my own doctor with food. Far out when I discovered at Findhorn that seeing could be healing. Far out when I realized that big-picture, all-the-views journalism could help heal the body politic. Far out when I learned to listen, and see, with the eyes of the heart.

The word for father in Norwegian is *far,* and the word for mother is *mor.* Your mother's parents are your *mormor* and your *morfar,* and your father's parents are your *farmor* and your *farfar.* Since my children are all boys, my grandchildren all call me *Farfar.* To them I'm Farfar Utne, or, you might say, Farfar Far Out.

Abuwa Edema certainly knew one thing about himself that last night in Oslo—he wanted to be seen and heard, and so he was. Where does this need come from? Is it basic human nature or something more recent, a response to the anonymity that comes with living in the techno-industrial machine?

The severest punishment a hunter-gatherer tribal people can inflict on one of their members is not expulsion or torture, or even capital punishment. For the indigenous San people of Southwest Africa, otherwise known as the Kalahari Bushmen, the worst punishment of all is to allow the person to remain among the tribe but treat them as if they are invisible, as if they do not exist. In other words, treat them the way most city dwellers treat most of the people they encounter every day—on the street, at the mall, in the parking lot, or just about anywhere else in the modern urban jungle. When we cross paths with people we don't know, most of us avert our eyes and navigate around them, as if they were impediments, obstacles in the way of our destination. Or we avoid them as potential threats to our life or property.

Everyone wants to be seen, and to be heard. It's human nature. That's how we know we exist. That's why we post pictures of our lives on Facebook and Instagram and tweet our thoughts in 280 characters. That's why we display messages on our T-shirts and bumper stickers. The subways and streets of Manhattan and every other metropolis are filled with people begging to be seen, and simultaneously avoiding seeing each other.

I started *Utne Reader,* and named it after myself, in part because I wanted to be seen. I am a Leo, after all. My greatest, most fundamental desire is to shine my light, to radiate the creativity that shines in and through me. Sometimes I forget that the source of this creativity is not me. The source shines through me, as it does through all of us. Each of us gives the source expression, in our own unique and idiosyncratic ways.

To be seen and heard—that's what a mentor can give a younger person. That's what a healer can do for a patient. That's what a teacher can do for a student. That's what lovers do for each other. They see past the tryout persona, the presenting symptoms, the vestigial negative patterns and self-defeating habits, to our essential being, our true self, our archetype, the person we were born to be.

I don't claim to be able to see with the eyes of the heart whenever I want. Though it's simple, it's not easy to see the essence of another person, whether they are a stranger on the street or family and friends. For most of us it takes years of practice and experience. And self-knowledge. All of which are in short supply these days. I'm guessing that it helps to have been raised in a family and community where people take an interest in each other and spend enough time together to see us at our best and our worst, and to hang in there with us nonetheless. But having a lot of history with the other person is neither a requirement nor a guarantee. Some people are just very good at seeing the essence of other people, even on first meeting.

Seeing with the eyes of the heart is not something you can just decide to do, and then "Bingo!" you have it. It's an intention, a disposition. I consider those times when I've been able to see with the eyes of the heart to be moments of grace. Rudolf Steiner called this way of seeing "faithfulness." The struggle to see, and remember, another person's archetype is faithfulness, Steiner said. "Striving thus for faithfulness we shall be close to one another as if endowed with the protective powers of angels." Perhaps seeing with the eyes of the heart really is a gift from the angels.

I've been fortunate to have several mentors in my life, people who saw something in me that I hadn't seen in myself—who saw my potential, helped me catch a glimpse of my essence, and challenged me to become my true self.

Brenda, Bob Schwartz, and Michio are all angels now. To them I say thank you for seeing me. May I do the same for others.

It is now February 5, 2020, a Wednesday, and it's one o'clock in the afternoon. I know because of the eerie, haunting wail of the civil defense siren blaring outside my window. It is fourteen degrees above zero, and there is a gentle, swirling snowfall. Sky and earth and lake are all the color of milk. As the sirens subside, the only sounds are the hum of the refrigerator and the occasional drone of a jet coming in low for a landing at the Twin Cities airport, five miles away.

I sit here in my big black leather La-Z-Boy, looking out the window. I ask myself, What have I learned for all my seeking? What, if anything, do I have to say? This is what comes to me:

I experience God or the divine in the wild world around and within me. My faith is experiential. I have learned a few practices that author Parker Palmer might call "habits of the heart" to remind and awaken myself to my connection to the divine.

I regard birds, rocks, flowers, trees, lakes, rivers, mountains, and the wind with awe and wonder. Since my vision fast on the edge of Death Valley, I consider all of them conscious beings, and I have had conversations with all these and myriad other creatures. I have experienced feelings of reverence gazing at the rose windows in Notre-Dame cathedral in Paris and standing under the canopy of the Amazon rain forest. I have howled for joy with neighbors in a community choir and with timber wolves in the echoing stillness of the Boundary Waters of northern Minnesota. I have felt life's unfathomable mystery in Death Valley at midnight under the wheeling stars, and in the heart of Manhattan, at Forty-eighth and Lexington, with a breeze caressing my cheek under the full moon.

I sense in nature a greater knowing, a presence with which I have become increasingly familiar. Even in the city, I have developed the "weather eye" and learned to read the clouds, and become intimate with the movements of the sun and moon. I have breathed the intoxicating tide of the apple blossom front as it sweeps through my St. Paul neighborhood each spring, and thrilled at the maple leaf front each fall. I know that despite my occasional feelings of separation and loneliness, all of us are intimately connected in the Great Mystery, the endless web of life.

"You don't have to be religious to experience transcendence, to experience 'the Mystery,'" writes Roger Housden in *Keeping the Faith Without a Religion*. "You just have to be human."

Or, as Paul Kingsnorth writes, "If anything is sacred, surely it is this thing we call 'nature.'"

I believe that all life is sacred. It is not random. It has meaning and purpose. As Brenda taught me, each of us is born to learn, to grow, to flourish, to become fully ourselves, and to give our unique gifts to the world. I believe our wounds (failures, handicaps, challenging life circumstances) are often gifts in disguise, if we can learn to live with them and possibly to transform them. As they say, "If something doesn't kill you, it makes you stronger."

I believe we can sense our own and others' essence, our archetype, our wholeness, our oneness with divinity, through opening, seeing, and listening deeply. I believe that sensing another's essential being is an act of love that can heal. And I believe that help is available, if we open ourselves to it.

I have been working since dawn, rising several hours before my beloved to write in the morning quiet. I am still wearing my frayed terry-cloth robe, unshaven, my hair disheveled. I need a walk badly and am comforted to know that if I don't initiate one, my sweetheart will. Around five o'clock we will get home from our walk, lie down on the living room couch, and take a nap. Then we'll rise, have a glass of wine and a bowl of stew, and get back to our writing for the evening.

And it is queer, I'm deep in "don't know" about what's next in life. But I feel strangely calm, more curious and interested than anxious. I find myself paying attention to synchronicities, to song fragments and random comments that move me, and to my memories and dreams. I'm listening for what is needed and wanted, and what is mine to do. I'm alert to the needs that arise around me, through direct requests from my family and friends, from complete strangers, and via news items in the media. Like Parzival, I'm learning to ask "What ails thee?" and "How can I help?"

ACKNOWLEDGMENTS

Many thanks to Jeri Maeve Reilly for climbing over barbed-wire fences, and for saying "Yes, please," when others might say "No way!" To Sherry Kasman Entus, who held my hand from the other side of the globe, and then from over yonder; to my sons Leif, Sam, Oliver, and Eli for still talking with me and being so much fun to hang out with; to Jim Levine for being such a great agent; to Richard Louv for introducing us, and to Aimee Porter for setting things in motion; to Cindy Spiegel, who bought the book before it was written, and to my editor, Annie Chagnot for her trustworthy moral compass; to Mary Carroll Moore and Elizabeth Jarrett Andrew for their expert guidance and evocative prompts; to the Anderson Center and the Ragdale Foundation for providing sustenance and sanctuary; to Perdita Finn, for reading everything and saying with such certainty, "this, not that"; to Clark Strand for his silver tongue; to Tove Borgendale for her deep listening, unflagging encouragement, and healing touch; to Jim Lenfestey, Tim Nolan, and Erik Storlie, gifted poets all, for their thoughtful readings and helpful suggestions; to Linda Bergh, Jennifer Fox, and John and Kerry Miller for being true Blue friends; to Gigi Coyle and Roger Milliken for their steadfast fire-keeping and hierophantic mirroring; to Buff Chace for the initial prod, and the support; to Josh Mailman and Richard Perl for being my soul brothers and friends; to Bryan Welch and Christian Williams for carrying the torch and keeping it lit; to Will Winter, Mark Odegaard, and Walton Stanley for their coyote howls and gifts of gab; to Thomas R. Smith for his sure ear and wise counsel; to Therese Stanton, for reading the cards with such insight and compassion; to Jostein and Gerd Matre for sharing their land and ancestors with my sons and me; to Jeffrey Huset for helping me find my Norse kinfolk; to Rob Steiner for his Luddish ways; to Charlotte du Cann for her penetrating questions; to Paul Kingsnorth for seeing so far and for sharing what he sees with such prophetic eloquence; to Ned Holle, Craig Neal, and Paul (Woolly) Strickland for their dog-yeared camaraderie; to Mary Branley for sometimes sleeping with her head in the mountains and sometimes sleeping with her feet in the sea; to Richard O'Beirne for sharing his family and his adventurous spirit; to Dennis and Marianne Dietzel for sharing their grief and their joy; to the Mud Lake Men, the Saturday Morning Walkers, the Outliers, the Linden Hills Jubilados, and the Inner Transitioners for communing with me; and to my parents, siblings, cousins, nieces and nephews, my sons and their life partners, and to my grandchildren, colleagues and friends, for hanging in there with me—your constancy and open-heartedness mean the world to me.

And, for their companionship along the journey and kindnesses too numerous to detail, thanks to Howard and Mary Rower, Robert and Penny Cabot, D. Wayne Silby, Margaret Lloyd, Mike Winton, John Cowles Jr., Gifford and Libba Pinchot, Mary Schoonmaker, April Wolff, Anne Riegel, Lenny Jacobs, Lily Kushi, Harua Kushi, Julie Ristau and Jay Walljasper, Debbie Cullen, Barbara Mischler, Jeanne Hoene, Helen Cordes, Elizabeth Larsen, Lynette Lamb, Jon Spayde, Tom McKusick, Mike Tronnes, Sarah Jirik, Mark Simonsen, Cornelia Bremer, Kristi Anderson, Craig Cox, Andrea Martin, Tony Goshko, Stanley Moses, Kari Senjem, Carolyn Adams, Toby Roux, David Schimke, the Donuts, SVN, Sophia Christine & Finbarr Murphy, John and Tina Burke, Kevin and Ananda Callery, Michael Quirke, Karin Winegar, Nor Hall and Roger Hale, Anita Helland and Fredrik Kjus, Steinar and Vesna Bryn, Geir Lundestad, Lya Guerre and Erik Strand, Per Helge and Solvi Kristoffersen, Bjørn Myhre, Berit Cock, Isabell Haug, Ole and Christina Köppang, Sverre and Linda Köppang, Richard Leider, Mary Jo Kreitzer, Sharon Franquemont, Bobby and Cathy Utne, Bruce and Melinda Gardiner, Emily Utne, Christian Utne, Danielle Enblom, Lizzie Coventry Holzapfel, Rob Rulon-Miller, Kate Strickland, Kris Kiesling, Cecily Marcus, Kathryn Hujda, Hannah O'Neill, Alberto Acosta, Anna Maria

Vera, John and Diane Sonsteng, Rick Ingrasci, Barbara McAfee, Ross and Bridget Levin, Hal Johnson, David Kupfer, Walter Pitt, Constance Pepin, Anders Christiansen, Jane Prince, Sonam Choden, Tashi Gyaltsen Gangzey, Chris Schaefer, Sally Bickford, Susan Lyon, Jim Billings, Stephanie Carpenter, John Danicic Jr., Dark Mountain, Amanda Hafics, Patricia Hampl, Jan Hively, Jo Holmwood, Richard Hruby, Tim Kershaw, Sonya Krimsky, Alice Kaplan, Jeff Linzer, Frank Miller, Edwin Funk, Bryce and Donna Hamilton, Kathryn Lundquist, Carrie Bassett, Laurie Savran and Cal Applebee, Lee Murray and Steve Clark, Ossian Or and Sandra Valle, Mary Beth Yarrow, CV Peterson, Darla Rayman, Douglas Rushkoff, Alan Rudy, Margaret Wheatley, Ben Whitney, David Minge, Rebekah Leonhart, George Johnson, Gary Smaby, Jim Dorsey, David Wagner, Jeff Staggs, Doug Baker, Catherine Ingram, David Pollard, Kristi Fackel, Redheart, Jonathan Flak, Paul Thompson, John Moser, Kevin Kane, Patricia Neal, Jeff Moen, Jennifer Holle, Deni Dantis, Mary Dymond, Grant Foster, Kree Ture, Aggie Hoeger, and anyone else I may be forgetting.

PHOTO CREDITS

Unless otherwise noted, photos are courtesy Utne Family Archives.

pages i, 185: Photos by John Danicic, Jr.
page viii: Cartoon by Noel Ford (c) Noel Ford Cartoons
page 39: Photo by Ramon J. Muxter
pages 47, 60, 65: Courtesy Haruo Kushi
page 80: Courtesy University of Minnesota Archives, Twin Cities
page 82 (both images): Courtesy The Estate of R. Buckminster Fuller.
page 84: Photo by Charles Brill. Courtesy Janice Brill.
pages 146, 257: Photos by Abbie Sewall
page 174: Photo by Art Hager. Courtesy Minnesota Historical Society.
pages 192, 193, 194, 203, 225: Photos by Tom McKusick
page 212: Poster by Will Winter
page 214: Photo by Will Winter
page 273: Photo by Gretchen Amis
page 290: Photo by Mary Ellen Niedenfuer
page 296: Courtesy Beyond Boundaries
page 314: Photo by Oliver Utne
page 318: Photo by Rob Steiner

INDEX

ABOUT THE AUTHOR

ERIC UTNE is a publisher, educator, and social entrepreneur. He has a BED (Environmental Design) from the University of Minnesota. He was founding publisher and editor of *Utne Reader,* of which he was chair for fifteen years. Eric was the seventh- and eighth-grade class teacher at City of Lakes Waldorf School from 2000 to 2002. In 2006 he was elected to the executive committee of the Nobel Peace Prize Forum. He is the father of four Waldorf-educated sons and has five grandchildren. He lives in St. Paul, Minnesota.